PRAISE FOR

WEAR AND TEAR

"Tracy Tynan uses the universal medium of clothing to tell the highly specific story of her bohemian British upbringing, and she does so with wit, candor, and yes—style. For anyone obsessed with the intellectual gossip of yesteryear—or just obsessed with the language of fashion—this book will be a cozy bedfellow."

—Lena Dunham

"A powerful concoction of famous names, famous fashions, and famous psychiatric disorders. Just the thing for a weekend in the Hamptons."

—*New York Post*

"An absorbing memoir well-told from a singular perspective. Master story-teller Tynan presents universal insight and wit in this striking volume that will have a wide appeal."

—*Library Journal* (starred review and Best Memoirs of 2016)

"In this wonderfully observed, elegiac, and least judgmental of memoirs, esteemed costume designer Tracy Tynan describes a society and personalities defined by style, and the ever-shifting self-perception that characterizes outsized lives—and talent. Moving effortlessly between the world where postwar American and British literature and cinema, theater, and politics converge, Tynan details a now-vanished golden age with wit, honesty, and that rarest of qualities—empathy."

—Hilton Als

"Tracy Peacock Tynan grew up in a tornado of glamorous, stylish eccentricity. So jealous!!!"

—Simon Doonan, author of *The Asylum:*
True Tales of Madness from a Life in Fashion

"Tracy Tynan takes on the paradox of style with unique flair in *Wear and Tear* by hanging her book on the clothes she wore at key moments in her life. But the life of the exceptionally stylish, charming, and resilient Ms. Tynan is like no other. *Wear and Tear* is poignant, surprising, and an enchanting inner view of what it is to come into oneself among the sacred monsters of the twentieth century."

—Joan Juliet Buck

"A page-turning memoir that affords an astonishing glimpse into rarefied lives in the now-extinct Anglo-American literary jet set. Tracy Tynan inherited both her parents' sartorial flair and their skill with words."

—Matt Tyrnauer, director of *Valentino: The Last Emperor*

"Tracy Tynan recalls her fascinating and difficult childhood during the swinging '60s in London and New York, and the legendary actors and artists who frequented her parents' life. She chronicles her growth as an artist, taking on myriad roles as lover, costume designer, stepmother, mother, and wife, with honesty and insights that make for can't-put-down reading."

—Wendy Goodman, design editor of *New York* magazine

"The first book that reveals style as a successful survival strategy. Tracy's familial chaos required much dancing backward in heels and looking good in the part. Written with compassion, she pulls no punches; her observations are not casual chic. A fascinating read about a creative clan."

—Deborah Landis, author of *FilmCraft:*
Costume Design and *Hollywood Costume*

"Her vivid descriptions reflect her love of clothes, designers, fabrics, and, not least, shopping. Star-studded, gossipy, and engaging."

—*Kirkus Reviews*

"Captivating . . . Tynan has written a moving, candid, and often hilarious account of her tumultuous childhood in England and New York in the 1950s and '60s."

—*The Wall Street Journal*

"Readers will appreciate the depth of Tynan's belief in the power of clothes to transform films and sets but also attitudes and impressions. Many worlds collide in this well-written, stranger-than-fiction, London and Hollywood who's who of a memoir, making it appropriate for a broad range of readers."

—*Booklist*

"Brilliant . . . makes you feel how painful it was to be the disfavored daughter of two exhibitionist parents."

—David Hare

"As you read, you marvel at the author's resilience; the girl with the apple-green shoes acceded to a bigger role than she had ever expected, and found that she knew how to dress the part."

—*The New York Times*

"Tracy Tynan has allowed us a glimpse into a world both fascinating and heartbreaking. An engrossing tale that I won't soon forget."

—*LA Explorer*

"Tracy Tynan's memoir is a wolf in sheep's clothing . . . Rich in humor and observation, its stylish tone belies the often harrowing nature of her formative years, and it details with bravery and precision exactly who she was and what she wore."

—Anjelica Huston, *author of A Story Lately Told and Watch Me*

"What makes a memoir a good read is . . . compelling characters, a plot that propels said characters to a place far from their point of origin, and an ability to create a sense of identification for a reader. Check, check, and check."

—*Los Angeles Review of Books*

"Tynan combines insightful sartorial analysis with delicious gossip and celebrity tidbits to create a compelling memoir of her life and times. A dressing-up box of delights."

—Andrew Wilson, author of *Alexander McQueen: Blood Beneath the Skin*

"Tynan conveys [this memoir] with unflinching vividness."

—*The Washington Times*

"Clothes may make the man but in Tynan's *Wear and Tear*, they tell the story of finding one's place in the world and creating a family with grace and, yes, restraint."

—Forbes.com

WEAR
AND TEAR

The Threads of My Life

TRACY TYNAN

SCRIBNER

New York   London   Toronto   Sydney   New Delhi

Scribner
An Imprint of Simon & Schuster, Inc.
1230 Avenue of the Americas
New York, NY 10020

First Scribner trade paperback edition July 2017

SCRIBNER and design are registered trademarks of The Gale Group, Inc., used under license by Simon & Schuster, Inc., the publisher of this work.

For information about special discounts for bulk purchases, please contact Simon & Schuster Special Sales at 1-866-506-1949 or business@simonandschuster.com.

The Simon & Schuster Speakers Bureau can bring authors to your live event. For more information or to book an event, contact the Simon & Schuster Speakers Bureau at 1-866-248-3049 or visit our website at www.simonspeakers.com.

Interior design by Jill Putorti

Manufactured in the United States of America

10 9 8 7 6 5 4 3 2 1

Library of Congress Control Number: 2015031108

ISBN 978-1-5011-2368-9
ISBN 978-1-5011-2369-6 (pbk)
ISBN 978-1-5011-2370-2 (ebook)

Excerpt from "Calypso's Song to Ulysses" by Adrian Mitchell is reprinted with the permission of United Agents on behalf of the Estate of the late Adrian Mitchell.

Chapter opening illustrations by Andrea Dietrich; Introduction photo © *Daily Mail*/ Solo Syndication; Chapter 25 photo by Douglas Kirkland; Chapter 33 photo by Alexander Ruas; Chapter 35 photo by Kara Fox.

For Jim, without whom . . .

Clothes make the man.

Naked people have little or no influence in society.

—MARK TWAIN

Contents

CONTENTS

WEAR
AND TEAR

INTRODUCTION

Why Clothing?

My earliest clothing memory is my mother's silky, soft sealskin coat. I must have been about four or five. We were at a party. It was a grown-up party and I was the only kid. Bored, I wandered into a bedroom and saw an inviting pile of coats heaped on the bed. I climbed on top and immediately recognized my mother's coat. It smelled of her—a mixture of her perfume, Ma Griffe, and her cigarettes, unfiltered Pall Malls. The idea that my mother could be present in a piece of clothing where she otherwise was not was a revelation. I pulled the coat off the bed and wrapped myself up in it. The glossy brown fur had a velvety touch, like the baby rabbits that she had allowed me to pet at my friend's house. I spread the coat out on the floor and lay on top of it, luxuriating in the feel of the fur

1

against my bare legs and arms. The fur had a nap to it, becoming darker or lighter depending on which way I rubbed it. For a while I entertained myself by tracing patterns on the coat. Eventually I fell asleep. I was awakened by a group of adults whispering above me: "Shhh, don't wake her . . . isn't she adorable?"

I saw my mother bending toward me. "Come on, darling, it's time to go home."

"Can I wear your coat? Please," I begged, reluctant to leave my cozy nest.

"Don't be silly, it's way too big for you," my mother said as she handed me my scratchy blue wool coat, which I reluctantly put on. She slipped on her coat and held out her hand. I took it, nuzzling into her furry sleeve as we said our goodbyes and left the party, and even today, over fifty years later, whenever I think of my mother, I remember the touch, the feel, and the smell of her fur coat.

I think I was destined to be obsessed with clothing, genetically speaking. My middle name is Peacock—from my father's side of the family. (He was a bastard: His mother's name was Tynan, and his father's name was Peacock.) My father, Kenneth Peacock Tynan, was a writer and theater critic, but before he had ever published a single sentence, he was known for his unique style of dress. In 1945 he fled provincial Birmingham and arrived at Magdalen College in Oxford with trunks filled with outlandish clothing: a cape lined in blood-red satin and a suit of purple doeskin flannel. Later, the British theater critic Alan Brien spotted my father rushing around Oxford, wearing a bottle-green suit purportedly made from the baize that covers billiard tables. The writer Paul Johnson, in his book *Modern Times*, described my father as a "tall, beautiful, epicene youth, with pale yellow locks, Beardsley cheekbones, fashionable stammer, plum-colored suit, lavender tie and ruby signet-ring." Everyone noticed not only what my father said but also how he dressed.

My mother, the writer Elaine Dundy, was no slouch in the clothing department, either. She was a petite gamine with blond curly hair and a curvaceous figure well suited to the cinched-waist fashions of the times. Born in 1921, she spent her late twenties in Paris, and there she discovered that the fashion houses had sample sales where designer clothing could be bought for a fraction of its original cost. Her best friend, the writer Judy Feiffer, described how glamorous my mother looked in an off-the-shoulder orange-and-brown silk Schiaparelli dress, which she wore on her first date with my father in 1950.

Fifty years later, in my mother's memoir, *Life Itself*, she described what my father was wearing on that memorable first encounter at the Buckstone Club, in the heart of London's theater district: "A double breasted camel's hair jacket, plum colored trousers, yellow socks and black shoes, and a Mickey Mouse wrist watch." Impressed with each other's attire, their mutual passion for theater, and their strong attraction, they married three months later.

In 1957 the *Daily Mail* did a feature on my parents and their flat in London called "New Décor in a Victorian Flat." There is a photo of them, lounging on a faux-zebra-skin chaise longue, wearing matching faux-leopard-skin pants, white shirts, and string ties, gazing into each other's eyes. I was only five years old and probably oblivious of how outrageous their outfits must have appeared, but as I grew older, I became aware that they, particularly my father, dressed very differently from my friends' parents.

From an early age, I had firm ideas about my own clothing. Going shopping with my mother was frustrating for both of us because I always knew what I wanted and wouldn't settle for less. When I was fourteen, she abandoned the struggle and gave me a clothing allowance, and that was when my interest really took hold. I enjoyed the hunt, searching for the perfect piece that matched what I had envisioned. Unlike most of my friends in the early 1960s, I liked shopping. I liked exploring different stores, checking out various styles, and trying on assorted outfits. This was before the days of swinging London and Carnaby Street; there were no malls, just a handful of department stores and boutiques, and for most people, shopping was a chore. There was no "retail therapy," and the concept of "fashionista" did not exist. But for me, shopping for clothing was my art, my body was my canvas, and in those stores I could decide the shapes and colors through which I would express myself.

Trying on clothes gave me an opportunity, albeit briefly, to test out different identities. With the pull of a zipper or the buckle of a belt, I could change the way I looked: jeans and a jeans jacket and I became a tomboy; a short skirt and a tight top, I was a femme fatale. I could make myself look younger or older, ingénue or sophisticate, according to my mood or the situation.

My parents' work put them in contact with many famous people who became their friends. They were the center of a group of writers, actors, and directors that included Kingsley Amis, John Osborne, Laurence Olivier, Vivien Leigh, and Tony Richardson. Appearances were important. Not only were my parents' friends famous, many were glamorous, and they set a high bar, in my mind, for what I ought to be.

As a young girl, I was not particularly striking or beautiful, but I had a nice, well-proportioned body, and clothing (when I stood up straight) looked good on me. I had a knack for finding unique, inexpensive clothing. Friends would comment, "You look nice . . . that's a great shirt . . . where did you find it?" I was shy, and those words of praise eased my anxiety. Clothing offered me a way to be noticed and accepted.

After high school, I went to Sussex University and studied social anthropology. I quit in 1972, attempted to become a ceramicist, decided I wasn't cut out to sit in a studio making cups and saucers, returned to school, and finally graduated from Sarah Lawrence with a degree in liberal arts. I still had no idea what I wanted to be when I grew up. I dabbled in photography; I did the stills on a PBS film. I moved to Los Angeles, attended UCLA film school—where my aunt, filmmaker Shirley Clarke, was teaching—and made a short documentary about octogenarian ceramicist Beatrice Wood, who dressed in exotic Indian saris. Two years after that, in 1978, fascinated by the phenomenon of the Dallas Cowboy cheerleaders in their sexy blue and white outfits, I codirected and coproduced a documentary film about them called *A Great Bunch of Girls*. I wrote a couple of scripts, but nothing seemed to click. Then I married film director Jim McBride, and he gave me an opportunity to work on his film *Breathless*, and I discovered what had been staring me in the face all the time: I could make a living using my fascination with clothes.

I realized that costume design enabled me to combine many of my interests: I was part artist, part historian, part shrink, part nanny, and part accountant. I learned how to read a script, break it down, and imagine the world in which the characters lived. How old were they? Where did they come from? How much money did they earn? Where did they shop? Would this young man be flashy or understated? Did this young woman start life as an ugly duckling and emerge as a swan? Or vice versa? I collaborated with directors, cinematographers, and production designers, helping to create the look of the film. I worked with actors, helping them to interpret their roles, and gradually all those eclectic talents I had that hadn't seemed to gel came together. But it all started out with my childhood obsession with clothing.

CHAPTER 1

The Lemon-Yellow Underpants

Nineteen fifty-eight. I was six years old, standing on a cold London street outside my parents' flat, waiting for my father to let me in. In the car on the way back from the circus, my three friends and I were daring one another to do silly things—cross our eyes, burp, and stick our tongues out at strangers.

"When we get to my house, I'm going to do something really different," I announced in a loud whisper. I don't know why I suddenly had this idea—this desire to shock. I was usually a shy, quiet, unobtrusive girl who didn't do unusual things and was fairly obedient. Maybe inspired by watching the clowns drop their multicolored trousers at the circus, or maybe like the teetotaler who inexplicably takes a first sip of alcohol, I just wanted to test-drive a new, bolder personality.

7

"What are you going to do? C'mon, tell us!" Sarah demanded. She was the friend who always challenged me, while Julia rolled her eyes and silently disapproved.

"It's a secret," I said, pressing my finger to my lips, and I could see their eyes widening. They were waiting.

Standing outside my family's flat—a tall Victorian building in the posh Mayfair section of London—I rang the doorbell, turned, lifted my dress, pulled down my lemon-yellow frilly underpants, and mooned my friends. I could hear their shrieks of approval from the car as Sarah's mother quickly drove off.

Flushed with success, I turned around and saw my father standing in the doorway with a puzzled look on his long, narrow, handsome face.

"Tracy, what were you thinking?" he inquired, looking confused.

"It was a dare," I said sheepishly as I struggled to pull up my panties.

He shook his head in disbelief. "You can't go around pulling down your panties in the streets of London. What's gotten into you?"

"I don't know," I mumbled. "It seemed like fun."

"I think we need to have a talk," said my father as we took the circular elevator up to our flat. I sensed my father's disapproval. He was tapping his foot. But I didn't know what to expect. We didn't spend much time alone with each other. He was usually working or out.

I sat in an armchair in the large high-ceilinged living room, facing my father, who sat on a faux-zebra-skin chaise longue. Behind him, a huge twelve-foot black-and-white reproduction of Hieronymus Bosch's *Garden of Earthly Delights* covered the entire wall. The painting swam with naked and partially clothed people doing all sorts of peculiar things—men and women climbing in and out of egglike structures, entwined in weird ways, legs and arms akimbo. The painting had always frightened me. I tried to avoid looking at it too closely, but no matter how hard I tried to look elsewhere—the bullfight prints on the adjacent wall weren't exactly soothing—it always drew me in. I watched my father take a cigarette out of his blue and white box of Player's Navy Cuts, with the picture of a jolly-looking bearded sailor framed by a life preserver. He lit up and I smelled the familiar odor. He held his cigarette between the third and fourth fingers of his right hand—an affectation he claimed to have invented so that he could smoke and write at the same time. Later, when I read *Persona Grata,* the book he wrote with photographs by Cecil Beaton, I discovered that he might have appropriated the pose from a famous British impresario with the improbable name of Binky Beaumont.

"Sex is a wonderful thing," said my father expansively as he crossed and uncrossed his long, elegant legs. I stared determinedly at my black patent-leather Mary Janes and white ankle socks with lace trim as I swung my legs back and forth, just missing scuffing the floor with each swing.

"Are you listening?" demanded my father.

Not really, I thought. I didn't know what sex was, but whatever it was, I was sure I didn't want to know. It felt scary and inappropriate, like I was being thrown into the pool without learning to swim first. Besides, I was uncomfortable: My lemon-yellow underpants were new and scratchy. They'd been a birthday present. On my actual birthday, two months ago in May, my parents had been away in Spain watching bullfights. When they returned, my mother presented me with a large white box. Inside, covered in tissue paper, were two pairs of elaborate frilly underpants, one yellow and one orange. "Aren't they great?" my mother asked, impatiently running her hands through her short, curly blond hair. I smiled, trying to show her I was pleased, but I was disappointed. I wanted a stuffed animal or a doll. This was the first time I had worn them, and now I was in trouble. I decided I would never wear the other pair. I would hide them at the bottom of my toy chest.

"Can I go now?" I asked my father.

"I'm talking to you," he said, and he leaned forward. "Where do you need to go?"

"I have to pee," I cried as I ran out of the living room, down the gray linoleum-covered curved corridor, and past my parents' bedroom. I skidded into the bathroom, pulled down my underpants, sat down on the cool toilet seat, and felt a huge surge of relief as the stream of warm urine hit the bowl. Staring at the underpants around my ankles, I carefully lifted my legs out of them, leaving two holes. Crumpled on the beige carpet, the yellow underpants with their white frills reminded me of fried eggs. I didn't like fried eggs—the runny yolks contaminated everything else on the plate, and now these yellow underpants had made my father angry with me and contaminated his affection for me.

I heard my father calling my name from the hallway. "Tracy, where are you? Come out here right now!" I lifted the underpants, tossed them into the toilet, and flushed. I didn't answer. I didn't want to talk to him. I didn't want to hear what he had to say about sex or anything else. I wanted parents who weren't always going away or going out. Parents who did things with their children, like Sarah's parents. Parents who didn't leave me to celebrate my birthday with au pair girls who did their best—Barbara, the current one, had bought a small sponge cake from the local bakery and put candles on it, which I blew out, forgetting to make a wish, but it wasn't quite the same.

Finally, my father walked away, and I stayed in my room until Barbara called me for dinner.

After that aborted effort, neither my father nor my mother ever attempted to offer me any information about sex. The man who wrote about avant-garde theater, who would be the creator of the sex revue *Oh! Calcutta!*, who could hold a roomful of celebrities rapt with his stories about outrageous strip clubs in Hamburg where women blew smoke rings out of their vaginas, never talked to his own daughter about sex. And I never asked.

CHAPTER 2

My Mother's Fur Coat

As theater critic for *The London Observer,* my father saw every play that came out in London or nearby, and if they had no play to see, my parents always had a party or a dinner to attend. That meant they needed live-in babysitters to take care of me, so from the time I was a baby, I was looked after by a string of au pairs who quickly became my friends and allies, more like older sisters than conventional nannies. But sometimes I felt as if I were the older sibling.

The first au pair I remember was Dolly. I was three years old. She was a petite, blond Italian with almond-shaped brown eyes, and when I was four, I went with her to meet her family in Venice. I returned with a huge blond doll bought at a local market, and I promptly named her

Dolly. A few months later Dolly left, and Dolly the doll was my transitional object until the new au pair arrived. Her name was Barbara, and she came from Stuttgart, Germany. She had curly dark brown hair that she wore short with bangs, and unlike Dolly, who was reserved, Barbara was soft and gentle. I adored her.

Barbara took me to Stuttgart to visit her mother, who lived in a dark formal flat. For breakfast Barbara's mother prepared me a huge slice of pumpernickel bread with a thick wedge of unsalted butter on top. The sight and smell nauseated me, but I did not want to offend her, so I took a few bites, then rushed into the bathroom and spat them out. On my third visit to the bathroom, Barbara figured out what was going on and convinced her mother to feed me something else.

On the day Barbara was leaving us, we took photos. She and I sat beside each other on the zebra-skin chaise in the living room. I wore a pudding-bowl haircut and was dressed in my blue-checked kindergarten school uniform. In one photo, I am kissing her cheek; in another, I am valiantly attempting a smile, trying to cover up my sadness at her impending departure. These departures were hard for me to process. I felt I had no control over when one au pair left and another came to take her place. My parents tried to reassure me that everything would be the same: To them the au pairs were interchangeable, but to me they were very different. Each departure was a small heartbreak, and each new person meant going through the process of falling in love only to have her disappear again.

Christina, an older spinsterish Italian woman, came to take Barbara's place, but she couldn't do that. She smelled of the olive oil she used to condition her long black hair, which she pulled tightly into a bun, and she wasn't warm and cuddly, like Barbara. Still, Christina was kind to me. She was a devoted Catholic, and I loved going to church with her. It was back in the late fifties when Mass was still in Latin. I couldn't understand a thing they were saying, but the strange sounds and the musty smell of incense created an atmosphere that, with my atheist background, I found very exotic, particularly since there was never any mention of religion in my family. Christina cooked delicious food with olive oil; I specially adored her french fries. I still have a small round scar on the top of my right hand from hot oil that splashed on my hand as I reached out to grab one of her tasty fries.

I never visited her family in Italy, but after she left us, I did go to see her in a dingy bed-sitter in Earls Court, where she was eking out a living as a seamstress. She kept in touch with me and sometimes, when my parents were out of town, I would stay with her. She served me instant Nescafé, diluted with lots of warm milk, and toast.

When I was seven or eight, I often sneaked into my mother's closet to look for her fur coat. If I was lucky and she hadn't worn it that night, I would pull it down from the pink satin hanger and take it back to my bedroom. I would spread it on top of my bed and curl up inside it. Though my mother told me it was sealskin, it bore no relationship to the wet shiny seals that I saw flapping and barking when Christina took me to the zoo. Nor was it like the seal perched on the headboard in the Thurber cartoon book that my parents had given me, which I had used as a coloring book, not keeping inside the lines.

My mother's fur coat had been given to her by her mother, my grandmother, Florence Brimberg. Florence, a plump, good-natured woman whom I occasionally visited in New York, liked to wear fur and to give her daughters and granddaughters furs. Aunt Shirley, Aunt Betty, and cousin Wendy all had fur coats, thanks to Florence's largesse.

One night I fell asleep on top of my mother's coat and was awakened by the sound of my parents yelling and screaming. This night the screaming was followed by a clatter of feet running down the corridor. My bedroom door was flung open, and there, bathed in hallway light, stood my mother, naked and flailing her arms. "Your father's trying to kill me!" she screamed. My mother had never before said these words, but they barely registered: I was too busy staring at her body, transfixed by the contrast between the blond hair on her head and her triangle of dark pubic hair. How was it possible that she had such startlingly different shades of hair?

A moment later my father, dressed in a suit, appeared behind her. He put his hand on her shoulder and said very calmly, "C'mon, Elaine, you're disturbing Tracy." He tried to steer her out of my doorway, but she jerked away from his touch and repeated, "He's going to kill me, he's going to kill me." I just lay there, unable to move or say a word, trying to disguise the coat beneath me, worried that my mother might be angry if she discovered I was sleeping on it.

After a few minutes of prodding, my father managed to usher her away. I huddled there, wide awake, listening as their argument continued, punctuated by the sounds of crockery breaking. I wondered if I ought to get up and give her the coat. Why had she been naked? Did she need the coat? And why, I wondered, was she afraid of my father, who was so calm? The questions whirled in my head until at last their argument subsided and I fell asleep. The next day no one, including Christina, mentioned the nighttime activities.

Another night after their screaming and shouting woke me, I ventured out of my bedroom and climbed up a small flight of stairs that led to a long corridor separating my bedroom from theirs. Along one side were windows that looked out on an inner courtyard. On either side of the windows was a collection of bullfighting prints, lurid reproductions of brightly costumed matadors waving crimson capes and stabbing bulls. Ignoring them, I peered across the courtyard and saw my partially clothed father—white jockey shorts and an unbuttoned pale blue shirt—perched on their bedroom window ledge. With his long legs dangling and his arms flapping, he looked like some strange kind of bird about to take off. "I'm going to jump!" he screamed. "I'm going to jump!"

Then I saw my mother, naked, smoking a cigarette, moving through the room behind him. "Why don't you? Why the fuck don't you?" she said coldly as she turned away and climbed into their bed. I was shocked—why was my mother being so mean to my father? I felt badly for him.

My father, looking dejected, his body slumped, remained on the ledge. I stood still, unable to move, terrified, but not knowing what to do. Finally, I turned back to my room, jumped into bed, and buried myself under the sealskin coat I had purloined once again. I clung to my favorite teddy bear and waited until the yelling subsided and I could let myself fall asleep.

The next morning I woke up early and tiptoed along the corridor to their bedroom. I cautiously opened the door. The room reeked of stale cigarette smoke and alcohol. I peeked in and saw both of them lying fast asleep on either side of the bed, not touching. Relieved, I ran back to my bedroom, pulled the fur coat off my bed, dragged it up the stairs and along the corridor, and deposited it in a heap in front of my parents' room and ran back to my room. I gathered my small collection of stuffed animals and dolls and brought them into bed with me. I lay there wide awake, hugging them close to me, and after a few minutes I heard the clattering of pots and pans in the kitchen and realized that Christina was starting to make breakfast. I ran into the kitchen and stood by her as she stirred the oatmeal and stroked my hair.

"Go on, get dressed," she said. "You don't want to be late for school."

I never again borrowed my mother's fur coat, but that moment marked a change in me. I realized for the first time my own fascination with my parents' behavior—watching them was like watching a horror movie, scary but riveting. Without understanding the word, I had become a voyeur, mesmerized by my parents' dramas. As I grew up, I was attracted to drama outside of my home, too. And when it wasn't around, life seemed to be drained of color, to turn to black and white, ordinary, dull.

CHAPTER 3

The Pearl Necklace

As a thank-you from the guests of honor for the big bash my parents had thrown the night before, I was getting a cat. Not just any cat, a special cat. A Russian blue. Richard—Dick, as we called him—Avedon was going to pick me up at nine in the morning and take me to a small town outside of London where a lady bred Russian blues. It didn't have to be a Russian blue. I would've been happy with any kind of kitten—ginger, tabby, or calico—as long as it was small and fluffy. Dick had insisted on a Russian blue, claiming to my parents that they had a reputation for being very affectionate and good with children. He had signed my navy blue quilted autograph book with his initials and a caricature of a face with the word "boo" coming out of the mouth. The drawing was a quirk I immediately made part of my own signature for many years.

I was excited at the prospect of the special car ride, to the special place, to get a special cat. For the first time in my eight years, I was in charge. I was going to be able to select the kitten of my choice. I loved cats. My father loved cats. My mother was indifferent. Some families are dog families; we were a cat family—the kind of people who, when seeing a cat out on the street, started making mewing noises to attract its attention so we could pet it. I have pictures of me as a four-year-old, clutching a small tabby kitten and grinning happily, though the kitten looks as if it is struggling to escape my clutches. Unfortunately, when we went to live in New York City so my father could be the theater critic for *The New Yorker*, we had to give that cat away.

We lived in New York for two years, and we had been back in London for only a few months, but I had been pestering my parents for another cat, and my dream was about to come true. My parents had let me stay up late the night before for the big party. Our small flat had been crammed with people smoking and drinking. Everyone seemed to be shouting, struggling to be heard above the din of the music and hilarity. Chubby Checker was playing on the stereo. A tall, skinny friend of my parents, Tom, was teaching everybody how to twist. "It's like stubbing a cigarette out with one foot and drying your back with a towel at the same time," he said as he demonstrated the technique. I had fun imitating him, wriggling across the dance floor, trying to keep time to the music.

The party was in honor of Dick and his best friend, Broadway director and comedian Mike Nichols. They had just flown in from New York. Dick was in London on a fashion assignment, and Mike to plan his next production. One month earlier, just after we'd moved back, my parents had flown to New York as a surprise for Mike's birthday. They were smuggled inside a cardboard cake into a restaurant where the party was being held, and "just like in a gangster movie," my father told me, "we jumped out of the cake." I didn't know what gangster movies were, but it sounded like fun to surprise my friends and jump out of a cake.

Early in the evening, Sally Belfrage, my mother's best friend, had attached herself to Mike. Sally was a natural blonde with translucent skin and a curvaceous figure, and admirers always surrounded her. I didn't know it then, but she was an acclaimed writer and journalist whose parents had been deported from Hollywood for being alleged Communists. She had published her first book, about living in Moscow, when she was barely twenty-one, and in her twenties and early thirties, she wrote books about the civil rights movement in the States and "The Troubles" in Northern Ireland. Later that night, Sally and Mike seemed very friendly: I saw her sitting on his lap and laughing.

I wandered around the party, catching snatches of conversation— "Hated the third act . . . Of course, she's a bit long in the tooth for the part . . . He wrote the play just for her . . . It was only up for a week." I didn't entirely grasp the meaning of those conversations, but that didn't matter, because I was caught up in the excitement of the evening, sipping from my glass of Coke, sucking on the ice cubes, trying to make them last as long as I possibly could. There were no other children at the party, but I didn't care. I felt like I was watching a play, with the grown-ups as the stars. The women were dressed in shiny dresses or pencil-slim skirts with thick belts that accentuated their waists and busts; the men were in boxy suits, crisp white shirts, their ties undone and their jackets off.

A year earlier, while we were living in New York and attending another grown-up party, my mother was complaining to Dede—a former ballet dancer with a neck like a swan's and hair pulled into a tight chignon—about how often I got carsick. Dede was so taken by my plight that she removed her necklace, a gold chain with a single pearl pendant, and handed it to me, saying, "Here, honey. Suck on this next time you feel sick. It'll make you feel better."

Now, at my parents' party, I was wearing that pearl. In fact, I always wore it. I liked the way it felt as I rolled it between my tongue and the roof of my mouth; it had helped me many times when I'd felt carsick. I was sucking on that pearl when I noticed a lull in the music and heard Sally's distinctive voice shrieking, "Oh my God, it's all false," followed by a stunned silence. I could hear every ice cube clinking in every glass. I looked around the room and saw my mother leading Sally out of the room and Mike being escorted by my father in the opposite direction. Unseen, I followed my mother to the bedroom, where I saw her sitting on the bed next to a weeping, inconsolable Sally.

"I am so sorry," Sally said. "I feel terrible. It was such a shock . . . A trick of the lighting . . . I am so ashamed."

My mother offered Sally a pink tissue from a box by the bed. "We should have warned you," my mother said, "a childhood disease left him without a hair on his entire body."

"How awful," said Sally between sobs. Listening closely, I learned that she had touched Mike's hair while they were dancing, and it had moved. That was how she discovered he was wearing a wig.

I didn't know that Mike wore a wig. Since I wasn't aware of any of my parents' friends wearing wigs, I was just as shocked as Sally. I sneaked away before my mother discovered me eavesdropping.

Later, I saw my father and Mike standing at the front door. The director was hugging my father. "Great party, what an introduction to London. But I've got to get up early tomorrow . . ."

"Of course, I completely understand," said my father as he opened the door and let Mike out.

I stood there trying to process all this new information. I had met Mike many times, and I couldn't understand what my mother had meant by the childhood disease she'd described. I was a child, and I often got sick, so I began to wonder if this could happen to me. Would I lose my hair, too? I tugged on my hair to make sure it was still attached, and I wandered back into the party to get another Coke. Just as I was pouring it, my mother found me. "Time to go to bed, it's way past your bedtime," she said. "Tomorrow morning Dick's going to take you to get a cat." I let out a yelp of excitement, and my mother smiled. "You and your cats," she said, and shooed me off to bed.

Early the next morning, while my parents were still asleep, I walked around the flat. The acrid smell of stale cigarette smoke and alcohol seemed to be levitating from discarded glasses and ashtrays, and when I remembered the conversation about the fake hair, I felt a wave of nausea but quickly suppressed it by sucking on my pearl. I couldn't get sick. I did not want to do anything that might jeopardize the cat expedition.

Promptly at nine, the doorbell rang. I answered it, and there stood Dick. He and I agreed not to wake my parents, and off we went. Downstairs a car and driver were waiting for us. I climbed into the backseat of the plush Jaguar and inhaled the distinctive leather scent that seemed to exist only in cars. As we sped down the M1 highway, I sucked on my pearl.

The last time I had been in a limo, I was seven years old. It was after seeing *Peter Pan* with my mother in New York. It was a stretch limo, and I was sitting on a little fold-up seat opposite Mary Martin. We were on our way to dinner. I couldn't stop staring at this person who had so recently been a boy dressed in green and flying through the air and had somehow transformed into an elegant woman wearing a silver-sequined gown and a mink stole. Maybe it was from staring too intently, or maybe it was from sitting backward in the car, but I was suddenly overwhelmed by nausea. The Shirley Temple and salty peanuts I had so greedily consumed during intermission were coming back to haunt me, and as I felt the bile rising up my throat, I tried desperately to aim for the floor. The driver came to a sudden stop, and I wound up vomiting all over Mary Martin's lap. Handkerchiefs were quickly dispersed from all the evening bags. There was a brief discussion about whether it was better to use club soda or still water for removing stains—both were available in a little cabinet in the limo—and club soda was deemed more effective. After her initial shock, Mary Martin was gracious, but she insisted that for the rest of the ride I sit up front with the driver, next to an open window.

Sitting in the limo with Dick Avedon this time, I remembered that embarrassing moment and diligently sucked on my pearl pendant. I opened the window a crack and let the wind rush in as we whizzed past miles and miles of dreary semi-detached houses that became a gray blur indistinguishable from the gray sky. Dick talked lovingly about his son, Johnny, who was almost the same age I was.

Just as I began to feel I might not make it, we arrived at the cat breeder's house. Even before the driver had time to open the door, I opened it and jumped out, eager to be back on terra firma.

The breeder lived in a small redbrick house. It smelled faintly of cat pee and musk. An elderly woman greeted us at the door and led us into a parlor where three gray kittens and a mother cat were curled up in a basket. I was entranced and a little panicked; how could I possibly make a choice? I sat down on the rug and started to play with the kittens. They all looked identical—fluffy blue-gray creatures with blue eyes. One of the kittens seemed reluctant to play; he hung back from the other two. I ran my fingers up and down the rug until he finally took the bait and pounced on my hand. I quickly scooped him up and placed him on my lap. As I stroked him, he started to purr and dig his paws into my skirt. I felt his claws scraping the skin under my skirt, but the sensation was oddly pleasurable.

After a few minutes I looked up. "This is the one I want," I announced.

"Good choice," said the woman. "I like him, too."

"What are you going to call him?" asked Dick.

I thought for a moment as I looked down at the kitten's rhythmically pulsating paws. "Greytoes," I said as I kissed him lightly on the furry space between his ears.

Soon we were back in the car with the kitten ensconced in a metal carrier, speeding back to the city and my parents' flat, uninterrupted except by the occasional mewing noises as the kitten strained to push its paws through the grille of the carrier. I felt deeply grateful to Dick, but it was another four years before I discovered that the man who had made me so happy that day was someone famous.

In 1964, when I was twelve, just before my mother's second novel, *The Old Man and Me*, was to be published, she asked Dick to take her portrait for the book jacket. He took a glamorous photo of her in his studio in New York. It was a three-quarter profile showcasing her elegant neck and her pert nose. Her hand and little finger were coquettishly poised on her lips. The photograph was beautifully lit. Her skin looked flawless, smooth as a statue's. It was flattering, and she liked it. She had it framed and prominently displayed, and friends who came to visit told her they were impressed that she had an "Avedon portrait." Though I still felt affection toward the nice man who had bought me a cat, I never thought that photo looked like her.

I had the pearl necklace for many years, but when I was fourteen, I left it in a bag in a New York cab along with the entire summer's worth of money I had made babysitting. I was devastated. I now have another pearl necklace that a friend made for me; I wear it every day. And I still get carsick.

CHAPTER 4

The Pale Blue Chemise

Soon after Greytoes became part of our household, I suffered my first case of severe dress envy. My best friend, Janet Wolfson, had a pale blue low-waisted dress that her mother had brought back from a trip to Paris. The minute I saw it, I coveted it. It seemed perfect—robin's-egg blue with a white Peter Pan collar, buttons down the front, and a short pleated skirt attached with a sash. "It's called a chemise, it's French," said Janet proudly as she twirled around her bedroom. And as she spun, the skirt flew up. I wanted that dress like I had never wanted anything.

Janet, a freckled, slightly chubby girl with mischievous hazel eyes, came from a wealthy family and lived in a grand flat off Portland Place, complete with a nanny and servants. Rather than a series of ever chang-

25

ing au pairs like I had, she had a nanny who not only had been with them forever, she had also been Janet's father's nanny. Janet's mother was a tall, dark-eyed beauty with shiny black, perfectly teased hair styled into a chin-length bob. Her father, whom Janet more closely resembled, was a fair-skinned, rotund man who claimed to be overwhelmed by all the women in his family—Janet had a younger sister, Laura—although he was clearly in charge. He was a businessman who wore a bowler hat and worked in the city. I loved going to their flat; it was done up in soft beiges and pale blue damask wallpaper, with comfortable sofas and armchairs and plush carpeting. Everything seemed calm and organized, unlike our chaotic house.

I lived in a flat with my often irritable, unpredictable mother and my nervous, chain-smoking father who was forever struggling to meet writing deadlines. We never ate dinner, or any meal, together. I don't have a single memory of sitting down to dinner alone with my parents. My mother did not cook. The only food I remember her making was a boiled egg and toast. Very occasionally we ate together at restaurants, but these were usually large social occasions where I just happened to be included. Most of the time I ate alone or with the au pair, who probably would've preferred to be out with friends her own age.

When my mother and father were home, they were often fighting. Years later, Sally Belfrage described a typical scene at my house: "[I would] arrive at the door of the Mount Street apartment where the locks had usually been changed by one or other of the Tynans . . . ring the bell, sounds of screams and smashing crockery and tiny Tracy opening the door, trying to find out which lock was working. Ken shouting, 'I'll kill you, you bitch.' Smash, smash, a whimper from the au pair, and Tracy, poised and calm, saying, 'Hello, how nice to see you. Come in. Can I take your coat?' And taking one into the living room, and pouring drinks and sitting down, looking very interested."

Most of the time I was scared and confused and felt I was in a movie with lots of crazy people. I believed I was supposed to play the normal one, particularly since there was no other role available. I welcomed the compliments from my parents' friends, who always told me how well behaved and grown up I was. I was proud of my performance, too, and derived a certain satisfaction in playing my role to the hilt.

One night I was at home with the Norwegian au pair, Martha, and her boyfriend, Dave. We were watching TV in the dining room, a dark room filled with books and walls covered in black faux-marble wallpaper. There was a black lacquer dining room table and chairs, but I don't remember ever eating there; the au pairs and I always ate in the kitchen. There was a sofa in the dining room, where we occasionally watched TV.

That night we were watching *A Night at the Opera*. Dave was imitating Groucho, twirling an imaginary cigar between his fingers, shrugging his eyebrows, and rolling his eyes. Martha and I laughed at the real Groucho and then at Dave's version. Suddenly our fun was interrupted by a loud "Fuck!" We spun around. There was my mother, completely naked, clutching a bottle of champagne she was trying to pour into a glass and kept spilling. She stood in the doorway, gently swaying. Speechless, we stared at her as she slowly emptied the rest of the champagne bottle into her glass. I stared at the foam spilling down the side and watched her take a sip. I worried that she would stay there all night, and I held my breath, willing her to leave or, if she didn't, that the floor would split open and swallow her up.

After what seemed like an eternity, I heard Martha saying in her singsong matter-of-fact voice, as if talking to a child, "Don't you think you ought to put some clothes on, Mrs. Tynan? Aren't you getting cold?" I noticed the movie flickering in the background and waited another excruciatingly long pause before my mother turned, stumbled on the rug, and staggered off toward her bedroom. As soon as I heard the bedroom door slam, I let out a gush of air. Dave burst out laughing, but Martha told him to shut up, and I felt bad for him. As mortified as I was, I understood that someone not related to my mother might find the situation funny. We didn't say another word about it. Instead, in silence, we continued watching the movie, though the Marx Brothers' delirious antics no longer seemed quite so amusing.

On Friday nights Janet's parents celebrated Shabbat, and sometimes they invited me to join them. Theirs was a large family affair with grandparents, aunts, uncles, and cousins, another novelty for me, since I rarely saw my relatives. My mother's family, her parents and two sisters, lived in New York City, and my father was an only child whose father was dead. We seldom saw his mother, my grandmother, as she lived in Birmingham. I think my father was ashamed of his "provincial" mum.

Janet's family was not seriously religious, but they included some ritual at their Friday-night dinners. Her parents encouraged Janet to say the prayers in Hebrew as she lit the candles. Her faltering rendition of "Baruch Atah Adonai, Eloheinu Melech ha'olam" sounded mysterious and alien to my untrained ears.

I didn't learn that my own mother was Jewish until I was in my teens, and even then nobody actually sat me down and said, "You're Jewish." As with many things in my family, the information filtered through in bits and pieces. The invitation to my cousin Johnny's bar mitzvah when I was twelve was one big clue. Another was my American grandmother saying that she wished that I were around during the holidays, which turned out to be neither Christmas nor New Year's but Hanukkah and Rosh Hashanah. I think it was my eldest cousin, Wendy, who explained to me the then rather astonishing fact that Judaism is matrilineal, passed on through the female members of the family. I decided at that moment that I was proud to be a Jewish woman. It seemed exotic. Yet I never discussed what being Jewish meant with my mother; nor did I stop celebrating Christmas and start celebrating the Jewish holidays.

Back then I was only the daughter of atheists and seriously longing for a dress like Janet's. A few weeks after I first saw it, my parents announced that they were going to Paris, and I was beside myself with excitement. "Please," I begged my mother, "buy me a chemise." I gave her explicit instructions. "It's blue and it has a collar and the skirt comes to here," I said, pointing to six inches above my knobby knees. I drew her a little diagram.

A few days later, my mother called from Paris. She sounded excited. "Darling," she said, "I found your dress."

"My chemise," I corrected her.

"You'll love it—it's just how you described it," she enthused.

I immediately rang Janet and told her the exciting news, but to my dismay, rather than expressing her joy, Janet said testily, "You're copying me?"

I was crushed. I'd thought that by emulating her, I was paying her a compliment. Inexplicably, my plan had backfired, and now she was cross with me.

"I promise I'll never wear it at the same time as you," I said.

"You better not," she said. "I'm wearing mine to Angela's birthday party next week."

My desire for her dress had been so great that I had not taken into account the fact that for nine-year-olds, imitation is not the highest form of flattery. Maybe imitation never is. Even years later, in adulthood, when friends ask me where they can buy a piece of clothing I am wearing, I am initially flattered, but after revealing the information, I feel a moment of anxiety, realizing I will never again be quite so unique.

My parents returned from Paris with the dress, and it was beautiful and similar to Janet's, but by then I wasn't so sure I wanted it. As I opened the box, I couldn't hide my disappointment.

"What's the matter?" my mother asked.

"Well, it's different. I mean, it's not exactly like Janet's."

"But that's good," said my mother. "You don't want to be exactly like Janet, do you?"

I shook my head, but I felt yes, and I realized too late that I did want to be exactly like Janet. I wanted to live in her flat with her family and wear *her* pale blue chemise to a dinner populated by adoring aunts and uncles.

My mother insisted I try it on. It fit me perfectly.

"I've been thinking," my mother said as I modeled the dress, "it would be nice if you curtsied when you were introduced to people."

I took a moment to absorb this information. I hadn't noticed my friends curtsying, but then maybe they didn't meet a lot of new people, or maybe they didn't meet as many prominent people as I did. Our flat welcomed a constant parade of famous actors, writers, directors, and musicians. I knew these people were important because my parents made sure I knew. "Orson, a very famous director, is coming to the flat today," my father would announce. "Larry Olivier is coming over for a drink," he might tell me, barely containing his excitement, stuttering as he often did when excited. "Marlene said she might stop by," my mother would add proudly.

For many years I knew only that these people were essential to my parents and somehow connected to their work, though I didn't understand precisely how or why. I now realize that my parents were the original celebrity hounds. They relentlessly and unabashedly pursued famous people. Often I heard them on the phone, quizzing their friends about who would be at a certain party or an event, and I watched silently as they changed their plans, rearranging schedules to make sure they were attending the same event as someone they deemed important. I didn't grasp it then, but now I see that their celebrity seeking was a contact sport. They thought that if they were around famous people, they, too, would become famous. They had valid reasons for pursuing these people; my father's livelihood as a critic and a journalist depended on meeting, knowing, and writing about them. But their obsession with celebrity seemed less practical and more like an addiction, a need to fill some bottomless hole in their psyches.

Later, I learned that other people saw this, too. Sally Belfrage's description of a typical day with my parents confirmed what I had suspected: "Meet Elaine in the late morning at the French Club or the Colony, drinking, drinking, drinking, picking up people and discarding them. They would go back to Mount Street late in the afternoon and then go out to dinner with Ken until 3 or 4 in the morning. It would take me about a week to rest up. But Ken and Elaine were at it again the next day. There was this frenzied feverish activity all the time, and there was never any pause to allow anyone to think or reflect what it was about. The essential thing was to keep moving in as many crowds of amusing people as possible."

What I was fully aware of from the earliest days was that my parents lived on an entirely different schedule from mine. They were usually asleep when I woke up to go to school, and when I came home, they were either out or working. Sometimes our lives intersected for a brief moment while I was having my tea (early dinner), but they always went out again. They never stayed home to hang out and enjoy the kind of simple pleasures I saw my friends' families enjoying—playing games, taking walks, going on picnics. They equated ordinary with boring, and boredom was to be avoided at all costs.

My mother's curtsy request puzzled me. I knew people were expected to curtsy to royalty, so I reasoned that these celebrities who orbited around my parents must be royalty, worthy of curtsies.

"Give it a try," my mother encouraged me as she held out her hand for me to shake. I took her hand and curtsied. "Oh, you look so adorable," she cooed. For the next few months, whenever I met a new friend of my parents', I curtsied.

And then one day Janet was at our house and a new visitor came to the door. I was wearing my blue chemise, and when I curtsied, Janet could barely suppress her giggle. I saw her out of the corner of my eye, and I wondered what she found so funny. Later, when we were in my room and safe from the adults' prying eyes, she said, "That was so weird. Why did you curtsy? Who was that man?"

"A writer friend of my parents'," I mumbled. "His name's John Osborne."

"He isn't royalty, y'know," Janet said.

"I know," I said defensively. "My mother thinks it's polite."

"That's weird," she repeated, and I vowed to myself that I would never curtsy again.

To my relief, when I was next introduced to a guest and I didn't curtsy, my mother didn't seem to notice. As so often happened with my mother's edicts, she quickly forgot.

A month later, I wore my blue chemise to a matinee with my mother, but after that it hung in my closet, forlorn and unused. Sometimes I eyed it guiltily. I wanted to wear it, but I couldn't. It had become a symbol of so many things that were wrong in my life—my lack of originality, a threatened friendship, and my mother's "weird" demands. Eventually I grew out of it, and my mother gave it to the cleaning lady to give to her daughter. I breathed a sigh of relief when it was gone.

But it was that dress that taught me the power of clothing. Like most people, I can have a happy experience wearing an item of clothing and want to wear it over and over again; if I have an unhappy experience, I struggle to wear it ever again. Bad dates, arguments, failed job interviews—they can't be blamed on a piece of clothing, but sometimes I can't help myself, and sometimes I blame that blue chemise.

WEAR AND TEAR

I have a forties dress that I wore on the first date with my husband and a plaid shirt a good friend gave me, and both of these I am sure I will keep long after they become threadbare. I have a beautiful brown velvet dress that I wore to a friend's funeral, and I will probably never wear it again, like the blue chemise. I don't throw it out. I keep thinking, much as I thought for years when I looked at the chemise, if I keep it long enough, one day the curse will be lifted, and I'll wear it once again.

CHAPTER 5

School Uniforms:
Purple, Blue, and None

In the late fifties, during my father's stint as drama critic for *The New Yorker*, the city suffered two unusually dreary theater seasons. Often plays closed before my father had a chance to review them. The nights off gave my parents more opportunities to collect unusual and entertaining celebrities. While I stayed with the au pair, a young German woman named Gertrude, in our Upper East Side apartment around the corner from the Guggenheim Museum, they went to parties nonstop and hung out with the movie/Broadway crowd—Sidney Lumet and Gloria Vanderbilt, George and Joan Axelrod, Lennie and Felicia Bernstein, Betty Comden and Adolph Green—and the entire staff of *The Paris Review*, including George Plimpton, Norman Mailer, and Bill Styron.

My mother loved being back in New York. The way she put it in her memoir was succinct: "Everything is so lively and great and it's open all night."

Meanwhile, performances at home outdid anything on Broadway, and as an only child, I was a captive audience. The slightest thing could set either or both of them off—a misplaced shirt, a lost phone number. As my father wrote in his diary, "a small frown could make us savagely resentful and a small smile could dissolve us into fits of delighted tears."

I witnessed their savagery more than their delighted tears, but there was something almost comical about the determined way that they fought: oblivious to whoever happened to be around. One day they started fighting in the living room—I was sitting there, minding my own business, trying to read a book—and while they were looking for things to throw, they noticed a maid trying to ease her way into the room so she could clean. Without missing a beat, they moved the battle down the hall and into the bedroom, where the maid had just finished cleaning. In the bedroom they began to hurl ashtrays and books at each other, and from my perch in the living room, I watched as if it were a tennis match. When they had exhausted themselves, my father stormed out of the apartment, slamming the door behind him. My mother turned to me and said, "What did you think of that?"

"You've had that one before," I coolly answered, trying to give the appearance of a blasé bystander.

Those two years passed in a haze of melodrama. A friend of my mother's, the writer Judy Feiffer, told me about my mother arriving at her apartment late at night, her dress covered in spaghetti. "What happened?" Judy inquired. My mother said, "Ken and I disagreed about a play." Judy was understandably shocked but even more surprised that my mother had made no attempt to clean the food off her dress. "She wore it like a badge of honor," Judy said. "It was as though she wanted me to see the proof of what he'd done to her."

Fortunately, although I was shy, the social skills I had learned that helped me survive at home were useful for making new friends. And my friends became a way to escape my troubled home. At Brearley, the all-girls' school that I attended while we lived in New York, I met Susie Sanders. Susie was a petite redhead with an upturned nose. She had an impish quality, and we spent a lot of time giggling together. She and her parents soon became my adopted family, and I spent many hours at their nearby apartment. We played card games with her older sisters, Dee and Debbie, who were very kind to me and treated me like a younger sister. I liked hanging out with them, especially sleeping in the bunk bed, which was a novelty to me.

I was eight years old when we returned to London and our flat on Mount Street. My mother wanted me to go to the prestigious St. Paul's Girls' School, but I failed the entrance exam. They claimed that I was behind due to my American education. I was disappointed, more because I felt I had let my mother down than because I wanted to go to St. Paul's. They suggested that I go to another school, catch up, and then reapply. This pleased my mother, and I felt I had received an educational and parental reprieve.

My mother chose Glendower Girls' School. It was nearby, and when they accepted me, I was relieved—I don't think they required an entrance exam. Glendower was located in a large redbrick Victorian building in Kensington. The outstanding feature, as far as I was concerned, was the deep purple uniform we girls wore. At the two previous schools I had attended in London and New York, we'd all worn the more traditional blue.

The trouble with school uniforms was that my mother, not wanting me to grow too quickly out of them, usually bought a size larger so that

I could "grow into it." Thus the hem had to be taken up or the waistband rolled. And in my previous schools, just when the uniform finally fit, I had to give it up for another too-large one.

Also, a complete uniform involved numerous elements. There was the winter uniform, with its scratchy wool pleated skirt, cotton shirt, tie, cardigan, blazer, and beret, each piece begging for an opportunity to be lost or misplaced. We started wearing the summer uniform on a certain arbitrary date, regardless of the weather (and in London, we rarely had summer weather during the school year). This consisted of a purple cotton check dress, a lightweight blazer, and a straw hat. We also had gym uniforms: voluminous shorts, white shirt, and black plimsolls (British sneakers). If you forgot any part of this ensemble, you risked not being allowed to participate in PE, and since Glendower did not have its own gym, we did our PE running around in a nearby park, freezing our asses off. I often forgot some part of my uniform on purpose, but after I tried this trick once too often, I got detention. Too many detentions resulted in lowered grades.

For the most part, I liked Glendower and its purple uniform. I particularly liked my teacher, Mrs. Nichols, a soft-spoken woman with light brown curly hair who was sympathetic and understanding and made history fun. Her description of the Tudors and Stuarts made their story sound like a racy novel, with lurid descriptions of the beheadings of Henry VIII's wives. At Glendower, I quickly managed to make it to the top of the class and felt pleased with myself. I would have been happy to remain there, but my mother had other plans. One day midway through the second term, I came home to find her waving a piece of paper in front of me.

"We just got the application for St. Paul's. The exam is in three weeks!" she exclaimed.

"But I just got a ninety-five on my history exam!" I said, showing her the yellow slip of paper with my test results, signed by Mrs. Nichols.

"That's wonderful, darling," she said, barely glancing at the mark, "but St. Paul's is a much better school."

"I don't want to go to St. Paul's," I said quietly. "I want to stay at Glendower."

"You're worried about the exam?" she asked.

"No, it's not that . . ."

"This time it will be different, you'll see," she insisted. When my mother insisted, I usually fell silent. As I did that day.

She had read in a magazine that it was possible to hypnotize someone into doing better on tests, so for two weeks prior to the exam, while I read aloud from a textbook, she droned on in a monotone, repeating key phrases: "You will do better this time . . . You will be more confident . . . In fact, when you come out of the exam you will say 'That was quite fun.'" Though I felt kind of silly doing this, it never crossed my mind to refuse.

I have no memory of the actual exam except sitting in a large hall and managing to finish it. According to my mother, when she came to pick me up, I turned to her and said, "That was quite fun." A month later, I received the exam results: I had been accepted into St. Paul's. My mother was ecstatic. She was convinced her hypnosis had paid off.

St. Paul's had a boring blue uniform. Instead of the snappy beret, we had to wear a blue felt bowler hat that always seemed to be flying off my head unless it was secured under the chin with an elastic band, which was uncomfortable and, more important, uncool. The other problem was that I was constantly forgetting or losing the bowler, because unlike the beret, I couldn't fold it up and stuff it in my satchel the minute the beady-eyed teacher wasn't looking. Instead I would take it off, put it beside me, and promptly forget about it. The only positive about the St. Paul's outfits was the considerably more chic, in my nine-year-old view, navy blue culottes we wore for PE.

St. Paul's junior school was a modern building, by British standards, built in the fifties, with spacious grounds for playing rounders and netball. A hopeless, knock-kneed runner, I was usually picked last for rounders, but I fared a little better in netball. Though my shooting skills were appalling, since I was tall, like my father, I was useful for defense, which consisted mostly of standing around in my culottes and waving my arms.

Over the next couple of years, I grew to like St. Paul's and made some close friends. One, Carla Capalbo, continues to be close to this day. She's the daughter of Carmen Capalbo, who brought Brecht to Broadway and directed *The Threepenny Opera*. Since my parents never had much in common with my friends' parents, they were glad I had at least one friend whose parents had some cachet.

Outside of school, I continued to cope with my parents' relationship, which continued deteriorating. When I was ten years old, they decided theirs would be an open marriage. They deemed this the solution to their compulsive infidelity. However sensible and civilized the idea might have seemed, it never succeeded in quenching the jealousy, anger, and resentment that animated their interdependency.

One night, the poet George MacBeth, a small, wiry man with horn-rimmed glasses, showed up late at our flat, banging on the door, demanding to see my mother. When he wasn't allowed in, he leaned on the doorbell for two hours until the police arrived and carted him off. I stayed in my room, holding the pillow over my head to try to stifle the sounds as my parents, in the living room, went on yelling at each other.

Still, after that night, I would catch glimpses of George MacBeth creeping in and out of the flat whenever my father wasn't around. Always polite, I would say, "Hello," and he would reply, "Hello," and I would go off to my bedroom and try to do my homework.

One afternoon I came home from school and noticed, out the window, men's clothing strewn around the courtyard. I asked my mother whose clothes those were and what had happened. She turned to my father and said, "Why don't you explain it to Tracy?" and walked out of the room. He began to mumble something that made no sense, and I didn't pursue it. The clothing remained in the courtyard for months, gradually fading and disintegrating. Only years later, upon reading my stepmother's biography of my father, did I learn what had happened.

It turned out my father had come home that day and discovered George in the kitchen with my mother, dressed in nothing but a necktie. My father promptly ran to the bedroom, gathered George's clothing, and threw it out the window into the inner courtyard. It was a great gesture, except that when he insisted George leave, George had nothing to wear, and my father wound up having to loan him a raincoat.

While my mother was having an affair with MacBeth, my father was sleeping with a Chinese actress named Tsai Chin, who told me many years later that my mother thought nothing of showing up at her flat while my father was there and starting to harangue him. Tsai would watch in disbelief from the sidelines, then leave them alone to hash out their differences.

Close friends of my parents were often called in as witnesses, allies, and mediators. One rainy day, my mother dragged me to their friend Maria St. Just's house, and before our hostess could get out a word, she raged, "I'm leaving. I can't take it anymore. He's impossible!" A few minutes later, I looked up from playing with Maria's two girls to see her answering the door. There stood my father, his hair matted and disheveled, soaked to the skin and furious. "I've been next door to the police, and I am having you arrested for abducting my wife and child. Where are they?"

Having been through variations of this performance, Maria calmly said, "Don't be so stupid, Ken, they're in the kitchen. Why don't you come in and have a cup of tea?" A few minutes later, we were all sitting around Maria's kitchen table, sipping tea and munching on biscuits as if nothing had happened.

My parents frequently separated. My mother even got an apartment of her own for a while. I always stayed with my father and an au pair at the Mount Street flat. I think it was their attempt to give some consistency to my life. During one of their separations, my father went to Málaga for the bullfighting festival. A few days after he left, my mother followed, checking into the same hotel, the Miramar, and immediately taking up with a handsome Scottish laird, Peter Combe. I can only attribute her choices to the fact that both my parents seemed to revel in humiliation in front of each other and in public, trying their best to be the Scott and Zelda Fitzgerald of the '50s. Epic fights took place, which exhausted their friends. Once my father broke my mother's nose, driving her into the reluctant arms of Orson Welles and his wife, Paola, who gave her a cold compress and a drink and sent her on her way. "They were obviously having a terrible time together," Welles told my stepmother, "the nature of which we weren't interested in looking into."

Blissfully ignorant of all this latest drama, I reveled in peaceful solitude with my au pair. When they returned to London after that trip, my parents took a moment out from their sparring to consider my academic future with the headmistress of St. Paul's. Mrs. Oakley, a tall, lean woman with short gray hair, suggested that boarding school might be more suitable for me. I took this as a rebuke and searched my mind for what I might have done wrong.

I may not be giving Mrs. Oakley enough credit. Perhaps she recognized that living away from crazy parents might be a better thing for a potentially troubled teenager. As we left that meeting, I was terrified that my parents would explode; fortunately, my mother had just read an article by Penelope Mortimer claiming that London, or any big city, was not the best environment for adolescents. (Famous people often influenced my mother's schooling choices: Raymond Massey's daughter, the actress Anna Massey, had recommended my elementary school; Gloria Vanderbilt had suggested Brearley.) In her article, Penelope maintained that once a child was ensconced in boarding school, holidays became lovely events. That my parents spent most of their time traveling, and I seldom saw them even when they were in London, didn't seem to dim my mother's idealized vision of what our vacations might become if I went away to school.

She and I visited several schools together—my father seemed to stay out of the educational realm—and she concluded that Dartington Hall, a coeducational progressive school, was the place for me. For once, I was thrilled with her decision. I loved Dartington's bucolic atmosphere in Devonshire, and the idea of being surrounded by lots of other kids 24/7 also appealed—it was lonely being an only child. Much to my relief, Dartington accepted me with only an IQ test, on which I scored high in vocabulary. I attribute that to the inordinate amount of time I spent with clever adults, fighting or exchanging witticisms.

A few months later, I stood on the platform at Paddington Station, getting ready to board a train for Dartington Hall, dressed in slacks and a pullover, the first time since I'd started going to school that I didn't have to wear a uniform. The idea thrilled me. I'd gone clothes shopping with my current au pair, Moira, at Peter Jones. Fortunately, my mother was out of town, because Moira was much more patient and tolerated the hours I spent trying on sweaters and slacks, imagining what the other kids would be wearing and worrying about whether or not I would fit in. That day, as I glanced around the platform, I was relieved to discover that then, as today, all the kids were wearing similar versions of what I had on—sweaters and slacks. (Jeans hadn't come into fashion yet.) Even without a dress code, kids create their own uniforms.

The first week I was at Dartington Hall, after lights-out, I would hear the muffled sobs of my classmates. They were homesick. I wanted to be like them. I wanted to join in the conversations about missing home. I tried to force myself to cry, but I wasn't sad. Not in the least. I didn't miss my parents one bit.

I liked getting up each morning and going through the small wooden closet to decide what I wanted to wear. In retrospect, I see those mornings as the start of my independent clothing style, an independence that coincided with my independence from my parents and their peculiar world.

CHAPTER 6

The Brown Wellington Boots

By the time I was eleven, I knew the best way to deal with my mother's moodiness and tendency to rage was to go along with whatever she planned. So when she took me shopping on Oxford Street one late May day, I suspected I was in for disappointment.

"But I want black boots," I said stubbornly as a salesman placed a pair of ugly brown Wellingtons in front of me.

"They only have brown in your size," said my mother impatiently.

"But—" I began to protest, then stopped short. I knew better. Nothing I could say would change my mother's mind. I never won an argument; trying just aroused her ill temper.

We bought the brown boots, and two weeks later, I was in the middle of a Scottish loch in the middle of the night, going down, down, down into murky brown water. I knew if I didn't take off my boots, I would drown, but even though I hated them, my weird, irrational eleven-year-old mind argued that I would need them for when we returned to dry land. So I kept them on.

My mother, Moira, and I were spending the weekend in Scotland with my mother's lover, Peter Combe. I didn't know he was my mother's lover; she billed him as a "friend," though even at eleven, I sensed there was something different about this friendship from her myriad others. He was an attractive Scotsman with dark curly hair and a penchant for wearing kilts that showed off his shapely legs. He was warm and friendly and lived in a beautiful stone house, nestled in the highlands just north of the border, that had belonged to his family for generations. I liked being there—he made me feel welcome. My mother and I were just two parts of a house party that included Philip, a soft-spoken man with dark hair and a beard, a famous falconer who helped Peter train his birds; and Susan, a plump blond no-nonsense type in her mid-thirties who each morning invited us to take a brisk walk across the countryside, which we politely declined.

Peter and my mother were discreet, careful not to kiss or hold hands in front of me, but I noticed the intimate way they looked at each other, the way she listened closely to his concern for her comfort; "Are you cold, Elaine? Can I get you a wrap?" I watched, amazed, when she nodded and he pulled out a beautiful blue and yellow tartan shawl that matched his kilt. I sensed something more when he covered her shoulders with it. My mother seemed much happier and more relaxed around Peter than she was around my father, and I was glad to see her in a good mood; it made being around her easier.

The second night of our visit, I politely refused the offer of haggis. The sangfroid of the others with regard to this savory pudding, encased in an animal's stomach, may have been facilitated by what seemed an endless supply of special aged whiskey Peter kept bringing up from his cellar. The gaiety among the crowd was infectious. At some point, the grown-ups decided it would be "great fun" to go for a midnight sail in the nearby loch, and Moira and I, caught up in the excitement, begged to be included. So we were.

There was much laughter and high spirits as we piled out of the car and gazed at the water. To me it looked murky and forbidding, but the adults seemed unfazed. In the distance we could see dim lights from a couple of houses, and as we dragged Peter's tiny dinghy from the beach down to the water, he told us only a few farmers lived in the area.

We pulled the boat into the water, climbed in, and Peter hoisted the sail. We were barely half a mile from shore when the wind picked up, and since Peter was the only experienced sailor, we fumbled about, laughing, unaware of the danger; before we could stop it, the boat flipped on its side and capsized. Nobody was wearing a life jacket, and the water was freezing cold and pitch black.

We all struggled to right the boat but quickly abandoned our efforts— we were getting nowhere, and gaiety had turned to shock and misery. Peter, ever the well-mannered host, insisted he would swim to the shore to get help. Nobody argued with him. And assuring us he would return "in a tic," he swam away.

I listened to the splash of his arms hitting water until I could no longer hear it. Soon a fog descended and we could barely see each other. Even though it was June, the night was bitterly cold and windy. We glumly hung on to the dinghy and said little. It was clear that none of these adults had a clue what we should do.

My boots started to fill with water, and I could feel them pulling me down. Yet I felt strangely calm about my watery fate and determined not to shed those boots as I sank lower and lower. I felt a kind of submission to the forces of nature, or maybe what I felt was an unconscious death wish. Numb with cold, I began to think how nice it would be to disappear. No more parents fighting, no more turbulence. Just peace and calm.

Looking back, I understand that I must have been a depressed child, but at the time I had no idea what depression was. I had been away at boarding school for a semester by then, and I liked being surrounded by kids my own age and being away from the chaos of my London life. Still, minor incidents could trigger unaccountable lows—a misunderstanding with a friend, being left out of a group activity, frustration with schoolwork. When I felt low, I sought solace in a giant old oak tree at the edge of the school grounds. It was a favorite spot: The tree was easy to climb, and the views of the Dart River were spectacular. You could even see the large gray stone house where Agatha Christie supposedly lived and wrote her mystery novels. I would climb the tree and sit on a sturdy limb overlooking a field of wild grass. There I would sob uncontrollably, the only outlet I had for all the tension that had built up inside me. And when I finally stopped, I felt as though a big knot had been untied. I would head back to school, feeling better. Sometimes I secretly hoped someone would find me in the tree and comfort me, but that never happened.

Back in the loch, being pulled down to the depths, I was running out of air and incapable of doing anything about it, but suddenly, Philip, who was hanging on beside me, must have sensed or seen me going down, and he reached and yanked me back to the surface. Half-relieved, perhaps, if still uneasy about the consequences, I let my ugly brown Wellingtons slip off my feet and drift to the muddy bottom.

On the other side of the boat, my mother, increasingly agitated, kept calling out, "Are you okay, Tracy? Are you okay?"

"I'm fine, I'm fine," I kept replying, but as her anxiety grew, so did her pitch. Finally, after I had told her for the umpteenth time that I was fine, Susan cried, "Elaine, shut the fuck up!" and this was followed by stunned silence. Even in the bone-chilling cold, from the far side of the boat, I could feel my mother begin to sulk. I was sensitive to her mercurial mood changes and felt weirdly responsible for her. After all, she was my mother. I was related to her. Wasn't her difficult behavior somehow my fault? Still, secretly, I was glad Susan had stood up to her. Few people did.

Philip, normally shy and self-effacing, realized the group dynamics were deteriorating and decided he must improve our spirits. Under his leadership, we sang "Row, Row, Row Your Boat" in a failed three-part harmony, and he told corny jokes—"How many Scotsmen does it take to change a lightbulb? Och! It's no' that dark!" And whenever our spirits flagged and silence began to envelop the group, Philip insisted he could hear the sound of a boat coming to rescue us.

We were in the water for an hour and a half. It seemed like an eternity. The strong wind kept pushing the boat farther from shore, and the hull, to which we steadfastly clung, was gradually foundering. Despite the jokes and songs, there came a moment when even Philip fell quiet; it seemed we had all given up hope of being rescued. "Who should go for help next?" someone asked, and the grown-ups had begun to discuss the various possibilities when Susan cried, "Look, there!" and we turned and, through the fog, saw the outline of a rowing boat approaching us.

The boat was manned by a local farmer, with Peter directing him. With cries of gratitude, we clambered aboard. The tiny boat almost sank under our weight, but somehow we managed to make it safely back to dry land.

On shore, a small reception committee of locals was waiting with rough blankets to cover us, and they escorted us to a nearby farmhouse. As we sat inside the old stone cottage, huddled in those blankets by the fire, I continued to shiver uncontrollably. My teeth were chattering so hard that my jaw began to ache, and I felt as if I would never be warm again. But I listened as the farmer's wife told her story, in a strong Scottish brogue, about how Peter had created quite a stir when he had showed up at their cottage "stark naked" and babbling about a bunch of people hanging on to a capsized sailboat in the middle of the loch. At first they thought he was drunk, but he managed to convince them that the reason he had shed his clothes was in order to swim better.

Later that night, after we had returned to Peter's house, we all sat quietly, in a state of subdued shock. Finally, Moira and I stood to go upstairs to bed—we were sharing a room—and my mother stood to hug me. We seldom hugged, and this felt awkward. I pulled away but then realized from the look on her face that she had been truly shaken. I suppose I knew she loved me and wanted the best for me, but I found it hard to receive her love when so many other things about her were prickly and difficult and her moods were so changeable. We were like two partners in a dance that never managed to connect. It was a dance that would continue for the rest of our lives.

The next morning, although we all felt revitalized, I was still obsessing about my boots when Moira confided to me that Philip had tried to take advantage of the situation: He had complimented her on her bravery and the fact that she had remained so calm. Then he had tried to kiss her. She was deeply offended. I listened, not saying a word about the boots or the fact that Philip had saved me from drowning. I wanted to tell her to be nice to him, but instead I said nothing.

Before we left Scotland, my mother pulled Moira and me aside and made us promise not to tell anyone what had happened—"Even your best friend, Janet," she said pointedly to me. Particularly, we were not to tell my father about our "adventure."

Only many years later did I learn that the episode had occurred during a time when my mother was planning to divorce my father, and she knew that taking her daughter on a midnight sailing trip without life vests would not look good on her parental résumé. I never saw Peter again—he and my mother parted ways. I think she realized that a life in the Scottish highlands as the laird's wife was not for her.

When I was fourteen, she told me she had written a play called *Death in the Country*, based on this incident, except in her story someone actually drowned. I never read the play, so I never found out who drowned. By then the story had become her story, and not wishing to compete with her version of events, I stayed silent about what had happened to me on the other side of the upturned dinghy—about my near-death experience and my obsession with those ugly brown boots.

CHAPTER 7

Bikinis and Water Skis

My grandmother on my mother's side appreciated the finer things in life and taught me to do the same. Her father, Heyman Rosenberg, was a Latvian immigrant who, in 1913, invented the self-tapping screw—a metal screw that penetrates metal and does not need a bolt to keep it in place. This screw was ideal for hard-to-get-to places, like air-conditioning ducts. It quickly became the standard component for the sheet-metal industry. A job that previously required two men now required only one. It was used on Charles Lindbergh's plane and to repair the Statue of Liberty. This screw, along with his other inventions, became the cornerstone of my great-grandfather's considerable fortune.

My grandmother Florence, a plump, petite woman with beautiful white skin, met my grandfather Sam when he came to work for my great-grandfather. I rarely saw my grandfather, but I remember him as a small, bald man with deep-set brown eyes. He married the boss's daughter, and they had three girls, Shirley, Elaine, and Betty. This did not please my grandfather, who was desperate to have a son.

Although my grandfather was perfectly pleasant to me, he had a reputation as a difficult man with a bad temper. My mother claimed he was abusive to her, both psychologically and physically, and in her memoir she referred to him as a "rage-aholic." All I knew was that she never mentioned him, and they were not close.

The final years of my grandfather's life were difficult. He was injured in a botched robbery at their house on Long Island. One of the robbers was a former chauffeur. My grandfather was so enraged that a past employee would try to steal from him that he refused to give in to their demands, and they hit him over the head with a gun. My grandfather's eyesight was already failing, and this incident left him almost completely blind. One night at a party, his heart failed, and when he was seventy-five and I was twelve, he died.

The next year—1964—my parents, unclear about what to do with me for the summer, thought it might be a good idea for me to spend it traveling with my grandmother, who had always wanted to travel. My grandfather had a phobia about leaving America. He didn't trust "foreigners." But my grandmother had kept up her French and her dream of exploring the world.

I was glad to leave home. Earlier that year, during one of my parents' many attempts at reconciliation, I had gone with them to spend a weekend in Bath. I was fascinated by the elegant Georgian architecture, the curved terraces with houses made out of honey-colored limestone, and the Roman baths with the smelly restorative mineral waters meant to cure all ailments. But even at the age of twelve I knew that there was no cure for my parents' marriage.

After a pleasant day of sightseeing, we returned to the hotel, where they got into a fight. My father felt that my mother had drunk too much at dinner, and before I could do anything to stop them, they were screaming and shouting and throwing stuff around, and I was cowering in a bedroom. The phone began to ring, they didn't answer it, and then there was loud banging at the door, which they ignored. Finally, I heard loud voices and threats to call the police. When my parents eventually opened the door, I peeked out and saw an agitated manager in a pin-striped suit and tails. I listened as he informed them that they were disturbing the peace and preventing the other guests from sleeping. He warned them if they did not stop, he would call the police. Furthermore, they should pack their bags, as he wanted them out first thing in the morning. I remained in the bedroom, embarrassed and wishing I could disown them right then and there.

So the prospect of spending the summer with my grandmother was welcome relief. In the tradition of all good grandmothers, mine had discovered that the best way to bond with her grandchildren was to spoil them shamelessly, and I was the happy and willing recipient of her largesse. When we lived in New York for two years—while my father was drama critic for *The New Yorker*—my grandparents would pick me up, and I would spend the weekend with them on Long Island. I looked forward to these visits, when I was assured of presents: trinkets, stuffed animals, or frilly dresses. Just the mention of a doll I saw advertised on TV resulted in instant gratification.

In my grandparents' house, I had a special ritual. I would wake up early, hurry into the kitchen, grab a big blue bag of Wise potato chips with the friendly-looking owl on the bag, and station myself in front of their large TV to watch cartoons. At some point in the morning, my grandmother would try to enhance the nutritional value of my diet by offering me a bowl of Wheatena smothered in cream and brown sugar.

This, too, I happily devoured. England had barely finished rationing in those years, and America seemed like a land of milk and honey.

As I packed for the summer, I envisioned TV, potato chips, and an abundance of gifts looming, but when my grandmother arrived in London, I was disappointed to discover we were going to Cannes, in France, where the availability of TV and potato chips was uncertain. Still, I felt hopeful that there would be other amenities to make up for their losses.

We stayed at the Carlton Hotel, with its famous wedding-cake facade and tiers of gleaming white columns. It also had a fabulous beach, covered in shimmering golden sand, which, compared to the pebbly English seaside resort beaches I had experienced, seemed like a marvel.

Every day my plump grandmother, squeezed into a brightly colored swimsuit with a matching turban, and I, dressed in a red and blue bikini that barely covered my skinny frame, descended in the elevator to the beach. My grandmother insisted on buying me three bikinis at the posh hotel store so I would never have to wear a wet one, even though they were so small that they took only five minutes to dry in the hot sun of southern France.

My grandmother sat under a large umbrella to protect her alabaster skin, and from her deck-chair perch, she watched me like a hawk, admonishing, "Don't swim too far. Put on more suntan lotion. Come and eat something. I think you'd better rest for a while." Although she worried about my welfare, she also encouraged me to take swimming lessons and, best of all, waterskiing lessons. I was never much of an athlete, and waterskiing terrified me, but with her encouragement, I managed to overcome my fears enough to take a lesson. I was swamped in a bright orange life jacket. The instructor was on skis beside me, and as the boat sped up, I rose from crouching to standing. My arms felt as if they were being pulled out of their sockets, but after my instructor's supportive tap on the back, I was able to stand up and stay that way for a short amount of time. After a few more lessons, I learned how to zigzag out beyond the wake and back. It was exhilarating, and I still have the photos, my face buried in the life jacket, bravely attempting a smile.

Years later, when I was nineteen and visiting my boyfriend, Herky, who was working on the Amalfi coast on the Roman Polanski film "*What?*," I used my mediocre waterskiing skills to keep Roman amused. Never one to waste time, Roman had a speedboat on standby, waiting to take him waterskiing in between camera setups. He decided that carrying someone on his shoulders would make his experience more entertaining. Since he was quite small (my father, who collaborated with him on a film adaptation of *Macbeth*, used to refer to him as "the little Pole"), and I weighed just over a hundred pounds, he chose me as his lucky victim.

It was a complicated procedure: We started in the water, where he put on the water skis and I carefully climbed atop his shoulders, wrapped my legs around his neck, and shivered, a little embarrassed by the proximity of our slippery wet bodies. At Roman's signal, the boat sped up; we stayed upright only a few seconds before toppling into the water. I think the cast and crew found our attempts at becoming the Flying Wallendas of waterskiing entertaining if disastrous. After numerous attempts, Roman reluctantly accepted defeat.

On the Riviera with my grandmother, life was simpler. She took great pains to organize my social life, carefully pointing out the children in my age range on the beach and coaxing me to introduce myself to them. Sometimes she introduced herself to their parents, and through this latter technique, I met a boy named Adam. One night his parents said he and I could eat supper alone in the Carlton dining room. What they did not mention was that they would be sitting with my grandmother a few feet away from us, at another table. We must have looked comical, two twelve-year-olds out on a date, Adam in a classic madras-plaid jacket and bow tie and me in a red and white polka-dot dress I had convinced my grandmother to buy for me.

Although my grandmother found Adam's pedigree perfect—he was from "a nice Jewish family from Long Island"—I found him unspeakably dull and was hugely relieved when an attractive local boy, Jean Paul, managed to ingratiate himself with my grandmother. He convinced her not only to allow us to go out on a date but also to pay for it. I have no recollection of what we did; I think he was simply rehearsing for his later career as a full-fledged French Riviera gigolo. Unfortunately, the evening ended badly when we arrived back at the hotel half an hour after curfew. My grandmother was hysterical, on the verge of calling the American consul and sending the gendarmes to search for us. That was the end of my nocturnal outings with Jean Paul; thereafter our activities together were strictly daytime. Apart from that minor glitch, it was a glorious summer, which ended with a visit to the Venice film festival to see my aunt Shirley Clarke's provocative film *The Cool World*, about black kids in Harlem. In late August I arrived back in London brown as a berry, with an excellent collection of tiny bikinis—six in all—and a smattering of French.

For my grandmother, that summer was the beginning of her life as a traveler. Over the next twenty years she visited Greece, Italy, Spain, North Africa—all the places she had yearned to see. On a cruise ship she met David, fifteen years her junior and owner of an exterminating company (cruise ships apparently have huge rodent populations). They traveled the world together, always keeping separate rooms. He wanted to marry her, but she refused, saying she didn't want to take care of another "sick old man," though in truth I think she simply enjoyed her newfound independence.

Despite the lack of a marriage license, David became part of our family. Whenever I visited New York, he picked me up from the airport in his big black Cadillac, and he always took my grandmother and me to fancy restaurants. My grandmother was indifferent to food—her idea of cooking meant directing the housekeeper on what to make—but she enjoyed the pomp and ritual of going to expensive restaurants. When he was just sixty-nine years old, David unexpectedly dropped dead. My grandmother put up a good front, saying she was grateful that he did not have to suffer. But I think she missed him more than she had anticipated. She stopped traveling. She had a series of companions, one of whom alerted the family about my grandmother's failing mental capacities. A few years later she began a painfully slow fifteen-year decline into dementia. She made it clear that she did not want to leave her Palm Beach apartment. Fortunately, my grandfather had left her enough money so she could be cared for at home. When she was two months shy of her hundredth birthday, she died.

In the beginning I visited her in Palm Beach, but as the years went by, I have to confess that I visited her less and less. I was working and starting a family, or at least that was the excuse I gave myself. But I was able to bring my nine-month-old son to meet her, and I know that meant a lot to both of us. True to form, she made sure there was a gift for him. A soft, cuddly teddy bear that he adored.

CHAPTER 8

The Apple-Green Shoes

Although I was free to choose my own clothes from the closet of my boarding school room, free to select bathing suits from the hotel boutiques when my grandmother and I were traveling together, I was not free to create my own wardrobe: I had to contend with my mother. Whenever we went on shopping expeditions, we clashed. Her own clothing style was simple and chic, nothing flashy or provocative. That was my father's domain: He wore elegant bespoke suits with colorful shirts and ties.

My mother and I didn't know how to be with each other, as we seldom spent time alone together. Shopping for clothes was one of the rare occasions when we did, and those expeditions were awkward and uncomfortable. As I tried on clothes, she grew impatient, and that inspired me to become sullen. She did not seem at ease around me, and I was equally nervous. I felt she couldn't wait to get back to her own life—working on her novel, hanging out with her friends, having cocktails, and amusing others with her wit. (Her wit was another thing I never really experienced, but her friends always told me she could be one of the funniest people they knew.)

One day when I was ten, we were walking along Regent Street when my mother suddenly stopped, turned to me, and said—apropos of nothing at all, as far as I could tell—"Did you know that one of your legs is shorter than the other?" I stared at her and asked, "What?" "Go on. Walk ahead of me." I did as I was told, and after I had walked a few steps, I heard her say, "Yes, definitely, one leg is longer."

"I thought you said it was shorter?" I said.

"Don't argue," my mother said.

That day we bought nothing, and the next day, to my astonishment, she whisked me off to the doctor's office. The doctor inspected me, measured my legs, and seemed unconcerned. My mother was undeterred and insisted he take an X-ray.

A day later the results came back, and my mother proudly announced to me that she had been right all along. One leg was indeed a quarter of an inch longer than the other. The doctor insisted this was perfectly normal, but I felt diminished, one more piece of evidence that something was wrong with me.

A couple of years later, my mother and I went on what turned out to be our final shopping trip together. We were at Harrods to buy a shirt, and there, as I browsed through the racks of clothing, I sensed my mother's increasing irritation. She tapped her foot and lit a cigarette and called out loudly, "Excuse me! Please, can someone help us?" When no one responded immediately, my mother raised her voice a notch and cried, "Is there anyone here?"

"It's okay," I mumbled. "I'm not quite ready to try anything on."

"Well, when will you be ready?" She sighed, lit another cigarette, and looked around. "Look, there's a whole rack of shirts, just pick one."

"I know," I told her, feeling my stomach tighten. "I just need time to look through them."

"Oh, for Christ's sake!" she said as she flung her cigarette ash toward the ashtray, nearly missing, just as a saleslady approached and timidly asked, "Can I help, madam?"

"About time, we've been waiting here for hours," my mother said. The time that had elapsed since we walked into the store had been perhaps five minutes.

"Can I start a dressing room?" the saleslady asked.

"But I'm not ready," I insisted, looking imploringly at my mother and the saleslady, hoping they would give me some time. The rack of shirts looked enticing, but as usual with my clothing choices, I was looking for something specific, but I didn't know what it was yet.

"Do you have to be so picky, it's only a shirt," my mother said, then turned to stare down the saleslady. "Can't you help her?"

The woman lifted shirt after shirt from the rack, but each one looked wrong. I knew what I wanted, and so far she hadn't shown it to me, but each time I shook my head, my mother shook her head at me until I had hunched myself up like a turtle, wishing I could make my head disappear inside a shell.

At last the saleslady lifted a green plaid shirt with a Peter Pan collar and I agreed to try it on. I slipped into the dressing room and put it on, then walked out to show my mother.

"Can you stand up straight for once, Tracy?" She sighed as she puffed away. My mother was short and petite, with perfect posture, while I was built like my father, tall and gangly, and tended to slump.

"Do you have this shirt in blue plaid?" I asked the saleslady.

"I'm sorry, everything we have is out on the rack," she replied.

"Get the green," my mother said.

"But I don't like the green." I knew what I liked, and I refused to settle for something I didn't.

She glared at me. "Fine, don't get anything."

I glared back. "Fine!"

That day we ended, as on so many other days, empty-handed and frustrated with each other.

Soon after this unsuccessful shopping expedition, my mother came up with a brilliant solution: She would give me a clothing allowance. Four times a year, she would give me money, and I could go shopping and buy whatever I wanted on my own. I was pleased. She was pleased. Everyone was happy.

On a sunny day in May, I set off to find a new pair of shoes, overjoyed to know I wouldn't have to hurry to make a decision, wouldn't have to listen to instructions to stand or sit up straight. I headed toward Oxford Street, the nearest shopping Mecca to our flat in Mayfair. I felt positively exhilarated by the myriad of choices that lay ahead of me. I was on a quest for shoes. I walked all of Oxford Street, all the way to Oxford Circus, about a mile, stopping in store after store after store. Early on, I found what I decided was the perfect pair of shoes—bright apple-green leather with a small chunky heel and a bow at the front. I kept looking, just in case. I wanted to make sure I wasn't missing out on another pair, just ahead, that were even more perfect.

Besides, those apple-green shoes posed a dilemma. They were expensive—in fact, my entire clothing allowance for three months. I was growing fast, and I knew I would need more clothes soon. Besides, I could pair only a limited number of clothes with bright green shoes. I tried on a few other pairs in more conventional colors, black and brown, but they seemed so boring compared to the green shoes, which were so beautiful, soft, supple. They fit me like a glove. Still, I was too nervous to blow my wad. I walked back home to ponder the situation.

As usual, there was nobody to offer advice. My parents were out, and even if my mother had been around, I would not have asked what she thought—I knew she would only shake her head. That year Moira was obsessed with her new boyfriend, and my father's secretary, Rosina, was making her way through a mound of overdue bills. The cleaning lady, judging by her practical black lace-ups, didn't seem the type who cared about shoes. Besides, I knew no one would give me the answer I wanted, which was: "Go ahead, buy them! Who cares if you have nothing to wear for three months?"

For the next few hours, I lay on my bed obsessing about the shoes— I could think of nothing but apple-green shoes, apple-green shoes, apple-green shoes—they had become almost a mantra. I walked to my closet and studied my clothes, imagining each item paired with those green shoes. The gray skirt would look good with them; so would my blue slacks, although the green shirt might clash, I thought, but then I stopped. I had an epiphany: I was the only person who would be staring at my feet and enjoying them. No one else's opinion mattered. Furthermore, no one but I would know I couldn't buy new clothes for three months. I would be away at boarding school, and my parents wouldn't notice anyway.

I ran down the corridor, raced out the door and down the circular staircase, too impatient to wait for the elevator that took forever, and rushed back to Oxford Street. I arrived just as the store was about to close, and the saleswoman could barely contain her irritation as she brought out the shoes for the second time that day. I could see she was sure I was only wasting her time.

I tried them on. I paraded around the store a few times. I checked them in every mirror, turning this way and that, studying them at every angle. I noticed out of the corner of my eye that the employees were waiting for me to finish, but I wasn't quite ready. I loved the way they felt. I loved the way they looked. Finally, I turned to the woman and said, "I'll take them."

"Check or cash?" said the laconic woman, and I saw she was still not convinced that I was going to buy them.

"Cash," I said proudly, and at the cashier's counter, I carefully counted out my entire clothing allowance, twenty pounds.

She warily counted each bill, placed them all in the till, and slammed the drawer. Then she looked up at me with pursed lips and said sourly, "You know, they're nonrefundable. If you return them, you'll receive only store credit."

"I know," I lied, and resisted the urge to tell her I wanted to wear them out the door. I thought that would be gauche. I simply watched quietly as she popped the shoes into a silver box and the box into a shiny black paper bag with black ribbon handles.

I took the bag and waltzed out of the store, trying to affect an air of nonchalance. I wanted her to believe I bought expensive shoes every day. The sun was setting as I walked home, swinging the shiny bag containing my treasure. It was almost spring, and a few trees in Grosvenor Square were starting to bud. The large gilded bald eagle perched on the top of the American embassy gleamed as it caught the last rays of the sun.

I sometimes wonder if that was the moment when my sense of style was firmly established. I would always choose how I presented myself to the world. Forever after that day, I would concoct an idea in my mind of what I wanted. Part of the fun was the hunt, the mystery as to whether or not I would find it, and when I did, the sense of accomplishment and deep satisfaction. In a world where most everything else felt out of control, having control over the clothes I wore filled a hole. I wore those green shoes for over two years. It turned out that my feet grew more slowly than the rest of my body. Those green shoes were only the beginning of a long love affair with shoes. They also were the beginning of walking on my own two feet, walking away from my parents and toward freedom.

CHAPTER 9

The White Cotton
Circle-Stitched Torpedo Bra

At boarding school, my best friend was Lizzy. She was smart, spunky, and had long blond hair and something I coveted: breasts. She had budded by eleven, and at twelve, she had sufficient frontage to require a bra. Lizzy proudly displayed those bosoms, encased in a new white cotton bra with circle-stitched torpedo cups. They jutted out from her black-and-white-striped T-shirt like, well, torpedoes.

I was flat as a pancake and insanely jealous. Besides the breasts, Lizzy had an older brother—another thing I envied, because I presumed having one put you on the fast track to boyfriends. He had told her that boys only liked girls with big breasts. Hearing this, I resigned myself to a life of spinsterhood, like Elizabeth Bennet in *Pride and Prejudice*.

The downside of attending our coed school was the boys—boys like blond-haired, blue-eyed Tim, who loved to swipe his finger down the backs of girls in gym class, checking to see if there was a bra strap. When he got lucky, he gave the bra strap a quick snap, an action usually greeted by hysterical giggles from the girl. Rather than feeling humiliated, the lucky girls with bras beamed with pride at their desirability. Each gym class became a study in torture for me—waiting, hoping, and praying that Tim or one of his cohorts wouldn't notice me. When I wasn't able to escape his scrutiny, Tim snarked, "Oh, still not wearing a bra, Tracy? Maybe by the time you graduate," followed by huge guffaws. Lizzy's popularity with Tim—not to mention all the other boys—was clearly due to her breasts. And I became obsessed with trying to figure out how to compensate for the cruel hand that nature had dealt me.

That year, on winter break, I flew to New York to visit my grandmother, and I persuaded her, with little effort, that I needed some new underwear. We went to Bonwit Teller, where the lingerie department had beautiful lavender floral wallpaper that matched the shopping bags. When I perused the bra rack, I found one exactly like Lizzy's—white with circle-stitched torpedo cups. I pulled out the smallest size–32 triple-A. I held it up to admire it. It was perfect. I slipped into the dressing room to try it on, and even though the torpedo cups sank like crushed paper cups around my peanut-size breasts, I convinced my grandmother to buy it for me. When the saleswoman, scanning my flat chest, said, "It might be a few years before you grow into it," I was unfazed. I had a plan.

Back at school, I unpacked my trunk, removed the bra, and took out the other tool I would need to fight off embarrassment: a box of Kleenex I had pilfered from my grandmother's bathroom cupboard. I put on the bra, opened the box of tissues, carefully wadded several into a ball, and stuffed them into the cups. I checked myself in the mirror: I was quite impressive. I buttoned my shirt and made my way to school and to my first class, shop, maybe not the ideal place to test-drive my newly acquired pulchritude.

No matter. I felt great, and I was sawing away at a piece of wood, already getting some admiring glances from the boys. Unfortunately, halfway through class, I noticed that my breasts had become lopsided. Asking permission from the teacher to go to the bathroom, I tucked away my project—a collapsible breakfast tray—and dashed down the hall to rectify the balance. In the stall, I discovered that one breast was in trouble—the Kleenex was gone. I surmised it was lying on the floor of shop class, but I replaced it with a wad of the school toilet paper, which was rough and scratchy, and returned to class. I could barely work, I was so distracted by my uncomfortably itchy left breast. The teacher, Bernard, a smarmy man who always leaned too close when he gave instructions—and who, many years later, would be brought up on charges of pedophilia—asked me what was wrong. I meekly told him I wasn't feeling well, and with a possibly inappropriate pat on the back, he let me out early. Back in my room, I removed the toilet paper and put on an oversize sweater to cover up my diminished chest.

The next day, I decided to make one more attempt with my tissue-enhanced breasts, but all day the tissues slid down at inopportune moments and places—in the cafeteria, walking to classes, or just when I thought a boy was walking over to talk to me. The bra, with no weight to hold it down, kept riding up, forcing me to surreptitiously hook my finger under the elastic and yank it back into place. That night I tucked the bra into my bureau drawer and reluctantly concluded that the saleslady at Bonwit's had been right: I would just have to wait.

Meanwhile, voluptuous Lizzy continued to be a boy magnet. Her waist-length hair and curvaceous body were exactly what the older lads lusted after. She was the first to develop and the first to be deflowered.

When she was fifteen, she "went all the way" with her boyfriend. She told me he had promised that he would "pull out in time," but he didn't, and a few weeks later, just before bedtime, she pulled me aside and whispered, "Tracy, my period's late." I knew this was serious. In those days, since there were no over-the-counter pregnancy tests, the only way we could find out was by going to a doctor.

I promised I would help her find one. We scoured the Yellow Pages and, by lying about her age, managed to find a doctor in nearby Torquay who agreed to do a pregnancy test after school on a half-day Tuesday. After we deposited Lizzy's urine at the doctor's office, we walked outside and strolled the palm-lined promenade—Torquay being one of the few places in England where the temperature is mild enough for palm trees to grow—eating greasy fish and chips and getting dizzy from chain-smoking Woodbines while we waited for the results. There was no question of her having the baby; if she were pregnant, Lizzy said, she would have an abortion. Although abortions were not legal at the time, Lizzy was convinced her parents would support that decision if necessary. I couldn't imagine telling my parents that I was pregnant. Not having a boyfriend, I could barely imagine having sex. In my naive teenage mind, having sex and becoming a parent were strangely unrelated. I just kept hoping that Lizzy wasn't pregnant, that maybe she had miscalculated her dates or there was some other explanation as to why her period was late.

After an hour, I stood waiting outside the red phone booth while Lizzy called the doctor. I watched the sun set over the English Channel and worried about hitchhiking back to school in the dark before curfew. The minute Lizzy opened the glass-paned door and I saw the stunned look on her face, I knew the news was bad. I had no idea what to say or how to comfort her. My stomach churned, and with a sickening feeling, I realized that there had been a seismic shift in my worldview. It had been irrevocably altered. This was no longer about wearing a bra or having a boyfriend. In the blink of an eye, Lizzy had been transformed from a teenager to a woman. My dearest friend was pregnant. In silence, we hitchhiked back to school.

Once we had returned, I stood outside the phone nook, with its yellow peeling paint and phone numbers scribbled on the wall, while a sobbing Lizzy called her parents. I'm not sure what I expected, but I heard no screaming or shouting. Everything was managed with the utmost discretion. Lizzy's father arranged for her to visit a private clinic, and since her parents were good friends of the headmaster's, she avoided expulsion.

I was sworn to secrecy and told that if anyone questioned her temporary disappearance, I was to say she was having her appendix removed. It was a role I knew well, having been trained by my family in dissembling. I never did say a word to anyone. But the whole experience put the fear of God in me, and as soon as I had a boyfriend, even though we weren't having sex, I found a doctor who would prescribe the pill—the father of a friend of mine—and I took it diligently as a precautionary measure.

I also never wore my torpedo bra again. By the time my breasts had developed, I was seventeen and at boarding school, but I had become a full-fledged hippie. My friends and I, Lizzy included, eschewed bras. We considered them anti-feminist, akin to Chinese foot binding. We adhered to the credo that everything had to be natural. We refused to shave our armpits or legs—not a pretty sight for those, like me, who had dark hair. And we used to wander around Totnes barefoot, wearing long skirts and see-through peasant blouses, handing out flowers to bewildered locals, solemnly preaching "peace and love."

CHAPTER 10

White Jeans
and White Denim Jacket

On my thirteenth birthday, just before bedtime, I was in my room in Chimmels when I heard the housemother, Kim, calling from down the hall to let me know there was a phone call for me. In my pale blue brushed-nylon nightgown, I ran down the long green linoleum corridor to Kim's sitting room, where she handed me the receiver. "It's your mother," she whispered. I thought my mother must be calling to wish me happy birthday; it was late for a phone call but I was glad she had remembered. Often she was a few days off.

I could barely hear her over the static on the line. "Hi, darling, I'm in Mexico." Her voice seemed to crackle. "I've just divorced your father."

I stood beside Kim, holding the phone in my hand, not knowing how to respond.

"Are you still there?" she asked after a few moments' silence.

"Yes," I replied. I knew I was meant to say something, but no words came. "I have to go to bed," I finally managed, and I handed back the phone to Kim.

"Is everything okay?" Kim asked.

"Yes," I told her, and I ran back to my bedroom.

"No running, please," Kim called to me. "Lights out, everyone!"

The house went black. I lay down on my bed and stared up at the ceiling. I didn't cry. I felt numb. So, it was finally over. All the years of fighting and drama: over. I thought about my friends. I knew no one whose parents were divorced. How was I to feel? What could I expect? I thought about my birthday and wondered why my mother had forgotten to wish me a happy one. I squeezed my eyes tight as I pondered: Maybe she meant the divorce to be my birthday gift.

Lying there in the dark, I began to hope that with my mother out of the way, I would have my father all to myself. I had received a birthday card from him, a floral affair probably selected by his secretary, but it did have his spidery handwriting on it, wishing me a happy day. Recently, I hadn't spent much time with him, but now maybe things would be different. Although I rarely saw him, when we were together, I felt a bond with him that I did not feel with my mother.

When I was much older, the actor Kenneth Haigh told me that my father had an ability to focus his attention on you in a way that was so laserlike, it lasted even after he was gone. "Ken would do to you what he did to all of us," Haigh told me. "He would say, 'Tracy, you mean you haven't seen this? We're going!'" And although I don't actually remember going a lot of places with my father, I do remember being in his thrall while he told me the stories of the plays he had seen or the books he had read. But the most important difference between him and my mother was that he was seldom impatient or bad-tempered around me. (Although that would change when I became a full-fledged teenager.)

During the brief times I spent with my father, he made me feel special. At dinner one night, we had a discussion about our ideal house, and on a napkin he drew a sketch with a swimming pool on the roof and a special run for the cat. For years I treasured this sketch, hoping that the fantasy house would one day become a reality.

A year before their divorce became final, while my parents were virtually living apart, my father began an affair with the woman who was to become his future wife, Kathleen Halton. She was twenty-eight, ten years younger than my father, and extremely beautiful. Later, he would refer to her in an interview as the Rolls-Royce of women. When they met, she was an aspiring journalist at *The Observer*, where my father worked; she was unhappily married to a brassiere factory owner, eager to leave and, with the help of my father, to climb the socio-literary ladder and join the ranks of the intelligentsia. I was twelve when they met, so I wasn't aware of any of this, but as I got older, I came to understand that they were a perfect match. Here was a young woman willing to be molded into my father's version of the perfect wife. She was Oxford-educated, smart and well read, and all he had to do was advise her on what to wear to enhance her natural beauty. A trophy wife, but with brains.

My father first introduced Kathleen to me as his "friend" on the eve of a trip he and I were taking to Switzerland. (It was Christmas vacation, and my mother had moved out.) Kathleen joined us for dinner at the Italian restaurant around the corner from our flat. I noticed only that she was conventionally dressed in a beige skirt and sweater set and that she had shoulder-length honey-blond hair, brown eyes, and high cheekbones. She seemed nice enough. I never could have imagined the threat her presence posed to my fantasy life with my father. At dinner that night, she offered to give me a reward if I brought back a photo of my father on a toboggan or skis. Since my father hated any kind of athletic activity, Kathleen and I laughed at this unlikely prospect.

The trip to Gstaad was one of my father's last attempts to spend time with me. I stayed with friends in a rented chalet while he stayed at the posh Palace Hotel in Gstaad. Unfortunately, he had not been apprised of the dress code, which was extremely formal, so throughout that week he had to sneak in and out of the hotel. I never got the photo. The nearest my father got to a toboggan was waving at me, cigarette in one hand and drink in the other, from the terrace of our friend's chalet as I slid down the hill on one.

After my parents divorced, my mother moved to New York, and my father stayed in the Mount Street flat. He lived alone for a few months. I came home from school for half-term and discovered that we had a new pet, a slow loris—a small, furry primate about the size of a large cat, with a round head, a narrow snout, large raccoon-like eyes, and little round ears. The loris—I don't remember it ever having a name—lived in a large cage in the living room. It moved very slowly, making little or no noise. My father told me we couldn't hold it because its bite was toxic. Many times I walked into the living room to find my father smoking, listening to his favorite Miles Davis or Duke Ellington records, and staring glumly at the odd creature as it swung lethargically from one branch to another on the tree inside its cage. It crossed my mind that maybe he missed my mother, but that seemed unlikely. I wanted to comfort him, but I didn't know how.

When I came back for my spring vacation, the loris was out and Kathleen—her divorce had become final—had moved in. My father never attempted to explain the new living arrangements. Although I was usually comfortable around adults, I felt awkward and tongue-tied around Kathleen. She wasn't old enough to be my mother, but she was too old to be my sister or a friend. Should I shake hands or hug her? Was I meant to call her Kathleen, or Mother, or what? Many questions were left unanswered, but we muddled along, doing our best not to get in each other's way. We did share a love of cats, and one holiday, when I brought home a kitten I had adopted at school, she seemed very happy to include her in the household. I think she found it easier to relate to the cat than to me.

Now my father seemed to have less time for me than ever; he did nothing to reassure me that Kathleen wasn't taking my place. She politely asked me about school and my friends, and took an interest in the music I liked, but it all seemed forced. Plus, I was embarking on my own teenage rebellion, the kind in which all parental figures become the enemy, and she became yet another name to add to the list of those I didn't trust. True, she was young, but she was firmly ensconced in the adult camp. Besides, most of the time I was away at school or with my mother, so Kathleen and I had few opportunities to get to know each other. I am sure she was as perplexed by our relationship as I was.

Meanwhile, my mother was trying to reinvent her life in New York. During my summer vacation just after her move, I visited. She was renting a duplex in a small brownstone on Charles Street in the Village, a flat that belonged to the film director Sidney Lumet. I liked the apartment, and the narrow streets and brownstones felt familiar, more like London than did the rest of New York. I liked walking around on my own, and exploring my new neighborhood, and people-watching. Women wore elaborate bouffant hairdos and sack dresses. Men wore dark narrow suits and white shirts. Kids my age were sporting the preppy look, slacks and skirts with button-down shirts, but hemlines were definitely on the rise. And jeans were starting to become a fashion staple. I spotted a couple of people wearing white jeans and matching jean jackets and thought they were very cool and very different from anything I had seen in England. The full-on hippie revolution had a few years to go before it engulfed the Village.

While my mother and I waited for the larger pieces of furniture to arrive from London, I helped her decorate the new apartment. Inspired by a purple and red embroidered Casa Pupo rug she had brought from England, I bought bright purple and red felt and covered crates to use as tables. As my mother's self-appointed interior decorator, I became obsessed with art nouveau bric-a-brac. Through ads I read in *The Village Voice*, I found exquisite lamps and statues. The dealers were disappointed to discover that the person they had been speaking with on the phone was a teenager with little money, but I did manage to haggle one guy down in price on a beautiful lamp with a woman holding a globe, and I proudly carried it back to the apartment. My mother seemed to genuinely appreciate my decorating efforts, using my purple and red color scheme when she eventually bought new furniture.

On that visit I discovered my favorite new American food, toasted Thomas' English muffins (despite the name no such item exists in England; the closest thing is a crumpet, a completely different kind of muffin) covered in mustard and slices of bright orange American cheese that tasted vaguely of plastic. Soon that was all I ate. My skin began to break out, probably prompted in part by this diet. My mother took me to see the famous Hungarian cosmetician Dr. Erno Laszlo; she was already using his complete line of cosmetics.

Laszlo was a small man with a thick accent. Wearing a white smock, he inspected my skin under a large magnifying glass. When he had finished, he prescribed his special formula for oily skin. I loved the sea mud soap that made the water look black, and the square art deco–styled bottles all the lotions came in. I don't think they helped my skin much, but I felt better: I liked the idea of using special products.

My mother had a boyfriend, a rotund, bearded actor named Severn

Darden, one of the original members of the Second City troupe in Chicago. He had a twinkle in his eye and was always willing to share a joke. I looked forward to his visits, for he seemed to cheer her up. He was great at improvising and doing funny accents; one of his mainstays was a German know-it-all professor.

My mother spent the next couple of summers in the Hamptons. The first year, we shared a house in Westhampton with the editor of *New York* magazine, Clay Felker, and his then-wife, the glamorous movie star Pamela Tiffin. Pamela was a brunette Jayne Mansfield type with a soft, breathy voice. She wore tight capri pants, sandals, and a shirt tied at the waist. She looked casual but chic. I liked her; she was friendly and seemed to take an interest in me. But Clay and Pamela came out only on weekends, and the rest of the time I was alone with my mother.

The days weren't too bad, since I could entertain myself at the beach, perfecting my tan and bodysurfing. But at night, back at the ranch-style house, my mother would start drinking and begin to ramble on about how much she hated my father and how he still loved her. As proof of my father's undying devotion, she presented me with love letters he had sent recently. I pretended to read them, but I didn't want to know the details of their sordid obsessions with each other. Although I was uncomfortable with Kathleen, at least things were calmer with her, and the thought of my parents reconciling was not appealing.

One night I decided to make dinner. Of course, I made the only thing I was interested in: hamburgers. I carefully laid them out on plates with lettuce, tomatoes, and pickles. I was proud of my culinary efforts and called out to my mother to let her know that dinner was ready. She staggered into the kitchen, took one bite, and announced, "Not enough pepper!" and proceeded to pour an entire container of peppercorns over both plates, ruining my perfect little meal. She picked up a large carving knife and started waving it around, yelling, "I'll show you how to prepare food." I backed away, terrified that in her drunken condition, she might accidentally fall and hurt herself or me.

When I saw a clear path to the door, I ran out of the kitchen and across the living room to my room, where I barricaded myself in by wedging a chair under the doorknob—like I had seen in the movies— and prayed she would eventually give up and collapse in her own room. She pounded on my door, demanding that I come out and finish my dinner, but I curled up on my bed, refusing to move or say a word. Finally, she gave up and I heard her footsteps moving toward the kitchen. I could hear her thrashing about in there, scattering plates and pots and pans.

Eventually, the noises subsided. I phoned my friend Stacy in East Hampton and invited myself to stay at her house beginning the next day. I didn't tell her what was going on in ours. I never spoke to my friends or to anyone else about my mother's drunken episodes. I was humiliated by her outrageous behavior. I feared it would reflect badly on me if anyone, including my father, knew about it. Besides, being an only child with uncommunicative parents, I had become accustomed to keeping things to myself. By this time I had learned how to stuff unpleasant feelings down into the deepest reaches of my body and psyche. This was my unconscious survival technique, which a therapist much later would tell me was called "splitting off," a behavior common among children of alcoholics.

Later that night I heard my mother shuffling down the hall toward my room; I heard her outside the door, trying to apologize. But I also heard the slur in her words, and I refused to let her in. I lay there, silent, pretending to be asleep. I wasn't taking any chances.

The next morning I woke early, threw some shorts and T-shirts in a duffel bag, and knocked on my mother's door. When she answered, I walked in and told her I was going to stay with Stacy for a few days. She was groggy, barely awake, and she asked no questions. "Keep in touch," she mumbled, and I handed her a slip of paper with Stacy's phone number. I left the room, quickly closing the door behind me.

Outside, I stood on the front steps, waiting for the cab to take me to the bus station. Stacy lived about an hour away. I watched the sun rise over the eastern edge of the ocean and inhaled deep breaths of the salty air.

I stayed with Stacy's family for the next two weeks. During the day we went to the beach, and at night we made money babysitting. Occasionally, I spoke to my mother on the phone, but neither of us mentioned what had occurred; we just carried on as though nothing had happened. I saw her briefly in New York before I returned to England and the relative calm of boarding school.

Before I left New York, I fulfilled an obsession I had been thinking about all summer: I was desperate for a pair of white jeans and a white denim jacket. Stacy had told me that some friends of hers had found their jeans at the Army/Navy store on Fourteenth Street. With money I had made from babysitting, I took the subway to Fourteenth Street and started exploring. Most of the Army/Navy stores sold jeans, but not many sold white jeans, and fewer still sold them in small sizes. But with perseverance, I managed to find both the jeans and the jacket.

I proudly wore my brand-new, rather stiff outfit on the train back to school. All my friends thought it was "fab." The next time I went to visit my mother, they all pestered me to bring them cool stuff from America. I began to have a reputation as someone who was ahead of the fashion curve. As a friend told me years later, "We all wanted to see what you wore, because we knew it would be something different and new." And I didn't need to tell anyone about the difficult behavior I had to endure with my mother for this fashion payoff.

CHAPTER 11

My Mother's Pucci Dress

As part of my parents' divorce agreement, I remained at boarding school and divided my vacation time between their homes. I never seemed to be in the right city at the right time. When my friends were in London, I was in New York and vice versa. But as the years passed, I preferred London no matter the other circumstances, because I preferred being away from my mother as she sank deeper and deeper into depression. By the time I was fourteen, she had added pills to her alcohol consumption.

Every time I visited, we attempted to narrow the widening gap between us. I knew she genuinely missed me: She wrote to me how much she did, and how much she looked forward to being together. But after those weeks in the Hamptons, I was wary.

I was in New York at the end of winter vacation when a big snow-storm practically shut the city down, and my mother was insisting I'd have to stay. Perhaps indefinitely.

"I don't want to stay in New York," I said, trying to stay calm. "I want to go back to England and school." (I was probably one of the few teenagers who looked forward to boarding school.) Before she could reply, the doorbell rang, and I rushed to let in my mother's friend and occasional lover Mike McDonald. He was a tall, laconic guy, probably ten years younger than she was, with a shock of dark brown hair that was always falling over his eyes. He surveyed the scene—the apartment was freezing cold (the storm had done something to the heating). I was so cold I was wearing my mother's new mink coat—a recent gift from my grandmother—on top of my traveling outfit. In those days you dressed up to go on a plane, so I was wearing a short gray skirt, a purple sweater, and brown suede boots. We were eating caviar—my mother's special farewell treat— and she was opening a bottle of champagne, though it was only ten in the morning.

Mike and I had nicknames for each other: He was M squared because both his initials were M; I was T squared because mine were T. He grinned at me and said, "Well, T squared, what's happening?"

"Elaine says I have to stay in New York, but I want to go back to London." I looked imploringly at him, certain he could talk sense into my mother. I moved closer and whispered, "M squared, please! You've got to help me get to the airport."

He clapped a big hand on my back and winked. "We'll figure some-thing out."

I knew Mike was fond of my mother, but he could also see how upset I was, and I suspect he also understood she had a drinking problem. She had already downed quite a lot of the bubbly and was in no condition to physically keep me from going, so Mike waved away my mother's importunings and took me downstairs. We stood side by side in the raging blizzard. He frantically waved at passing cabs until he managed at last to stop one. He loaded me and my bags into the cab and gave me money for the ride. I arrived at JFK and managed to get on the last plane to London before the airport shut down.

Soon afterward my mother and Mike broke up, and she was feeling lonely. I was fifteen by then, and she wrote to say that she wanted to take me on a cruise during my summer vacation. I pleaded with my father to let me stay with him, but he and Kathleen were going away, so I had no choice.

I was nervous. Traveling with my mother would not be easy, but I figured once we were on board a ship, surrounded by a lot of people, she couldn't misbehave too badly. The itinerary sounded pleasant enough, starting in Yugoslavia, proceeding through the Greek Islands, ending in Venice.

We flew from London to Dubrovnik. There, as we looked over our schedule, we realized I hadn't packed enough dresses to wear for the rather formal dinners. My mother had brought along an extra dress—a jersey-knit Emilio Pucci shift that was ideal for traveling because it never creased. It was purple, blue, and green in a bold, swirling graphic design, and when I saw it, I was skeptical that it would look good on me. To my surprise, when I tried it on, I liked it. A lot. It was form-fitting and clung in the right places and showed off my small waist. It was the only time, since her fur coat, that I'd worn something of my mother's and liked it. It was modern and chic, and I realized if I took up the hem four inches, it would hit that perfect mid-'60s sweet spot: high thigh.

When I told my mother about my plan to shorten her expensive Pucci dress, she nervously agreed, as long as I promised not to cut any of the fabric. Using an entire hotel sewing kit of various-colored threads, I sewed a rudimentary hem. If you didn't look too closely, the dress looked great, and I looked great in it.

The cruise was another matter. The cruise line was German; consequently, the schedule was rigid, and the ship brimmed with hearty, robust German tourists. Each night there were lengthy lectures about the places we were going to visit the next day, translated into English by a heavily accented woman and difficult to understand. Everything was incredibly efficient and incredibly boring. After my mother had scoped out the situation on the first night and realized there was absolutely no one on board with whom she had anything in common, she retreated to our cabin with a bottle of vodka and a pack of cigarettes.

I was left to fend for myself, which was fine with me. There was plenty for a teenager to do, including a swimming pool and deck chairs with large fluffy towels. I was content to slather myself with olive oil and work on my tan while reading through my collection of Agatha Christie murder mysteries, chomping on salty peanuts and sipping sickly sweet fruit concoctions. The real problem was mealtime. We had been assigned to a large table filled with an assortment of families, single men and women, and each night at dinner, I had to make excuses for my mother's absence: She was tired, she was sick, she was seasick. I wasn't lying; my mother was sick, but her illness was alcoholism, a term I didn't yet know existed. All I knew was that she drank, a lot.

My mother remained in our cabin almost the entire week: There seemed to be an unlimited supply of duty-free vodka and cigarettes. I was left to deal with the Germans and their progressively persistent inquiries. People kept offering to send a doctor, while I continued to maintain that, really, she was fine, on the verge of recovery. They lamented all the wonderful sights she was missing—the oracle's cave at Delphi, Palaio Frourio, an old Venetian fortress in Corfu, and St. Mark's Square in Venice, excursions I diligently attended and sometimes even enjoyed.

The coup de grâce came when the cruise ship staff discovered, via her passport, that it was my mother's birthday. At lunch the purser informed me that at dinner there would be a big celebration. I think it may have been a ploy to see if my mother was still alive.

Panicked, I raced to our cabin, shook my mother from her drunken stupor, and explained the situation. "You have to come to dinner tonight," I pleaded. "They know it's your birthday. There's going to be a cake and everything. Please, I can't make up any more excuses." Taking pity on me, my mother agreed to make an appearance. I dug up a frock from the bottom of her suitcase for her to wear—a turquoise number with white trim—and I decided that this was the night for me to wear the Pucci dress.

At the dinner table, we made a striking impression—my mother, pale-faced in her turquoise dress, me dark bronze in the neon-colored Pucci that barely covered my underpants. Everyone solicitously inquired about my mother's health, and she looked blankly at them, barely concealing her boredom as she pushed her uneaten food around on her plate. I was becoming more and more nervous, but the captain came to the rescue with a bottle of champagne, and everyone in the room toasted my mother. The band played "Happy Birthday," and the purser presented her with a large cake. She obligingly blew out the candles and even ate a small slice. When she was drinking, food seemed to be an afterthought.

The next thing I knew, my mother was whirling around the dance floor with some equally intoxicated Germans. Relieved that things were going so well, I slunk back to our cabin, exhausted by the whole episode. I prayed my mother wouldn't become so inebriated that she would embarrass me by falling down or, worse, calling the Germans Nazis, as she referred to them in the privacy of our cabin.

Many hours later, my mother returned while I feigned sleep. She slept the entire next day and remained in the cabin for the duration of the cruise. The boat made a stop near Athens, and since I had by then run out of clean clothes, I wore the Pucci dress to join everyone else as we piled into a hot bus and drove to the various historic sites. The ship's photographer took a picture of me standing in front of the Acropolis, wearing the Pucci dress with a wonky hem, looking like a teenager playing dress-up, clearly wishing I were anywhere but there.

When we returned to dry land, I took down the hem and returned the dress to my mother. "Maybe you should keep it," she said, perhaps out of guilt for having ignored me throughout the trip.

"No, thanks," I said. It was a beautiful dress, but I knew that every time I wore it, I would remember my mother's drunken stupors and the strain of all the lies I had to tell to strangers on that awful cruise.

CHAPTER 12

The Gold Flapper Dress

Even though I considered boarding school a respite from parental strife, it was becoming the new battleground for my latest obsession: boys. During my teenage years, I spent an inordinate amount of time trying to attract boyfriends—usually older boys who were not that interested in a physically underdeveloped teenager like me.

In ninth grade, I was obsessed with Duncan and determined to snag him. His best friend had told my best friend, Jenny, that he was interested in me, but Duncan was shy and probably wouldn't make a move until the end-of-term party. That was all the encouragement I needed. The party was three weeks away.

Duncan's family lived near the school, so he didn't board there but was a day pupil. He wasn't particularly good-looking—medium height and medium build, with long, greasy, dark brown hair parted in the middle and a nose like a beak. But he seemed kind. He had a quiet, sardonic way about him that appealed to me. He hung back from the crowd and observed from a distance what was going on. He was sixteen, two years older than I was, and that meant a lot, since all my girlfriends had boyfriends who were older. Duncan smoked cigarettes that he rolled himself, and that made him seem cool. My lame excuse for making contact with him was to ask for a light, and these smoky encounters usually ended with Duncan's casual "See you around," a phrase that filled me with hope for our future. With the dance, our future was at stake. I needed something special to wear, something that would make me stand out.

In a thrift shop, I found an old *Vogue* magazine that had an illustration of a flapper from the '20s wearing a fringed dress. The minute I saw it, I knew it was perfect for my long, skinny frame. I set out to find that dress, but not surprisingly, none of the local stores had anything even approximating my vision. I decided I would make it myself.

I hitchhiked fifteen miles to a fabric store in Torquay, ignoring the elderly driver who picked me up and gave me a long lecture about how dangerous hitchhiking was. This was the '60s, and all my friends hitchhiked everywhere, fearless and too broke and impatient to wait for buses.

At the fabric store, I spent most of my pocket money on yards of gold satin. After much searching in the upholstery department, I found the perfect gold fringe. Back at school, I discovered a sewing machine stashed away in a closet in the art room, and despite my limited sewing skills, I cut the material and stitched together a basic tank dress to which I pinned rows and rows of overlapping fringe. So far, so good. The only problem was that when I tried to sew the fringe on the dress, the sewing machine needles kept breaking. Once I had gone through an entire packet of needles, I realized I needed professional help.

On the main street in nearby Totnes, just below the medieval clock tower, I found a small alterations shop where I presented my half-finished creation to the owner, a middle-aged woman with a rosy face, wire-framed glasses, and a pincushion wrapped like a bracelet around her wrist.

"My, my," she said as she held up the lopsided dress, "what have we got here?"

I explained my problem.

"Mmn," she half hummed as she inspected the dress, "when do you need it?"

"In a week?" I replied hopefully.

"I expect we can manage that," she said.

One week later, on a Saturday, I returned to pick up the dress. When the seamstress brought it out on a hanger and I saw the neat rows of gold fringe, I was overjoyed. "It's beautiful," I said as I fingered the fringe.

"You'd better try it on," she said. "You didn't leave any room for a zipper, so I just sewed up the sides. I hope there's enough room for your head to go through the neck hole."

I slipped into the dressing room and quickly changed. The dress slid effortlessly over my head. I closed my eyes, took a deep breath, and when I opened them and looked in the mirror, I gasped with delight. She had essentially remade the entire garment, transforming it from a sack into a dress and giving it shape by cutting out armholes and a neckline. It was just as I had imagined, and it fit me perfectly. When I shook my body, the fringes swayed suggestively. I would have the best dress at the party. Duncan would find me irresistible. I thanked the owner, paid, and left the shop, swinging my precious cargo in a brown paper bag, eager for that night.

Before the party, Jenny and I swigged from a bottle of whiskey that her boyfriend, Rob, had smuggled onto campus. I hated the taste, but

I liked the buzz and the confidence that I began to feel. I slathered on the turquoise eye shadow and the black eyeliner I had bought at Woolworth's. When I stared at myself in the mirror, a raccoon looked back, but I thought I looked fantastic. Emboldened by the booze, we made our way to the auditorium. The fringe on my dress swayed with every step.

My plan, if you can call it that, was to sidle up to Duncan and do my routine "Have you got a light?" gambit. As it turned out, I tripped over a step entering the dance hall just as Duncan walked into the party, and he caught me. "Wow! Quite a dress," he enthused.

I beamed with pleasure. "I made it myself," I lied, and shook the fringe. Duncan smiled his crooked smile and guided me to the dance floor. We started to dance to the pulsating sounds of the school band's cover of "Gloria." The dress seemed to have a life of its own, the slightest movement provoking an undulation of fringed frenzy. It was the perfect dancing dress. Duncan moved closer and closer. I could smell his breath—a blend of his home-rolled cigarettes and whiskey. Everybody was looking at us. I felt like a star.

When the band took a break and Duncan suggested we go back to my room and drink some more whiskey, I happily agreed. Hand in hand, we meandered across the moonlit courtyard, carefully avoiding any inquisitive teachers. We sneaked up the stairs to my bedroom, which I had decorated with a combination of patterned Indian bedspreads on the walls and blue fishing nets suspended from the ceiling. It was like a cave. We lay down on my narrow bed and swigged from his small bottle, smoking cigarettes and snogging to the distant throb of the band as they began to play again. I felt very sophisticated. After twenty minutes I said, "Maybe we should go back?" I wanted to show off my dress and the way it shimmied when I danced. And I wanted to show off Duncan.

"Sure," said Duncan, offering me a final sip.

But when I stood up, I suddenly felt uncontrollably nauseated. I made it to the tiny sink in my closet just in time. Duncan stood at a respectful distance as I vomited into the sink. I knew that this incident would not endear me to him. As soon as my retching had subsided and I turned to look at him, he casually waved and said, "See you around," and he was gone. I knew he meant "Goodbye," except that because we were in school together, I was doomed to run into him all the time and each time to relive my embarrassment.

I lay back down on the bed. The room was swirling, and the fringes on my dress seemed to be swirling, too. I took it off and saw that it was splattered with vomit and probably ruined. I stuffed it into my bulging laundry bag, burst into tears, and cried myself to sleep.

The next morning I experienced my first full-on hangover—a throbbing headache and a queasy stomach. The episode didn't deter me from further alcohol consumption, though to this day the smell of whiskey arouses nausea in me. It didn't remind me of my parents' drinking, and I was never inspired to think twice before imbibing. I was young and invincible. I was going to be different from them.

Despite the humiliation of losing Duncan and my pride that night, the gold flapper dress started me on the path of creating my own clothing. My next effort, a pair of black light wool bell-bottomed pants with a matching sleeveless vest, didn't snag me a boyfriend, and I did have to keep tightening the belt because the pants continually stretched out, but I looked cool, and though I wasn't fully aware of it at the time, I had found a creative outlet for all those longings and dreams I harbored.

CHAPTER 13

The Silver Chain and the Poncho

I was thirteen when my mother moved back to New York, where she valiantly tried to reinvent her life without my father. He was a tough act to follow. Gradually, over the next three years, she spiraled into deeper and deeper depression, fueled by generous amounts of Dexamyl and vodka.

After the lease on her Charles Street apartment ran out, she selected a high-rise apartment building on East Seventy-Second Street, lured by the proximity to her pal Tennessee Williams, who lived in the building.

From the minute she moved into the new place, her behavior began to deteriorate. Maybe having Tennessee so available hadn't been such a great idea. I would hear them on the phone assessing their drug choices.

"Which ones are you taking today, Ten? The little yellow ones or the green capsules?" she'd ask as she toyed with a selection of brown plastic pill containers. A tough decision, but add a bit of booze into the mix, and it didn't make much difference. Each time I visited, she seemed in worse shape, more depressed and often incoherent.

During one winter vacation—I was nearly fifteen by then—I began doing some of my own drug-and-alcohol dabbling. On New Year's Eve, I went to a party with a group of friends, wearing jeans and a cream crepe de chine top with long bell sleeves and a high gathered waist. I had made it from a pattern designed by Rudi Gernreich—famous for his topless bathing suit—and although it didn't look quite like the illustration on the pattern, I was proud of my efforts.

At the party, I experimented with marijuana for the first time: The result was only a bad headache and an excruciatingly sore throat. Early on New Year's Day, nursing that sore throat, I returned to the apartment, where my mother was passed out in her bedroom, surrounded by empty vodka bottles, empty pill containers, and ashtrays filled with cigarette butts. The stench was overwhelming, but the sight was familiar, so I didn't panic. I shrugged, walked to my room, and crawled into bed. When I woke, it was late afternoon, and hearing no sounds in the apartment, I went to her room to check on her.

She was still in bed, her hair in disarray, her face puffy. She was moaning. "I feel terrible."

This was worrisome—usually, after one of these binges, she would wake up and seem more alert. "What should I do?" I asked, feeling helpless and confused.

"Call my doctor," she said, waving toward her multicolored floral address book. I found the doctor's number and called. Considering this was New Year's Day, he was surprisingly understanding and promised to come right away. Before long, a pale gray-haired man in a gray suit, carrying a black doctor's bag, arrived; I showed him to my mother's room. He told me to wait outside. A few minutes later, he reemerged. Seeing my concerned expression, he reassured me: "Don't worry, she'll be fine tomorrow. I gave her something to help her sleep." I thanked him and showed him out.

When he was gone, I felt momentarily relieved, but I also began to wonder what would have happened if I hadn't been there. Would she have called the doctor on her own? Would she have remained in bed interminably? I couldn't imagine; I didn't know what was wrong with her or what to do. But as usual, I said nothing to anyone. I had become expert at acting as though nothing was wrong. I even took a certain pride in my ability to sweep these unpleasant events under my mental rug.

Since this kind of behavior was becoming more frequent, I just accepted that it was how my mother was. I didn't like it, but I didn't feel there was anything I could do. I just wanted to escape from her. So I did what most self-involved teenagers do—I hung out with my friends, going out late, coming in late, waking up late, and going out again. In some ways, I was imitating my parents' lifestyle. One of the advantages of having a mother who was out of it was that, unlike my friends', my life was fairly unsupervised. I could wear or do pretty much anything I wanted to.

A few months after this incident, back at school, I received a letter from my mother telling me she was moving to Stockbridge, Massachusetts. She had voluntarily admitted herself to the Austen Riggs Center, where she could get "psychiatric help," as she described it. I read the letter several times. The decision lifted a weight that I had been carrying without even being aware of it. It was odd to be relieved that my mother was in a psychiatric hospital, but that was how I felt. I would no longer be responsible for her. I had a nagging concern that eventually, one of her vodka-and-pill cocktails would end up being fatal. At the time, I had no idea that my mother's self-destructive behavior was a cry for help, but I did sense that she longed for someone to save her. And when I was with her, I felt that the someone was meant to be me. It made me extremely uncomfortable, and sometimes I found myself wishing she would die so I wouldn't have to deal with her anymore. The minute I felt this, I would be racked with guilt. How could I want my mother to die? What kind of person/daughter did that make me?

A few weeks later, in her next letter, she asked if I had ever heard of a singer named James Taylor. He was a fellow resident at Austen Riggs. I shook my head as I read this. Had I heard of James Taylor? I was a huge fan, and now, instead of worrying about my mother, I began to fantasize about meeting him on my next visit. As I sat in my room, smoking Woodbines and morosely playing and singing along to "Sweet Baby James," I convinced myself that he and I were destined to be together. I imagined that when we met, there would be this incredible physical attraction, and he would sweep me up into his arms and kiss me passionately. Without words, we would know that we were meant for each other. It was the classic Prince Charming fantasy, probably influenced by the tawdry eighteenth-century Georgette Heyer historical romances I was reading at the time. Instead of me saving my mother, James Taylor would save me.

That spring, as I sat on the bus driving up the Taconic State Parkway toward Stockbridge, passing through the lush wooded landscape and the quaint New England towns, I was nervous, not knowing what to expect or what shape my mother would be in. I was wearing jeans and a thick navy blue sweater (dubbed a fisherman's jersey, as they were supposedly worn by Irish fishermen), which were all the rage at school but were rather stiff and scratchy. In those days I was prepared to sacrifice comfort for looks.

When I arrived in Stockbridge, nestled at the foot of the Berkshires, the snow had just melted and the trees were beginning to bud. It was crisp, cold, and beautiful. The sun was shining, and I began to feel hopeful that this bucolic spot might be the solution to my mother's problems.

Stockbridge's other claim to fame—besides the Austen Riggs Center—was that it was the home of Alice's Restaurant, made famous by the hugely successful Arlo Guthrie song. It was a Mecca for hippies who were coming to the countryside to start communes and "tune in, turn on, and drop out." This was a new scene to me, as the hippie revolution had a few more years to go before it hit England.

My mother looked sober and better. I hugged her and said, almost without waiting a beat, "Can I meet James Taylor?"

My mother shrugged. "Oh, he's gone," she said. She must have seen the devastated look on my face. "I'm sure he'll be back," she said glibly. "Those Taylor kids are always bouncing in and out of here."

Hoping that he would bounce back while I was visiting, I took stock of her new home, familiarly referred to as Riggs. It consisted of two large white clapboard buildings surrounded by a white picket fence. One building housed the patients and the other offices where patients met with their doctors. It was benign-looking, more like a sanitarium than what I had imagined a mental institution to be. Instead of visible bars or locks, there were verandas with rocking chairs. The patients were free to come and go as they pleased. If they felt up to it, they could work in the large garden on the grounds behind the buildings. The only giveaway that this wasn't a holiday spa was an occasional white-uniformed orderly or nurse walking the hallways.

I stayed alone at a hotel within walking distance of Riggs. It was a large Gothic structure perched on a hill. It had thin walls, and at night, I could barely sleep because of the loud grunting and groaning from my sexually active next-door neighbors. But what most disturbed me about the place was that the owners bore an uncanny resemblance to Ruth

Gordon and Sidney Blackmer from the film *Rosemary's Baby*, which I had recently seen. During the week of my visit, I became obsessed by the resemblance. My room was just above the front desk, and I would lie awake, imagining that they were planning devilish deeds, trying to figure out how I could elude them. I barely slept for three days, until I convinced my mother the hotel was too noisy, and she let me move.

The new motel, a brown one-story building off Route 7, seemed nondescript and just fine, but after I checked in, I noticed that the shower in the bathroom was almost identical to the one in *Psycho*, another film that had kept me awake. I'd always been afraid of the dark and of being alone at night. One of the reasons I liked boarding school was that I was always surrounded by other kids. Nighttime felt safer that way. I knew I could not explain these irrational fears to my mother and move to yet another motel, so I devised a complicated ritual. Every night when I unlocked my motel room door, I switched on the light, dashed to the bathroom, and threw back the shower curtain. Having convinced myself that Norman Bates was not lurking there, knife in hand, waiting to murder me, I walked back into the room, turned on the TV, and tried to find some innocuous show to distract my fertile imagination. This was no easy task, as most of the late-night movies were horror-filled, but that was when I discovered Johnny Carson, and thereafter I watched him religiously. (Ironically, ten years later, my father became fascinated by Johnny Carson and wrote a *New Yorker* profile about him.) With the TV blaring and the lights on, I eventually fell asleep.

During the day, I visited my mother and ate bland institutional food with her and the other inmates in the dining hall. They were actually a jolly lot, considering they were in a mental institution, and most of them were closer to my age than to my mother's. I became friendly with a plump girl named Seabury who had a snazzy red Mustang convertible. She would get a pass so she and I could drive around Stockbridge with the top down. Another inmate, her gay friend Michael, a skinny freckled strawberry blond, came along sometimes, and we blasted Marvin Gaye and Jimi Hendrix songs from her eight-track stereo, checking out the hippies with their long hair and bare feet. The Indian tops, beads, and bell-bottom jeans were a whole new fashion concept to me, and I was eager to copy them. I started by collecting beads and threading them into necklaces that I draped around my neck.

Sometimes we just hung out in Seabury's room and listened to music and smoked cigarettes. She and Michael never told me why they were at Riggs, and I never asked, though now and then my mother would fill me in on a detail of someone's diagnosis—mostly depression, suicide attempts, and eating disorders. For the most part, the kids at Riggs seemed no different from my friends at school.

When I got bored with their company, or if one of them was having a bad episode, I entertained myself at the arts and crafts center: a pottery studio, a jewelry room, and a weaving room all located in a small house a few blocks away. Most of the time, the inmates were too depressed or disinterested to use the facility, though one or two Riggs outpatients usually were there and willing to teach me something.

My mother remained at Riggs for five years, and in those years I learned a great many different crafts, but on that first visit, I was focused on pottery and on a cute local boy.

Dale had alabaster skin and long, dark, curly hair. He supplied the center with clay, and we met one day when he was making a delivery. We flirted and he invited me to visit him in his large A-frame, where he lived with his mother and sisters. I did, and soon a romance bloomed. We did some heavy petting in the back of his pickup truck but nothing more. Along with pottery, it provided a good escape from spending time with my mother.

The next time I visited Riggs, I wove an ugly but cozy poncho in the arts and crafts center. Too late, I realized I had made a terrible selection of colors—brown and blue—but threading the loom was a complicated procedure, and learning to work it even more complex. The alpaca wool was soft and I loved the feel of it, and when I finished, despite not loving the result, I felt committed to wearing it. After all, it had taken me almost an entire vacation to weave. On another visit, I learned how to solder silver and make jewelry, and I made a series of silver chains, a time-consuming but satisfying venture. I wore those chains wrapped around my neck and was proud of my creation. It was in those rooms that I began to discover I enjoyed making things with my hands—the work not only took up my time and distracted me from my mother's unusual living circumstances, it also soothed me, and sometimes I was even proud of the results.

One Christmas holiday I flew to New York, but my plane landed later than scheduled, and I missed the last bus from Port Authority to Stockbridge. The only available bus going in a similar direction went to Pittsburgh, Massachusetts, a town about an hour and a half from Stockbridge, so I called my mother to ask what to do. Though she didn't have a car, she told me she would arrange for someone to meet me. I told her I was wearing my brown and blue poncho—it was the only thing I had that was warm.

When I reached Pittsburgh and got off the bus, I was greeted by one of the Riggs inmates I knew, Danny (whose foot was in a cast), and his friend Katie. After making fun of my "ugly poncho," Danny pulled me aside to whisper that he had accompanied Katie because she had taken a sleeping medication before setting out on the trip. He was worried that she might fall asleep at the wheel. As we piled into Katie's battered yellow VW Bug and drove off, I was nervous; we had driven only a block when the VW sputtered to a halt and refused to start again. With Danny steering and Katie and me pushing, we guided the Bug into a gas station, where we stood in the cold, shivering, while the attendant tinkered around and finally confessed that we had to wait until morning, when his brother who owned the place might be able to fix it.

We pooled all our money and realized that we had just enough for one hotel room. We trudged through snow down the road to the nearest place, a Howard Johnson's. This is perfect, I thought, another crappy Christmas. A reminder of all the happy "normal" families that I did not belong to.

"One room, please," I told the receptionist.

He was a dour New England type who surveyed our motley trio with suspicion. "For how many?" he asked.

"Three," I answered, trying to sound casual. I don't know why I was the designated leader of the group—Danny and Katie were a couple of years older—but I instinctively took charge. Maybe it was that I was the only person who wasn't a resident in a mental hospital.

"Okay," the receptionist said, but quickly added, "pay up front." We handed over our cash, and he reluctantly gave us a key.

When we were finally ensconced in our turquoise and orange HoJo abode, Danny called Riggs to explain what had happened. I could tell from his conversation that the administration was not pleased with the turn of events—two inmates and a sixteen-year-old girl sharing a room was not their idea of a good situation—but they were as helpless as we were to do anything about it. When I tried to call my mother, she had already taken her medication and was fast asleep. I left a message explaining what had happened.

Katie passed out on the bed we were to share and immediately began to snore. I tucked myself beneath my poncho for warmth and listened to Danny on the bed beside us. He had taken off on a talking jag.

"I'm seeing a new doctor. Dr. Phillips left. His wife went off to join a commune, and he had some kind of breakdown . . . Anyway, I like this new guy much better, but he has this weird habit of saying 'And how do you feel about that?' after everything I say, and I think, Well, I don't know how I feel, that's why I'm here!" After an hour or two of listening and pretending to be interested, I pulled the pillow over my head and managed to fall asleep.

The next day was Christmas. Luckily, the attendant's brother had figured out that the car's problem was merely a loose connection to the battery. Without further incident, we arrived back at Riggs, much to the relief of the staff. We were just in time for Christmas dinner, a low-key affair featuring the traditional holiday fare: turkey and all the trimmings. Everybody was medicated or depressed or both, including my mother. I ate as little as possible before fleeing to my room in town at the Red Lion Inn. When I unpacked, I realized I had left my poncho at HoJos. I called, but they couldn't find it.

The next day I mentioned to my mother that I had lost my poncho. "Probably just as well," she commented. "It was rather . . . unattractive." I was hurt. Despite the fact that I didn't like it, I still wanted her approval of my endeavor; I wanted her to appreciate all the hard work that had gone into it. Danny came up with another explanation: "Maybe the maid stole it?" I liked that better. I was chuffed that someone had thought my ugly handmade poncho was worth stealing. That was the best part of an otherwise dreary Christmas vacation.

CHAPTER 14

Sexcapades and the Plaid Pinafores

Despite being the daughter of notoriously libidinous parents and having been born into a pretty sophisticated universe, for years I was a naïf in the realm of sex. When I was twelve and in boarding school at Dartington Hall, I had a boyfriend, Patrick, and one day I proudly wrote to my best friend, Janet, in London to tell her I was "sleeping" with him. Unfortunately, Janet's mother happened to read the letter and swiftly phoned the headmaster and headmistress, Hu and Lois Child. They rushed into the junior school, pulled me out of my English class, sat me down, and demanded to know exactly what was going on between Patrick and me.

I looked blankly at them. "We know what's going on," said Hu sternly, "and we will not put up with such behavior."

I continued to stare, bewildered. After half an hour of grilling, they discovered that although I had "slept" in the same bed as Patrick, we had done little other than cuddle. I couldn't understand what I'd done wrong, and eventually, the Childs believed me and let me return to class. Unfortunately, they concluded that Patrick, who was a year older and had already been in trouble, ought to have known better, and he was expelled. By that time we had split up; nonetheless, I felt badly and responsible for his expulsion.

I was severely scolded for disobeying bedtime rules, and all my weekend privileges were removed. A few days later, I received reprimanding letters from my parents telling me that I must "learn to behave appropriately." I had little idea what they meant, but I did know that from then on the headmaster and headmistress kept a careful watch over me. They needn't have.

A couple of years later, I was again at the center of an uproar, though this time it wasn't caused by anything I had done. It was my father. He appeared on a late-night TV show, and during a discussion about censorship with Mary McCarthy, he was asked whether he would allow a play featuring sexual intercourse to be produced at the National Theatre; at the time he was the theater's literary adviser. For my father, it was an invitation to be provocative: "Oh, I think so, certainly," he said. "I doubt if there are many rational people in this world to whom the word 'fuck' is particularly diabolical or revolting or forbidden."

Clearly, my father was looking for an opportunity to insert the word "fuck" into his reply—most things he did were carefully orchestrated. And this one wreaked havoc. No one had ever said the word "fuck" on British TV. Difficult as it is to imagine now, this was England in 1965, and there were very strict laws about the use of "obscene" language on TV. A barrage of headlines followed, and at school I became the daughter of the man who had said "fuck" on the BBC.

The story was impossible to avoid. Newspaper headlines followed for days: THE BBCENITY, SACK THE 4-LETTER MAN, IS THIS MORAL? Even French newspapers got in on the act and dubbed the event *"L'affaire du mot."* Mary Whitehouse, cofounder of the Clean-up TV campaign, announced that my father needed his bottom smacked. (This must have appeared ironic to those who knew my father and his S and M predilections.) There were even motions in the House of Commons, supported by both Labour and Tory back-benchers, attacking my father and the BBC.

Being the daughter of the man who had said "fuck" on TV meant I was guilty by association. After this, whenever anyone met me for the first time and discovered who my father was, that person assumed I must be both sexually liberated and an easy lay. Nothing could have been further from the truth. After my innocent sleepover with Patrick, two years followed without even a boyfriend. Then there was the brief interlude with Duncan. It wasn't until I was sixteen that I began to date Nick, a shy teenager two years older than I was.

That year during my half-term holiday, Kathleen and my father were planning a trip to Paris. I somehow convinced them to let me stay home alone in the flat and have a couple of friends over. Naturally, the minute word got out that there was an unchaperoned party in progress, kids stormed the place, and things rapidly spun out of control. The liquor cabinet was raided, the stereo was turned up to full volume, beds were filled with entangled, groping bodies, and bathrooms were filled with vomiting youth.

I was wearing my new favorite outfit, a short purple polka-dot dress that I had bought from a trendy clothing store called Biba (one of the first stores in London to have communal dressing rooms, and whose decor looked more like a living room, with sofas and armchairs). Nick and I were right in the midst of the party, making out and mussing up the new dress, when the maid walked in and, seeing the revelry, headed for the phone to call Paris and inform my father of the mayhem.

He and Kathleen cut their trip short and returned the following day. My father was furious with me, and I got the usual parent-to-teenager litany: "How could you lie to us? What did you think you were doing? How can we ever trust you again?" To which I had no good response.

That night my father eavesdropped on a telephone conversation I was having with Nick. He concluded, wrongly again, that Nick and I were doing it. "You're acting like a Lolita," my father said.

"Lolita?" I had never even heard of the book before that night. In truth, I think my father was more annoyed by my literary ignorance than by my behavior. I immediately ran out and bought the book—not a great choice as a sexual deterrent for a teenage girl, but I had to admit it was a good read.

A few days later, I came home late from a party, wearing my short-skirted Biba frock again. When I walked in the door, my father called me into his smoke-filled office, where he was sitting at a typewriter, working on an article. "You know, Tracy," he said, "you're acting like a whore."

I stared at him. I was hurt, and this accusation seemed particularly unjust, as I had barely gone beyond second base with any of my boyfriends. But I was angrier at my father's hypocrisy: The man who considered himself at the forefront of the sexual revolution couldn't cope with the prospect of his teenage daughter becoming sexually active. I said nothing and stormed off to my bedroom and slammed the door.

My father decided there must be some serious repercussions for my half-term weekend rave. On the final day of my holiday, he announced that after considerable thought, he had come to the conclusion that I was not getting a suitable education at my school. Furthermore, he added, "No one famous has ever graduated from Dartington." I was dumbfounded. This was one of the most absurd things my father had ever said to me. I returned to school angry at him and with an uncertain future.

The ironies were not over. A few weeks later, he took the train to

Dartington to remove me from school. He was carrying a briefcase filled with letters to him from famous people. He was planning to write a book based on them and wanted to work on it during the four-hour train journey. At some point he tucked the briefcase into the overhead compartment and went to get a pack of cigarettes, and when he returned, the briefcase was gone.

Consequently, he arrived at school in a terrible mood, tense and pale, chain-smoking his Dunhill cigarettes. He kept talking about those letters—they would never be found—until I felt the loss was somehow my fault. When he met with my tutor, Roger, he was persuaded that taking me out of school was not a good idea. I imagine Roger told him that a man who was living in sin with his girlfriend (they were not married) and who had allowed his teenage daughter to stay home alone in London was perhaps not the best moral compass. With my father in a weakened state—probably due more to the loss of his literary cache than to his concern for me—Roger convinced him to let me stay. My father returned to London that day, and I was allowed to remain at Dartington.

When he was gone, I was hauled yet again into the Childs' office and made to understand how very narrowly I had missed being expelled. Hu Child sagely puffed on his pipe while Lois sighed and wrung her hands and said things like "What is going to become of you?" and "What are we going to do with you?" I was mortified, especially since all my friends were having much more active sex lives than I was. But here I was, always the one in trouble.

"Look at how you dress," said Lois, as I sat there tugging at my cutoff jeans and pulling down the T-shirt that barely covered my midriff, wishing I were wearing something more conservative, when it wasn't any different from what my schoolmates wore.

What I wanted to do was scream, "I'm a virgin. My vagina is so tight I can't even get a fucking Tampax up me. Put that in your pipe and smoke it!" But of course I didn't dare, so I simply sat there silently, listening to their diatribe. When I realized that they expected me to say something, I simply mumbled, "Can I go now?" Shaking their heads, they released me.

The myth of me as slut continued. Though by then I did know the facts of life, the mechanics were still a bit murky. When my best friend, Lizzy, revealed that after her "first time" there were "buckets and buckets of it," I couldn't imagine what she meant until I questioned her further and discovered "it" was semen. The very idea horrified me. The logistics of changing sheets and getting rid of all this gooey liquid at boarding school, where we were given clean sheets just once a week, left me stymied.

The more serious problem was physical: I was literally tight as a drum. With one accommodating boyfriend, Philip, I did manage to experience a clitoral orgasm, but the minute he attempted penetration, I tensed up and made that impossible. This was hugely embarrassing, especially for someone who was assumed to be "liberated." And I knew nothing about masturbation as an option for sexual pleasure. In America women were reading *Our Bodies, Ourselves* and studying their vaginas in mirrors. In England sex was barely discussed among my friends. Our main concern was not about pleasure but about getting pregnant. Particularly after my experience of Lizzy's unwanted pregnancy, I was even more nervous about the unintended consequences of sex.

Yet as the sexual revolution progressed, I was not happy about being a virgin at nineteen. I was attending Sussex University, studying social anthropology, and living in Brighton, sharing a house with a group of friends, all of whom seemed to be hopping in and out of bed with everyone. I felt left out. I wanted to be sexually active; I had desires but was unable to fulfill them. One day I confided in my stepmother about my inability to use Tampax. Embarrassed, I muttered something about how it was affecting my sex life, and in an uncharacteristic moment of concern, Kathleen offered to find me a sex therapist.

I was grateful if self-conscious as I walked into Dr. Chandler's small mews house in Kensington. She resembled a plump, contented Cheshire cat, petite, in her mid-forties, with hair twisted into braids on either side of her head, Heidi-esque, and dressed in a plaid pinafore dress. I guessed that this casual, un-doctor-like style was meant to put me at ease—as if anything could. I was in my current uniform—jeans, T-shirt, and calf-length coat with silver buttons and epaulets—which, looking back, I can see that I wore as a kind of armor.

After a brief chat, the doctor diagnosed my condition. I had vaginismus, an involuntary tightening of the muscles surrounding the vagina, which made any kind of penetration impossible. I could only nod as she led me upstairs to her office and told me to undress from the waist down. Though uncomfortable with the idea, I was compliant, as always. But when she returned with a series of graduated glass tubes and lubricating jelly and inserted one tube, wiggled it around, and removed it, I grew rigid with embarrassment. I waited for her to explain.

"Take the rest of these tubes," she said, "and practice with them. That's your homework."

Too mortified to ask any questions but desperate to end my enforced virginity, I dutifully took the tubes and returned to Brighton. In our shared house, privacy was nonexistent, so I never did manage to "practice," though each week I showed up at my appointments with Dr. Chandler and told her I had. At each appointment, I noticed that she was wearing a pinafore made of a different-colored plaid. It was her uniform. I thought it more appropriate for a schoolgirl than a middle-aged sex doctor.

After a few sessions, I was able to insert a Tampax. I never asked what might have caused my problems, and she never offered an explanation except to say that it was "a more common affliction than you may think."

When I was in my twenties, I read in a medical journal that some contributing factors are "knowledge of sexual or physical abuse of others without being personally abused, or domestic violence, or similar conflict in the early home environment." I realized that many of my parents' fights had sexual undertones. Unconsciously, I think, I had absorbed a fear of sex that probably caused my physical tightness. Even after the treatment, I remained ashamed of my problem. I never talked about it with my boyfriends, who were often puzzled by my mixed messages: wanting to have sex, yet finding actual penetration virtually impossible.

Finally, at twenty, I was officially deflowered. The culprit was Tom, the thirty-something editor of a trendy London magazine. I was still at Sussex, this time living alone in a single room. I was unhappy, certain I had made a mistake in my choice of major. I painted the room mint green under the misconception that the vibrant color would lift my flagging spirits. I met Tom through mutual friends in London at a party. When he found out I lived in Brighton, where he was going for a business trip, he more or less invited himself over. I was flattered that this older, successful man was interested in me.

When he walked in the door, I noticed his crooked smile and how slight he was. He was wearing classic attire of the time—black velvet jacket, lacy shirt, jeans, and boots—and I thought he looked very cool.

I had dressed carefully in a vintage blouse and a long Ossie Clark skirt, cut on the bias and made out of panels of purple and red Liberty-printed fabric, covered in tiny roses. I loved this skirt. I wore it all the time and had even bought a second one made out of a different-colored fabric. I liked the way it moved when I walked. I hoped I would impress Tom and appear older and more sophisticated than I was.

Tom sat on the bed—there wasn't anywhere else to sit in the tiny flat—and we smoked a pipe of hash he'd brought. Soon we were making out, and for some reason—perhaps the effects of the hash—I relaxed enough that Tom was able to penetrate me.

I remember little else about the event. Certainly not pleasure. When I informed Tom that this was my first time, he looked at me with a horrified expression. "Wow! I just presumed, with your dad and all . . ." Once again I had to thank my father for this misunderstanding about my supposed sexual liberation. "I mean, if I had known that it was . . ." he continued, "you know, your first time . . . I never would've . . . you know . . . done it."

After Tom left, I put on my beautiful skirt and wept. I never saw him again. This experience did not help my sex life, but at least technically, I was no longer a virgin and could attempt to join the ranks of the sexual revolution. It would take years before I was able to trust and relax enough to connect with someone sexually and discover the pleasures of intercourse. As the years went by, I was less defined by the assumptions that people made about me because of my father's famous utterance on TV and his controversial opinions about sex. I became more comfortable in my own skin and was able to shed the burden of being the daughter of the man who had said "fuck" on TV.

CHAPTER 15

Twenty-One in Ossie Clark

For my twenty-first birthday, my father announced that he wanted to give me a big bash. He told me in the kitchen, where he was eating one of his guilty culinary pleasures—Heinz mulligatawny soup, a spicy fermented smell that I will always associate with him. My first reaction was shock: a big party just for me? I was touched and flattered to have such a fuss made over me. I should have known better. What became rapidly apparent was that my birthday was the occasion, but the party was for him.

Using his clout as literary adviser for the National Theatre, my father persuaded the Young Vic to loan us their theater for one night. He determined that we should serve Indian food—his favorite—and made many forays to innumerable Indian restaurants until he found the perfect one that would supply the food at the perfect—cheap—price. The centerpiece of the entire event was the guest list. This wasn't going to be just a regular group of my father's family and friends celebrating his daughter's twenty-first birthday. This would be a testament to his ability to attract A-list celebrities into his life. For the next couple of months, creating the list, keeping track of who was coming and who was not, became the central focus of our lives.

I was at Sussex University, studying social anthropology. The events leading up to the party could have become a mini-anthropological thesis: party-giving among the British literary and theatrical intelligentsia circa 1973. Even though I only periodically came up for weekends, I found it hard not to get sucked into my father's celebrity obsession. Princess Margaret would be out of town. Should we postpone the event until her return? So what if the new date bore no relationship to my actual birth-day? But wait a moment, the Young Vic wouldn't be available after her return. Oh dear. Well, we would just have to have the party without her. Of course, it wouldn't be quite the same without royalty, but we would make do.

I had long known that the acceptance or rejection of a celebrity could make or break my father's day; usually, my reaction was to ignore it. I also had witnessed the other problem—the classic guest-list dilemma of the noncelebrity sort—if you invite Larry and Joan (Olivier and Plow-right), you have to invite Robert and Maggie (Stephens and Smith), as each will be offended if he finds out he hasn't been invited and the others have. The agonizing questions of whom to slight amused me because, really, the question was moot: My father had offended virtually all of his friends at one time or another.

As we sat in his smoke-filled office, going over and over the list of two hundred guests, I knew, too, that my stepmother had her own concerns about the party. They were already living beyond their means, and this event would only add to their overextended overdraft. I felt guilty, but every time I suggested cutting back on the numbers, my father insisted that the place would feel like a morgue if we didn't have enough people. And as so rarely happened, Kathleen and I bonded as the foot soldiers, carrying out while simultaneously resisting my father's increasingly grandiose demands.

"What, no champagne? What's the point of having the party?" my father declaimed.

"It's too expensive," Kathleen and I answered, almost in unison.

"There must be a way to find good cheap champagne," my father insisted, dispatching Kathleen and me out into the wilds of London to find it. When we returned from a warehouse in Henley, he tasted it and deemed it too inferior to serve. Kathleen and I were left muttering under our breath that maybe beer would be a more authentic and much cheaper beverage to serve with Indian food. Finally, a compromise was reached: an acceptable white wine that would go with the spicy Indian food.

As for entertainment, I had been thinking along the lines of a band and dancing, like my friends had at their parties. But no, that would not do. It was a theater, there was a stage, there had to be entertainment. With all his showbiz contacts, my father felt he had a direct line to top-notch talent, and one day, as we sat in the living room and he smoked the inevitable cigarette and sipped his favorite drink—gin and ginger ale—he announced that he had solved the entertainment problem.

"He's brilliant, he's available, and he's agreed to do it for a nominal fee." He glowed with pleasure at the thought.

"Who?" Kathleen and I nervously inquired.

"Max Wall."

We looked blankly at each other and then at my father.

He rolled his eyes. "I can't believe you haven't heard of him! He's one of the most brilliant vaudeville comedians ever. I just saw him. I laughed so hard I wept."

Kathleen rearranged books on the coffee table, and I slumped further into my chair. Great, I thought, an ancient comedian no one's ever heard of.

"It's a major coup," continued my father. "We may be single-handedly responsible for resurrecting his career."

"What about the music?" I asked tentatively. "I really want people to dance."

My father didn't dance, so he didn't care; miffed that we weren't genuflecting over his idea, he said, "Get whomever you want."

I had heard Shakin' Stevens and the Sunsets (a band that specialized in covers of danceable '50s music) at a venue near my college and tracked them down and convinced them to drive up from Brighton to London to play at my party for not much money.

Meanwhile, my father was pressuring Kathleen to convince her friend John Wells (an actor, satirist, and the writer of *Private Eye* and the popular British TV comedy *That Was the Week That Was*) to perform at the party.

"You should definitely ask John," insisted my father.

"The invitation will be better coming from you," Kathleen countered. "If I ask him, he'll expect to be paid."

"But if I ask him, he'll be offended that I want him to do it for free."

Round and round they went until they retreated into their separate corners in huffs. I returned to college, relieved to be going back to the relatively unstressful task of writing a term paper on the anthropologist Claude Lévi-Strauss.

As the party drew closer, I became increasingly anxious. Luckily, my new boyfriend, Michael, was very supportive and kept reassuring me that everything would be fine. Michael was from Scarsdale, New York,

Jewish and shy, super-smart and very political, with long, wavy red hair. In high school back in Scarsdale, he had been a leader of the Students for a Democratic Society. We met during my second year at Sussex, where he had gone to take a break from active politics and to focus on intellectual pursuits. He was knowledgeable about all kinds of literature, from William Blake to Raymond Chandler, and introduced me to the pleasures of American cinema—John Ford's westerns and Howard Hawks's screwball comedies.

At home, the tension over the party and its costs were becoming too much to tolerate, so I began to spend more time with Michael at his parents' house. They had recently moved to London to sell art and antique jewelry. Michael claimed they had moved to follow him; they certainly were very involved in his life. Unfortunately, as the party neared and they heard my discussions with Michael about the party, they became more and more excited at the prospect of the gala event that would introduce them to *le tout* London. I didn't want to disappoint them by revealing that I knew barely anyone coming to the party and therefore wouldn't be able to introduce them to any of the famous people they longed to meet. They hadn't met my father, and I was nervous that he would find them a bit provincial, compared to his more high-powered friends.

These concerns paled beside the real burning question of the moment: What was I going to wear? Some people find shopping for clothing stressful, but I found wandering the streets of London, checking out all the boutiques and trying on clothing, strangely calming. I always did it on my own; most of my friends didn't have the patience. I ended up at one of my favorite stores, Quorum, a small boutique off Fulham Road that mainly sold designs by Ossie Clark. In the late '60s and early '70s, Ossie Clark was the quintessential London designer. His clothes were beautifully made, often in crepe de chine or silk fabrics designed by his wife, Celia Birtwell. The clothing he created had a '40s flair: broad shoulders, cinched waists, and bias cuts. Everybody from Mick Jagger to the lowliest college student was wearing his clothing, because an Ossie Clark design made anyone look stylish and chic. In the shop, I picked out a long cream crepe de chine wrap-around dress with a cutout back, flattering and sexy, perfect for dancing. I was confident about nothing else, but I knew I would look good in my Ossie Clark frock.

A couple of days before the party, my father told me that our friends George and Joan Axelrod had a special birthday present for me. (George was the writer of many classic screenplays, including *The Manchurian Candidate* and *Breakfast at Tiffany's*, and Joan was an interior designer.) They wanted to give it to me on the evening prior to the big bash. Their pal Sammy Davis Jr. was in town, and they had arranged to screen his personal copy of *Deep Throat*, the infamous porn film that had come out the previous year in the States but was still banned in Britain.

I'd never seen a porn film and was, frankly, terrified at the thought. It became clear to me that George and Joan really intended this gift for my father's pleasure. He was famous for his pornographic predilections. He had, after all, created the sex review *Oh! Calcutta!* (The title is taken from a painting by Clovis Trouille, itself a witty pun on "*O, quel cul t'as!,*" French for "Oh, what an ass you have!") I would've preferred to stay home and leave the grown-ups to their fun. Still, the Axelrods had always been nice to me, and I liked them. I knew they meant well by offering this gift, so as we walked into the small screening room at a private club in Mayfair, I smiled and pretended to be looking forward to seeing the film.

There were about twenty of us, including the Axelrods, a few other friends of my father and Kathleen's, and Mike and his parents. My father was in high spirits as he greeted people walking into the plush red velvet room. He looked very stylish in a navy double-breasted jacket with gray piping around the lapels and pockets. He was immensely pleased with himself for having brought off this coup.

I was wearing a beige linen jacket and a short skirt that I realized, too late, looked crumpled and worn. I was nervous about the film. Despite my deflowered state, I was pretty inexperienced, and so was Mike. Our sexual activity was very limited and often consisted of not much more than cuddling in bed. I had never even given a blow job, and the thought of having to laugh or cheer—or, God forbid, derive pleasure—while watching a woman endlessly sucking a man's penis seemed akin to torture. As we took our seats, I could barely look at Michael. Sammy dropped by to introduce the film and said he "hoped we'd have a good time." As I watched him, I could only think how incredibly small he was and wonder what kind of a person traveled around the world with a personal copy of *Deep Throat*. I supposed he did it to impress people like my father—and this night he had clearly succeeded.

As soon as the lights went down, part of me was riveted and part horrified. The plot was preposterous: Linda Lovelace plays a sexually frustrated woman who seeks advice on how to achieve an orgasm. Outside of that room, surrounded by people I trusted, I might have identified with her plight. Linda discovers via the help of a doctor that her clitoris is located in her throat, and so she develops oral skills and ultimately becomes a sex therapist. I squirmed in my seat during the longest hour and a half I had ever spent in a theater and was hugely relieved when I heard the final line: "And Deep Throat to you all."

When the lights went up, I was so embarrassed I wanted to flee. But as the daughter of Kenneth Tynan, important critic and writer and über-cool purveyor of all things sexual, I felt compelled to hang around, chat with the guests, and act nonchalant, as if I'd been watching this kind of thing since I was a toddler. After profusely thanking my father, Michael and his parents quickly left. Actually, I think everyone felt a bit awkward, and as soon as they could, they, too, escaped. When I got back to the house, I was so wound up I couldn't sleep; I had to take a Valium. Nonetheless, I had nightmares about being pursued by large swirling penises.

The next day, the day of the party, I woke up barely recovered from the trauma of *Deep Throat* and gripped with anxiety about the party. I forced myself out of bed and rushed off to meet a college friend whom I had convinced to score me some cocaine. I rarely did cocaine, but I felt I needed extra oomph to get me through what was becoming a terrifying prospect. With the cocaine tucked safely inside my purse, I went to Kathleen's hairdresser and had my hair washed and set, something I never did. When it was finished, I took one look in the mirror and realized I looked ridiculous with curly hair. On the subway ride home, I combed it out.

Tension was high at the Tynan household as we dressed for the party. My father always had a lot of input on Kathleen's outfits, but this evening she had selected her own exquisite black-and-white-striped glittery top and cream silk pants. She looked stunning, her cheekbones prominent, her long hair beautifully coiffed and falling in soft curls. My father, a famously flamboyant dresser, wore what I could only describe as a white safari suit with a wide collar and pockets on the front of the jacket over a black patterned shirt. Despite this strange ensemble, he somehow looked dapper and suave.

When I walked downstairs in my simple cream frock and by now stringy hair, I felt like a poor relation of the glamorous couple. Suddenly, the dress I had so carefully picked out looked drab by comparison. I hated my dress, I hated my hair, and I hated the way I looked. My father must have complimented me, but I don't remember that he did, or if he did, I didn't believe him. At that moment I was so filled with self-loathing that I wished I were going anywhere but to my own birthday party. Instead of a celebration, it felt like I was facing an ordeal. We piled into a taxi and drove in silence across London to the theater.

We arrived at seven, a little early. Seats had been pulled out to create a dance floor. A few people were milling around, sipping wine and nibbling Indian appetizers. Most of them were my parents' friends, whom I barely knew, so I awkwardly stumbled around the room, wishing my pals—fashionably late, of course—would arrive. Gradually, the theater filled up. The mood became more festive, and I began to feel hopeful that the evening would turn out all right.

At eight thirty my father felt it was time to start the entertainment. He climbed onstage in his white suit, grabbed a mike, and said, "Welcome, welcome, everyone. Let's give a big hand to Max Wall." There was brief applause as the venerable vaudevillian, a tiny man in a lank wig, black tights, and ungainly boots, walked onstage. He started by telling a few benign jokes that aroused a titter here and there. He even had a drummer who did a rim shot at the end of each joke—or perhaps I've only mentally supplied that drummer, I'm no longer certain. As the routine continued, the jokes became less funny. He began to tell anti-black and anti-Semitic jokes; mortified, I could only look at the floor. I could feel the audience squirming. When, at long last, he left the stage, he was followed by a faint smattering of applause.

Just when I thought the evening was doomed, John Wells (Kathleen had managed to persuade him to perform for free after all) took the stage, played some witty songs on the piano, and afterward brought Dudley Moore to join him. Their combined charm put everyone in a better mood, and by the time Shakin' Stevens and the Sunsets started to perform, I was feeling hopeful again.

Also, by this time I had consumed a fair amount of cocaine, which probably contributed to my elevated mood. I began to mingle among the crowd: Liza Minnelli and Peter Sellers, who had just started dating and seemed engrossed with each other; Lauren "Betty" Bacall holding forth to a group of admirers; Maggie Smith, Robert Stephens, and a small coterie of National Theatre people sharing inside jokes with my father.

Despite my concerns about my friends from boarding school and college mixing with my father's friends, everyone seemed to be enjoying the food and drink, the good dance music, and the celebrity spotting. My father beamed with pride at his accomplishment. I was happy that he was happy, and I began to relax and finally enjoy myself. As I took the dance floor with Michael—who had also partaken of my cocaine stash—and twirled around in my Ossie Clark, I even felt better about my choice of dress.

A little while later, as the night wore on, my father and I were standing together when he leaned in and asked if I knew anyone who had cocaine.

I looked at him and said, "I have some."

We sneaked up to the balcony—a secluded spot—and I pulled out my small glass vial. We spread the last of my stash along the wooden armrest of a theater seat and, using my father's credit card, chopped it up. We took turns snorting through a rolled-up five-pound note. He claimed this was the first time he had done cocaine and begged me not to tell Kathleen. I was sure she wouldn't care, but I agreed to keep it our secret. I swelled with pride at being the person introducing him to something new. Not exactly a traditional father-daughter moment, but that is about as good as it could get with my dad and me.

Surprisingly, Max Wall's career, if not invigorated by his performance at my party, survived, and he continued performing into the '90s. John Cleese even claimed that Max inspired his "Ministry of Silly Walks" from Monty Python. Photos and a blurb about the party ("Young Tynan and Young Vic") appeared in "Jennifer's Diary," a column in English *Vogue*. According to Kathleen, that made the whole event tax-deductible and thus lessened their financial pain.

I never again wore the crepe de chine dress. I had no other grand parties to go to. Soon after my birthday, I realized that Sussex, social anthropology, and I were not a good fit. Those hours doing crafts at Dartington and in Stockbridge had inspired me, and I decided to leave college to focus on my creative self. As usual, my parents were too wrapped up in their own dramas to discourage me. Even if they had, I am not sure it would have made any difference. With Michael's help, I found a craft school in Maine where I could take a six-week summer course in pottery, while he lived nearby in a house owned by friends of his parents. On the move to America, I lost the dress.

Twenty-nine years later, as I approached my fiftieth birthday, I was browsing in a vintage clothing store on Melrose Avenue in Los Angeles when I came across an Ossie Clark dress identical to the one I had worn at the party. Like so many talented people of the swinging '60s, Ossie Clark's meteoric rise had been followed by an equally spectacular fall. After years of struggling with drug addiction, he was found murdered in 1996 by an ex-boyfriend. My dress was now a collector's item.

I pulled it off the rack and admired again the cut, the fabric, and how contemporary it still looked. As I held it, I was hit by a wave of nostalgia. I felt again the intoxicating brew of anxiety and excitement, and I thought of trying it on. To recapture my youth? I looked at the price tag: a thousand dollars! I returned it to the rack. My elegant, complicated father was long gone, my youth was gone, but I hoped someone would buy it one day and wear it for a memorable event.

CHAPTER 16

The One-Size-Fits-All
Clothing That Fits in a Bag

After a summer of making pottery in Maine, I realized that spending my days sitting in a studio throwing pots was not going to satisfy my intellectual side. Besides, I probably wasn't talented or dedicated enough to make a living at it. I decided to go back to school to finish my degree. I applied to Sarah Lawrence College in New York and was accepted.

Soon after, I met a tall, soft-spoken young filmmaker named Ken Locker. We started to date and then moved in together. He was the first man in my life to be gentle and patient enough to help me overcome my vaginismus problems. It was a huge relief after all those years of sexual anxiety, and we settled into a relatively easeful life. During that time, Ken directed a film for PBS, and I worked as a still photographer and editing assistant and became acquainted for the first time with the exciting world of filmmaking. Around the time I graduated from Sarah Lawrence in 1976, Ken began to feel that there were more opportunities for his film career in L.A. Since I didn't have firm ideas about what I wanted to do, and I liked being with him, and liked movies, and was still very much in an exploration mode, a move seemed like a good idea.

We arrived in L.A. in late August, and through a connection from my aunt Shirley Clarke, who was teaching film and video at UCLA, we managed to find an apartment in West Hollywood on Fountain Avenue. It was in a large white stucco building, built in the '20s in the French château style. Shirley also invited me to join her class at UCLA. "I'm sure no one will notice another body," she insisted, and because I was curious about film and video, I eagerly accepted.

Shirley was not only an accomplished filmmaker who had made groundbreaking films like *The Cool World*, *The Connection*, and *Portrait of Jason*, she was an encouraging and generous teacher. But there was a problem: She was allergic to video equipment, or maybe it was vice versa. The minute she walked into the studio at UCLA, some piece of previously functioning equipment would break down. The students took bets on which deck or light would stop functioning when she arrived. Still, her students managed to overcome this aberration and, under her idiosyncratic tutelage, turned out dozens of interesting films and videos.

After a few weeks of attending Shirley's class, I noticed a girl who always seemed to be stylishly dressed: brightly colored shirts, narrow leather belts over tailored slacks, and oversize jackets with padded shoulders in bold prints. It was a more sophisticated look than I was accustomed to, with my jeans and vintage patterned shirts, or '40s dresses made out of rayon, cinched with a belt. By now I had become a clotheshorse, always lusting after new items. Some people first notice eyes, hair, or skin, but I always noticed what people were wearing and, from a mile away, could pick out a fashionista. This girl, I saw, was just that, so I decided I had to know her. Her name was Mary Ann, and we became good friends. She worked part-time for a fashion designer named Harriet Selwyn, and she had access to a lot of cool clothing.

One day as we sat in the studio, waiting for yet another piece of equipment to be repaired, Mary Ann told me that Harriet was looking for someone to work in the PR department at her company, Fragments. She asked if I might be interested, and I leaped at the chance. I was worried that I might not be qualified for the job, but Mary Ann assured me that my lack of experience was not a problem. Harriet hired according to her gut, and if she liked me, she would hire me. I could learn what I needed to from her and her staff.

A year before, Harriet had discovered a lump in her breast and had a mastectomy. For her thesis project, Mary Ann had made a documentary about this traumatic experience. In the early '70s, there was a lot of shame and secrecy surrounding breast cancer, and few people knew what a mastectomy looked like. We watched Mary Ann's film in Shirley's class, and when Harriet bravely removed her shirt and revealed her scar, I was shocked, disturbed, and impressed by her brave approach to her disfigurement. Harriet refused to wear a prosthesis. Her courageous attitude reminded me of the myth of the women warriors of the Amazon who removed their breasts to make firing a bow and arrow easier.

I was nervous when I went for my interview at Fragments, housed in a building on Melrose Place (way before it became the trendy spot it is today). Harriet greeted me wearing one of her designs, a loosely fitted dress made out of a silky fabric that fell flat on one side of her chest. It was hard not to stare. Despite my gawking, Harriet took a liking to me and hired me to do PR.

The truth of the matter was that Harriet didn't need a PR department; she was her own best salesperson. She had a dynamic personality coupled with a distinctive New York accent. She treated everyone who worked for her equally, from sales executives to seamstresses. She ran the business like a family. At the same time, there was no question that she was the boss, and when necessary, she was tough.

The company's line was based on the Fragments Bag, a soft tote that could also be worn as a hat and/or scarf. The bag held six basic separates made out of washable, wrinkle-free Qiana jersey in a range of bright mix-and-match colors; when combined, they supposedly transformed into a hundred different outfits. (I never managed more than fifteen.) Also in the bag was a chic silver necklace with a stainless-steel tube that contained a toothbrush. The main selling point of the Fragments Bag was that it offered multiple wardrobe options for the on-the-go modern woman. After discoing the night away at Studio 54, she could head out to a weekend jaunt on Long Island and never lack for clothing (or a toothbrush). Also, because of the stretchy nature of the fabric, there was no sizing: It was hailed as one-size-fits-all clothing. A brilliant concept and way ahead of its time.

My job—apart from calling newspapers and magazines and following up on interviews—was to show off the amazing Fragments Bag to prospective buyers. This actually required some serious performance skills, as I whipped out the dress, skirt, pants, and tops and modeled how the skirt transformed into a dress, how it could be layered with the pants, how the shirt became a jacket, how the bag became a scarf or a hood or a belt. After a month, Harriet deemed me sufficiently competent and assigned me a low-level buyer to whom I was supposed to show off my stuff.

A small man entered the all-white showroom, where I offered him the requisite tea or coffee. He declined. We chitchatted. I stalled, avoiding the moment when I would have to begin the show. He looked at his watch, mentioning that he had another appointment after me. Forced into action, I brought out the bag and began. At first I was at ease, but after a few minutes of wrapping, tying, and stretching, I managed to tie one knot too many (or perhaps I pulled one drawstring too tight) and became hopelessly tangled in a web of stretchy Qiana. In a panic, I yanked, but the harder I pulled, the more entangled I became. As I hopped around the room, I caught the buyer's eye and realized that he was struggling to suppress his laughter. "It's okay," he said softly. "I think I get the idea."

But I was determined to finish what I had started, and after a few more pulls, I managed to disentangle myself, stuff the clothing back in the bag, and jauntily throw it over my shoulder. Smiling at him, I said, "And there you have it—a complete wardrobe, crease-free, ready for any occasion."

The man looked at me, momentarily at a loss for words, and then clearly eager to leave the world of Qiana before he was permanently trapped in its web, he leaped up and mumbled, "Ah, thank you. Must be going now . . . very interesting. I'll have to think about this." As he rushed out the door, he added, "It might be, well . . . a little complicated for my clients."

I realized that the Fragments Bag and its goodies would not be sold at this man's store, and I felt terrible for losing a sale. From that point on, I avoided show-and-tell. Eventually, Harriet created a video with an attractive model successfully showing off the line. All I had to do was insert the video and add commentary. That suited me much better than modeling.

The main bonus of working at Fragments was the virtually free clothing. Harriet liked to have her employees show off her collection. We were allowed to buy clothing at cost, but since no one was guarding the store, we could also "borrow" items, which we seldom returned. In addition to the less expensive Qiana line, Harriet had another, more luxurious line made out of expensive silks and chiffons—dresses and blouses and skirts. This line was not so readily available to the employees, but I coveted the clothes. Mary Ann, an old pro working the system, told me to befriend Eddie in shipping.

Eddie was a flamboyantly gay man with tattoos, studs, and long streaked-blond hair. He took great pride in ruling the roost of the shipping department, located at the back of the building, at the top of a flight of stairs. He was in charge of any clothing returned from the stores with minor flaws. I learned that if I lurked around the shipping department on certain days of the week and flattered him—"You look cute today, that shirt looks really good on you, have you lost weight?" (Eddie was on a permanent diet)—some of that returned clothing would miraculously find its way into my expandable Qiana bag.

Over the course of several weeks, Eddie gave me a black-and-white-check silk jacket, a cobalt-blue silk shirt, and a tiered tiger-print chiffon skirt. Unfortunately, in the flush of my joy at my wardrobe expansion, I got careless and wore the cobalt-blue silk shirt to work one day. Harriet's eagle eye immediately spotted it. "Oh," she said, "I thought we'd sold out of that style. Where did you get it?" I quickly muttered something about a sample and ran off to the workroom.

The next time I visited Eddie, he chastised me for being so stupid and threatened to cut off the flow of clothing. This was tantamount to withdrawing drugs from an addict. I begged him to reconsider and promised never to make such a stupid mistake again. He relented, but he was never quite as generous as before.

After five years, someone copied Fragments, and Harriet began to sell her clothing for less. Also, with the onslaught of AIDS, a line that promoted carefree sleepovers became less fashionable. Undaunted, Harriet reinvented herself and teamed up with different collaborators to produce lines of clothing and jewelry that I spotted in department stores everywhere, long after I stopped working for her. Occasionally, I would see Harriet at a party or a farmers' market with her beloved terrier, proudly displaying her single-breasted torso.

One item of pilfered clothing left over from that era—a chiffon tiered skirt in a brown and black tiger print—I still wear, and it's still fashionable after forty years. When Harriet died in 2012 at the ripe age of eighty-one she was surrounded by family and friends. Mary Ann told me that just before she died, she gave her close friends signature pieces of her jewelry. I like to think of us all wearing keepsakes of this brave, indomitable woman.

Before working for Harriet, I had no experience of the business of fashion: how it worked, the seasons, the collections, and the marketing. Much as I loved clothing, it made me realize that I had no desire to be part of the fashion industry. But through Harriet, I got to know other designers like Mary Kay Stolz (professor of costume design at Fashion Institute of Design and Merchandising), David Wolfson (president of Maker's Row), and Rosemary Peck (jewelry designer), and I became intrigued with the idea of dressing other people besides myself.

CHAPTER 17

Pierrot

I was enjoying living in L.A., auditing Aunt Shirley's class, and working part-time for Harriet. Taking pleasure in the endless sunshine and allowing my olive skin to turn nut brown (no one knew about the damaging effect of UV rays in those days). Expanding my clothing style to include the trendy but ubiquitous jumpsuits. I had one in periwinkle blue and one in raspberry pink. I loved the idea of zipping yourself up into an outfit and that was it, you were dressed. No need to find any other matching elements. (What was not so much fun was that when you went to the bathroom and unzipped your jumpsuit, you were virtually naked—particularly as, during this time, I didn't wear a bra.) I cut my mousey-brown hair short and tinted it red with henna, sometimes adding streaks of Pepto-Bismol pink for a special occasion or a party. I liked my new look: I thought myself stylish and original. But just as I felt I was coming into my own, my father and his family—Kathleen, my half sister, Roxana, and my half brother, Matthew—decided to move to L.A.

During the early '70s, when he was in his forties, my father's health began to deteriorate. He constantly suffered from bronchial infections and had trouble breathing. He was diagnosed with a hereditary form of emphysema (Alpha-1 antitrypsin deficiency, which had caused his father's early death), exacerbated by his nonstop smoking. Doctors advised him to move away from England to a more salubrious climate and to quit smoking. Characteristically, he selected Los Angeles, with its air filled with pollution and parties filled with celebrities, neither offering a particularly healthy lifestyle. He claimed he was a "climatic émigré."

They rented a beautiful Spanish-style house, complete with swimming pool, on Kingman Avenue in Santa Monica Canyon. In order to support their new California lifestyle, my father wrote profiles for *The New Yorker*, which he often dismissed as trivial and taking too much time to write. But I think it belied the tremendous satisfaction he got from researching and writing these pieces, not to mention the accolades that he received. (They remain, in my view, some of his best writing.) Meanwhile, he struggled to find backers to direct a screenplay he had written about a ménage à trois. He also continued to smoke at least two packs of Dunhills a day, refusing to cut back. "If I can't smoke, I can't write" was his justification.

I had mixed feelings about being in such close proximity to my father. I hadn't lived in the same country, let alone the same town, as my father for more than four years. I barely knew my young siblings, Roxana and Matthew, now nine and five, respectively, and I did not feel part of my father's new family. I had an uneasy relationship with Kathleen. She wasn't a mother, but she wasn't exactly a friend. We were polite but guarded with each other.

I loved my father, but at this point in our lives, we had a contentious and complicated relationship. A few years before the move, when I had visited him in London, my friend Rosie Boycott (then editor of the feminist magazine *Spare Rib*) and I had gotten into an argument with him about feminism. Many years later, I read about that encounter in an entry he made in his diary:

> *After three hours of this strident nitpicking, I slink off to bed. Their need to attack me is, of course, identical with the tribal assault traditionally launched by the sons of the chief; the king must die. What is sad is that the new woman should turn out to be no more than the old Adam writ large (but perhaps if I were not such a prominent figure they would be gentler with me).*

Of course, I remember the evening quite differently. With Rosie's support, it was one of the few times that I felt emboldened to stand up to him, and I was quite proud of myself for doing so. When I read the diary entry, I was surprised and pleased that it had affected him. Needless to say, the differences in the way we looked at our encounters and at the world had reached a nadir. Now, one year after I had moved to L.A., a few weeks before Christmas, he showed up at my apartment in West Hollywood holding a white box: an early Christmas present, since he would be out of town for the holiday. He was very excited and wanted me to open it immediately.

I invited him inside and eagerly opened the box and pulled out a two-piece white polyester outfit. I looked at him, puzzled. "It's a Pierrot costume," he announced proudly. There was a long-sleeved top with see-through sleeves and a pair of wide-legged trousers. For the pointed clown's hat, he had substituted a wide-brimmed floppy white felt hat. "It was really hard to find," he explained. "Judy [his secretary] had to search all over Los Angeles for it. I hope it's the right size."

I tried to act grateful, but I'm sure my disappointment showed. What was I going to do with a clown costume?

"Don't you like it?" he asked.

"It's great," I lied.

"Why don't you try it on?" he pressed.

Reluctantly, I went into the bedroom and donned it. I took a tentative glance in the mirror: I looked ludicrous, lost in a sea of white polyester. I walked out to the living room to show my father. A broad grin spread across his face. "It's perfect, it fits perfectly, just as I imagined." I was floored. Was this how he imagined me? A comic yet pathetic persona swathed in white?

Several weeks earlier, at dinner one night, he had systematically criticized my emotional life. "You always have a sadness about you, Tracy," he said. "You wear your heart on your sleeve. You should cover up how you feel more." I thought about those words as I looked down at the costume. Though he wanted me to disguise my feelings, he had given me the costume of a sad clown and wanted me to wear it.

Gifts were never simple with my father, because nothing was ever simple with my father; he had a way of saying or doing things that he thought would reassure me but often had the opposite effect. Once when I was a teenager, he said to me, "It doesn't matter if you're not beautiful." I think that was his backhanded way of saying looks didn't matter, yet his life was filled with beautiful, glamorous people, a testimony to the precise opposite. And if I was neither beautiful nor glamorous, I thought in those days, surely there was no hope for me. His words, meant to be soothing, hurt me to the quick and undermined my already fragile self-confidence.

Another time he said, "You know, maybe you could become a presenter, like Joan Bakewell." Joan was a famous English interview host who had a kind of British bluestocking look, lank brown hair, and glasses, verging on dowdy. She was not exactly someone a young girl would want to emulate, but he seemed bent on assuring me I would be fine. "I don't care what you become," he announced when I struggled with my college applications. Yet all his friends "did" something, so it was clear to me that he did care. I wanted to please him, to live up to his high standards, but I felt doomed to failure, and despite his facility with words, he seemed unable to find the right ones to inspire confidence.

Now here I was, in my rented West Hollywood apartment with its postage-stamp pool, dressed up as a sad white clown. And my father was sitting opposite me in his pale blue *guayabera*, blithely telling me about his affair with Nicole, a young actress whom he had met in London through mutual friends. She shared his predilection for sadomasochism, he said. This was the first time he had ever spoken to me about his sexual obsession, but I don't remember being shocked. I think my mother may have said something in one of her drunken rages, and when she said something negative about my father, I instinctively took his side. Now, longing for unconditional love and approval from him, I was willing to accept anything he told me.

He did not go into graphic detail; rather, he described his interest as if describing someone with a foot fetish. He extolled the virtues of their mutual sexual satisfaction. When I look back on it, the conversation seems almost ludicrous, but at the time it sounded perfectly normal to me. Besides, from an early age, I had learned to accept my parents' aberrant behavior with a kind of voyeuristic fascination.

"Does Kathleen know?" I asked.

"Yes, and she's not happy about it," he said. "Don't tell her that I told you."

There was something thrilling about my father confiding in me. It made me feel special, though I knew I was entering treacherous waters. If Kathleen found out that my father had told me his secret, she would be upset with me. And I knew she would find out. She always did, because my father always told her. He couldn't help himself—he had to create drama.

When I first learned about his emphysema diagnosis, Kathleen swore me to secrecy. "You mustn't tell anyone," she insisted, "because if the press finds out, it will mean the end of your father's career. If people know he has a serious illness, no one will hire him."

I tried to reassure her that since my contact with the press was nil, the likelihood of my talking to the press was equally nil. She was not appeased. "Just swear to me that you won't tell anyone, not even your friends!" I agreed, though at the time I thought she was being paranoid. Later, as I came to know how Hollywood works, I realized she may have had a point, but at the time, her caution set up an atmosphere of secrecy around my father's health. As his disease progressed, that secrecy was hard to maintain.

That day in West Hollywood, as my father said goodbye, he lit up a cigarette and coughed violently. "Don't tell . . ." he spluttered. I nodded. I knew the drill. As I waved goodbye, I caught a glimpse of my reflection in the pool—the gauzy sleeves of my top blowing in the breeze, the floppy hat half covering my face. I looked sad. I felt sad.

CHAPTER 18

The Brown Fedora and the Gold Lamé Jeans

I first met Jim McBride a year before I moved to L.A. I was twenty-four and living with Ken in New York. We were having dinner with friends at a Greek restaurant; one of them, Jack, had invited Jim. He arrived late. Jack had already confided in us that Jim was devastated because his girlfriend, Clarissa—the mother of his child—had abandoned him not for another man but for a woman. I imagined that must be a terrible affront to the male ego. From the moment I saw Jim, I thought he was very attractive, and I was surprised that anyone would leave him. He was wearing a brown fedora that partially covered his cornflower-blue eyes, and he had a laid-back attitude that I found appealing. He sat at the far end of the table, smoking cigarettes, observing the situation, but not saying much. We were part of a large group, and I barely said a word to him, but he made an impression on me. I remember thinking that if I weren't with Ken, I would make a play for him. And that surprised me, since when I was with Ken, I usually didn't think about other men.

Six months later, after Ken and I had moved to Los Angeles, Jim kept popping up in our lives. He, too, had moved to L.A. and our mutual friend Jack was staying at his apartment. He invited us over for drinks, where we met Jim's four-year-old towheaded son, Jesse, whom Jim was raising by himself (Clarissa had remained in New York). In those days, single fathers were a rarity, and Jim's devotion and commitment to his son impressed me. It was touching to see their affection for each other. Jesse sat nestled in Jim's lap. He reminded me a little of myself at that age; he seemed very at ease around adults. Jim didn't remember me from the Greek restaurant. I was miffed that I hadn't made the same kind of impression on him that he had made on me.

Several months after that visit to Jim's duplex off Fairfax, Ken and I gave a belated housewarming party at our apartment in West Hollywood, and we invited Jim. The night of the party, I was wearing my recently purchased skintight gold lamé Fiorucci jeans. (Fiorucci had just opened a flagship store in Beverly Hills in an old art deco building filled with shiny disco clothing and music from *Saturday Night Fever* blasting away.) The jeans looked great, but wearing them was like wearing a plastic bag. Jim arrived wearing his trademark fedora. Despite my sweatiness, he looked at my jeans and broke into a grin, saying, "Never thought I'd go for a girl in gold lamé." This time I knew I was making an impression.

Kathleen was also at the party, and at some point as I was serving drinks, she asked me who Jim was. I told her what little I knew—that he was an avant-garde film director who had made a few films. One of them, *David Holzman's Diary,* a faux documentary, had won a prize at the prestigious Mannheim film festival and was considered by many

cinephiles to be an underground masterpiece. Kathleen seemed interested; since moving to L.A., she had gathered more film people into her
social circle. Later that night, I noticed them dancing together. They
were close in age—both ten years my senior—and I felt a twinge of
jealousy, particularly since my relationship with Ken was failing, and
although we were struggling to make it work, I was losing hope.

Ken was frustrated with his work situation, trying to raise money
for various film projects. His frustration led to arguments between us
that sometimes frightened me. As time went on, I realized that he was
not the man I was destined to be with. In April, eight months after we
had moved to Los Angeles, we split up. I never would have admitted it
to myself, but Jim's appearance in my world, and the fact that he was
single, were probably factors in my decision to move out.

A couple of weeks after Ken and I separated, my friend Jonathan
Demme invited me to a screening of his new film, *Citizens Band*. I
decided that this was a perfect excuse to call Jim and invite him to the
screening. I knew it was a bold move, but I had never felt the kind of
obsession for someone that I felt about him. Jim sounded pleased that
I had called. He said that he had been thinking of calling me but had
thought maybe it was too soon after my breakup. He was probably right,
but since things had not been going well with Ken for a while, I was
impatient to start the next phase of my life.

As part of my film class with Shirley, I was making a documentary
about the famous octogenarian ceramicist Beatrice Wood. On the day of
my date with Jim, I was scheduled to film Beatrice at her house in Ojai, a
couple of hours' drive away. Her autobiography, *I Shock Myself*, revealed
that she was an eccentric and talented woman who had hung out with
famous artists from the '30s and '40s—men like Man Ray, Picasso, and
Duchamp—and had slept with many of them. Wood's signature outfits
were brightly colored saris. She insisted that the keys to longevity were

chocolate and sex. Apart from her beautiful Lustre glazed bowls, she also made charming figurines engaged in pornographic activities. She had never been married but seemed to have lived a fulfilled life. She had a young male assistant who was devoted to her. In many ways, she had become an inspiration to me, and that afternoon I left her house wishing that my life could be so free.

Beatrice was very gracious, and the interview went well, but I was nervous about making it back to L.A. for my date with Jim. After battling traffic from Ojai, I made it just in time to meet Jim at my apartment but not in enough time to change into my carefully planned first-date outfit—a pink and gray '40s vintage dress cinched with a belt—and we rushed to Paramount for the screening.

After the movie, we went to Nickodell's restaurant with its iconic flashing blue neon sign in distinctive cursive writing: a classic '20s hangout for Paramount actors and technicians. We sat in a red leather booth and sipped cocktails; me a martini, him Scotch on the rocks. In my interviewing mode after filming Beatrice Wood, I quizzed Jim about his life. He had grown up in New York and lived on the Upper West Side, not far from where Ken and I had lived. He had traveled in Europe and spoke French and Portuguese; we even had some mutual film friends in Europe.

"You know Herky!" I exclaimed. He was an ex-boyfriend and a beloved friend since childhood.

"He was one of the first people to show *David Holzman's Diary* in London."

"Then you must know Bernardo [Bertolucci] and Clare [Peploe]," I continued. Indeed he did. Even though he had grown up on New York's Upper West Side and I had grown up in Mayfair in London, I felt like we had common connections.

He told me about his life in New York with Clarissa (also British, a good sign for me—maybe he had a thing for British women), where they had briefly housed one of the members of the Weather Underground. As young hippies, they had driven across the country looking for a commune to join and wound up spending a year in Northern California, living in a log cabin, where Jesse was born.

We also shared similar tastes in film: John Ford westerns, Howard Hawks comedies. And a love of Andrew Sarris's seminal opus, *The American Cinema*. But the most amusing connection was that we were both half Jewish/half Irish. Both our mothers were Jewish, which technically made us both Jewish. Despite the fact that neither of us was religious, this coincidence secretly convinced me that we were destined to be together.

As we continued our conversation in Jim's beat-up tank of a car—a late-'60s muddy brown Buick—outside my West Hollywood apartment, talking and smoking cigarettes, I found myself more and more attracted to Jim. And when he leaned over and kissed me, I was gone. We started making out, and though I needed little encouragement to jump into bed with him, I was trying to maintain my Beatrice-inspired independence. So I announced that I never slept with anyone on the first date. I leaped out of the car before my resolve melted, and I ignored the question he shouted out the window after me: "What about the second?"

In reality, much as I was attracted to Jim, I was terrified that my vaginismus might return. On our next date, in a misguided preemptive move, I presented Jim with an article that I had written about vaginismus for *Ms.* magazine (it was never published). Understandably, he was rather taken aback, but he dutifully read the article, and we proceeded to have somewhat awkward sex. After that initial hurdle, our sex life greatly improved. I was in love with him, and I couldn't think about anyone or anything but him. My mood hinged on whether or not he called and whether or not I was going to see him that day. I wove elaborate fantasies about our life together. I imagined we would make a new family—me, Jim, and Jesse.

Jim had other ideas.

A few weeks into our dating life, I traveled to New York to investigate a teaching course for a body alignment method called the Alexander technique, which I had studied at Sarah Lawrence. (I was accepted but ultimately decided I did not want to move yet again.) Back in L.A., I called Jim several times, but he didn't return my calls.

When I finally reached him, he sounded offhand and was vague about getting together. After a few more days of silence, rather than take the hint, I called him again and demanded to know what was going on. There was a pause during which I must have stopped breathing. And then he spoke: "Well, er, um, I don't think we should see so much of each other . . ."

"Oh," I said, trying to hide my disappointment. "Why?"

"Well . . . I just don't think I'm ready—"

I interrupted him. "You know, if you're trying to break up with me, you'll have to come over and say it to my face."

"Okay," he said, "I'll be right over."

My stomach tightened. I thought I might get sick. The moment he hung up, I burst into tears.

Half an hour later, Jim showed up at my apartment. It was one of those late-fall afternoons in Southern California when the combination of a setting sun and smog create a beautiful orangey-pink haze in the sky. I opened the door and he walked in, sat on my sofa, and lit up a Marlboro. He was looking particularly good, tan and with a new short haircut (that I later discovered Clarissa had given him), dressed in a short, faded pink western jacket trimmed with black and white piping, and faded jeans. I was more attracted to him than I had ever been to any man, and the fact that he was unattainable just made him more desirable, as though he were emitting seduction pheromones that were intoxicating me. In his soft, gravelly voice, he reiterated what he had said on the phone, rolling out the classic trope: "I like you a lot, but just not in that way."

"Oh," I said, trying hard not to burst into tears.

"And," he continued, "I think I'm still in love with Clarissa."

I knew Clarissa had been visiting L.A. to see Jesse, but I hadn't known that Jim was seeing her, too. This was a serious blow.

Clarissa and I had never met, but I had seen her in Jim's movie *My Girlfriend's Wedding*. She was a beautiful woman with long brown hair parted in the middle, chiseled features, and a charming smile. She had come to America to follow the radical-hippie trail. She met Jim and they started dating. In order to stay in the country, she needed a green card. Jim couldn't marry her because he was in the midst of divorcing his first wife, Fern. Clarissa found another friend, a yippie, who agreed to marry her. Jim filmed the wedding and was the witness.

The first time I saw the film, in the early days of our dating, I had a hard time watching it. It is clear from the way Jim looks at Clarissa in the film that he is besotted with her. The film is a visual testament to their burgeoning love affair. Even though it was made eight years before, I was consumed with jealousy.

Now here he was, sitting on my sofa, telling me that he still loved her. And then, poof, he was gone in a cloud of cigarette smoke, and I was left standing there, feeling like an utter fool. I drew the curtains, blocking out the last rays of the smoggy sunset, got into my pajamas, and spent the next few weeks, unwashed and weeping, in front of the TV, watching reruns of old movies.

At last I emerged from my cocoon and decided I had to get on with my life. I edited my film about Beatrice. I got a job working in an antique store owned by an old friend of my parents', Joan Axelrod. I dated a young photographer, Ira Resnick, who showed me photos he had taken of the Dallas Cowboy Cheerleaders. I was immediately taken by their sexy blue and white outfits and white boots: I had never seen anything like that. (In England there are no cheerleaders.) It was 1978, and they were at the height of their popularity. I thought a documentary about their tryouts would be an entertaining and informative piece of Americana. I partnered with my Texan friend Mary Ann from UCLA. A friend of my father's introduced me to the producer David Merrick, and he agreed to finance the film.

Since I had never made a feature-length documentary, I decided it would be helpful to interview all the filmmakers I knew. Or at least that's what I told myself when I called Jim and asked if I could talk to him about how to make a film. I hadn't seen him for over four months, and I was nervous.

He was gracious and agreed to meet me at Schwab's Pharmacy on Sunset, a hangout for film folk where Lana Turner allegedly was discovered in 1937, wearing a figure-revealing sweater. Jim and I sat at the counter and ate lunch. I have no idea what he told me about filmmaking that day, although I am sure it was helpful. I just kept staring into his blue eyes and trying to convince myself that I felt nothing. Absolutely nothing.

A few weeks later, just before I left for Dallas, Jim called and said he had a big favor to ask me. Things were not working out with Clarissa. I had a brief moment of hope, but that was quickly dashed: He was calling to find out if Clarissa could stay in my apartment while I was in Dallas and she looked for a place of her own in L.A. She couldn't pay rent, but she was good with cats and plants. Because the person who was meant to be staying had fallen through, I agreed to meet her and talk about it. Besides, I was curious to meet my nemesis.

A couple of days later, at the time of our appointment, I heard the clomping of heels on the walkway outside my apartment and a loud knock on the door. It was Clarissa. At first I didn't recognize her. In the eight years since *My Girlfriend's Wedding,* she had morphed from a beautiful young woman with long brown hair to a striking, somewhat older woman with short, spiky bleached-blond punk hair. She was dressed in black from head to toe: black leather motorcycle jacket, black skirt, black ripped fishnet tights, and black high-heeled shoes. The soft young face had hardened. She had clearly been through a lot. She was rail-thin. She resembled a younger, more attractive version of Cruella de Vil.

At first I was intimidated—the love of Jim's life, the mother of his child—but as we talked, I realized that despite our ten-year age difference, we came from similar backgrounds—British, theatrical, middle-class—and had similar educations—progressive coed boarding schools. Regardless of my misgivings and jealousy, I reluctantly admitted to myself that I liked her. We had a pleasant conversation, and I gave her the keys to my apartment.

I was gone for two months. It was an exhausting and exhilarating time. Trying to figure out which cheerleaders to follow and trying to guess which ones would make the cut to the final squad was very tricky. The judges had conventional tastes and preferred the "girls next door" to some of the more exotic-looking girls we favored. I developed a crush on our cameraman, Eric, the son of the famous architect Eero Saarinen, but it turned out he had a girlfriend back in L.A. By the end of the shoot, we had lots of sexy footage of the girls trying out to disco music, and a good selection of girls; three made the squad and one didn't.

When I came back to L.A., Clarissa had found another place to live. She came by to return the keys. She knew that Jim and I had previously dated and mentioned that she thought Jim might be ready to get into a serious relationship. I tried to act like I didn't care, but I couldn't help fantasizing about the possibilities.

A producer friend in Sherman Oaks invited Jim, Clarissa, and me to a Fourth of July party. I spent hours trying on and discarding different outfits, finally settling on a short purple-and-green-patterned '40s frock with padded shoulders that I felt showed off my legs to advantage. I completed the ensemble with one of the many pairs of '40s suede wedges that

I had discovered in the back room of a shoe store in L.A. I arrived at the party fashionably late, walked past actors Bill Murray and Dan Aykroyd playing basketball in the backyard, and sauntered into the living room. The first people I saw were Jim and another woman necking on a sofa. I had to summon all my willpower not to run out of the house in tears.

Fortunately, the next person I encountered was Sebastian, an old boarding school friend from England. He was wearing black jeans, a black shirt, black cowboy boots, and a red bandanna tied around his black curly hair. He looked ultra-cool, the perfect antidote to my crushed ego. He was an actor and part-time model and, I later discovered, a drug dealer. He was pleased to see me and showered me with compliments about how cute I looked in my short dress. Over drinks and a joint, we reminisced about boarding school and family. I made sure Jim saw me leave the party holding hands with Sebastian.

I was busy editing my film on the Dallas Cowboy Cheerleaders, and Sebastian needed a place to stay, so within days, he had moved into my apartment. He was generous with his unlimited supply of pure South American cocaine. We spent an evening with mutual friends at Jim's apartment, where Sebastian poured a pile of it onto a table, and we all snorted to our hearts' content.

But a few months after we began living together, Sebastian went out for a pack of cigarettes and never came back. At first I was worried that he had been picked up by some South American drug cartel and beaten into a senseless pulp or, worse, arrested. Then I was pissed. I had never been in love with Sebastian, but I'd enjoyed having him around. We had a shared history of family and friends, and his departure left me feeling one more humiliation. Many years later, I discovered he had hooked up with some drug dealers and gone on a crack-fueled binge and wound up a destitute heroin addict on the streets of Bangkok. There he had been arrested and deported back to England. Eventually, he got sober and reinvented himself as the executive director of the drugs charity Release. We are still friends today.

A few weeks after Sebastian disappeared, Jim called. I was surprised—I had been trying hard not to think about him.

"You sound down," he said.

"Sebastian seems to have disappeared," I said.

"I'm sorry. Why don't you come over for dinner with Jesse and me? I'll make my famous tuna casserole."

Happy for the diversion, I drove two miles to Jim's South Carthay duplex. There he was, looking good in his familiar faded pink western jacket, apologizing about the party. He confessed that he had been hoping to be with me that day, but when I didn't show up, he had gotten stoned and wound up with someone else. It was a lame excuse, but I so wanted to believe him that I did, and before long, he and I began to date again. I was finishing my documentary, Jim was working on a script, and we started spending time together. The truth was, I liked being with Jim and Jesse. We were like a family—the kind I had always looked for.

Clarissa had moved back to New York, and Jim seemed to be over her. Jesse was now six and in first grade at a nearby public school; he was pleased to have me around. The three of us settled into a domestic routine. With my rudimentary cooking skills, I'd make dinner—lamb chops, veggies, and baked potatoes—Jim would read Jesse a bedtime story, and then we would watch some TV—*Mary Hartman*, reruns of *Taxi*—and go to bed. It was a low-key life, but we were both working, and it suited us. When the lease on my apartment came up, Jim asked if I wanted to move in with him. Although he made it clear that he wasn't interested in marriage or more kids, things were going well, so I accepted his terms, hoping he would change his mind.

During this time my father's emphysema took a turn for the worse. It was clear that he wasn't going to live much longer. Kathleen told me that his doctor thought it was a miracle he had survived this long. When I moved in with Jim, I was in therapy, trying to deal with my complicated and ambivalent feelings toward my parents. My shrink pointed out that my situation with Jim was not ideal and that I deserved someone who was more committed to me, but I brushed away his concerns, determined to prove him wrong. Not wanting to acknowledge the reality of the situation.

Ill as he was, my father still loved to play games. One night after dinner at our house (Kathleen was away, so he had brought the actress Barbara Steele as his date), we played one of his favorites, Truth or Dare. We all sat around in a circle and asked questions of the person on the hot seat, trying to guess who was or wasn't telling the truth. If you guessed right, you scored a point. The person who accumulated the most points won the game. If, on the other hand, you chose "dare," you would have to perform an embarrassing or dangerous task.

When it came time for my father to ask questions of Jim, he chose "truth." "What are your intentions toward my daughter?" asked my father.

I stared across the room at him. What had started out as an amusing pastime had turned deadly serious, and I held my breath, waiting for the answer. I hoped Jim had changed his mind, but he turned red and then told the truth. "Well, I'm not going to marry her, if that's what you mean."

I looked down at the floor, flooded with humiliation, angry at my father for asking the question, angry at Jim for answering the way he had. I wanted to take Jim's brown fedora and cram it over his face.

CHAPTER 19

The Leisure Suit and Guayabera Years

With his increasing frailty, my father's taste in clothing seemed to take a bizarre turn, or maybe it was his idea of stylish attire for the Mediterranean climate of L.A. I remember the look of surprise on Jim's face when I introduced him to the man he had so admired. We were at my parents' rented house on Stone Canyon Road, where we had gone to swim.

"Is your dad wearing a leisure suit?" he whispered.

"Yup," I said, followed by a groan.

"Wow!"

This one was bright yellow, but my father also had a pale blue one, both made of polyester. This from a man who once wore bespoke suits made of the finest wool and silk, and custom-made shirts from the best haberdashers on Jermyn Street.

Due to his long, lean physique, he was able to carry off the leisure suits with some aplomb; I imagined that he associated the jacket with the safari jackets worn in the tropics by characters in Graham Greene novels. Besides, at the time—though it's hard to believe—leisure suits were quite fashionable. Since he worked from home and never had to go to an office, he must have thought they suited his new, casual California lifestyle.

His other adopted uniform was *guayabera* shirts in assorted pastel colors. *Guayaberas* were popular in Cuba in the '50s and '60s; I figured my father had seen them there when he visited after the revolution. Short-sleeved, the shirts have either two or four patch pockets and two vertical rows of *alforzas* (fine tiny pleats sewn closely together, running up and down the front and back of the shirt). The stylish ones are made out of cotton and can be quite elegant. But in Los Angeles in the '70s, polyester versions were worn primarily by working-class Latinos and waiters—not exactly the sophisticated set my father liked to be associated with.

Inevitably, the deterioration of his health put a great deal of emotional and financial strain on Kathleen and him. Kathleen continued to write articles for magazines and newspapers—interviews with actors like Dirk Bogarde and an article about the women of Cuba—to help bring in some cash. She also wrote a screenplay based on an idea of my father's that became a film called *Agatha*, starring Dustin Hoffman and Vanessa Redgrave. Although my father was proud of Kathleen, he also seemed to be jealous of her having gotten a movie made while he struggled to find funding for his own project, *Alex and Sophia*.

There were other pressures on their marriage. The affair my father was having with Nicole had intensified, and he spoke of leaving Kathleen. Partially in response to this liaison and as a result of the widening gap between them, Kathleen also started having affairs, though hers were more discreet: I learned of them only when my father decided to tell me about them.

My father's sexual escapades became more extreme the sicker he got. He hooked up with prostitutes who urinated and defecated on him, and he also engaged in other sadomasochistic activities. I knew because Kathleen told me, offering up details that I did not particularly want to know. I think she told me because she was desperate and hurt and needed someone to talk to. But when my father discovered that Kathleen had told me something about his affairs, he revealed stories of her infidelities as justification for his behavior. It was all rather sordid and sad. Often after I saw them, I returned home feeling depressed and wishing I were far away from their squalid drama.

My father increasingly relied on an oxygen tank to help him breathe and was frequently hospitalized to have a tube inserted in his trachea to help him breathe better. Doctors were amazed that he had survived as long as he had, considering the deterioration of his lungs.

Once, while Kathleen was away in Paris, he was rushed to the hospital, and the doctor called me. When I got there, I found my father hysterical and trying to rip the tubes out of his throat. The doctors declared that this was one of the most difficult intubations they had ever done, and they threatened to put him in restraints if he did not calm down.

Unable to speak because of the tube they had stuck down his throat, my father began to frantically write on a yellow legal pad. His usually elegant handwriting had been reduced to a spidery scrawl; from what I could decipher, he claimed that the doctors and nurses were trying to torture him. "Call the British Embassy and get help!" he wrote. "Save the notes. This is proof of what they are doing to me." He tore the paper

157

from the pad, crumpled it in his hand, and gave it to me to ensure that the doctors would not see what he had written.

Bewildered, I pulled the doctor aside and demanded to know what was going on. He assured me that my father was going to be all right. His paranoia was a side effect of too much carbon dioxide in his blood. As his breathing stabilized and his brain received more oxygen, the paranoia would diminish.

He was still writing feverishly when I told him I had to leave. He insisted I take the notes with me; otherwise, "they will steal them." Once again I tried to calm him and explain that he would be feeling better soon, but the fear and anguish in his eyes haunted me as I walked away.

The next day my father was out of intensive care and in a regular room. I was struck by his extraordinary powers of recuperation. He was still unable to talk, but he was much calmer. His first note to me was a request for a bottle of his favorite cheap champagne, Chandon Blanc de Noirs, and a bar of his favorite chocolate, Toblerone. I quickly agreed, although I suspected that he was not meant to have alcohol. All I wanted was to maintain his upbeat mood.

Despite having been ordered by his doctors to stop smoking, my father stubbornly refused to give up the cigarettes that were killing him. Although he had attempted to quit periodically, he always went back. He used to boast that he had gotten his money back from the Schick Center when their quit-smoking program had failed to cure him. Occasionally, when I visited him in the hospital, I caught him smoking. He would look at me sheepishly, as if to say, "What's the difference? I'm going to die anyway." The fact that he had tubes up his nose connected to an oxygen tank, and that he was in danger of blowing himself and a large chunk of the hospital to smithereens, seemed irrelevant to him.

During one visit, he looked particularly fragile, his face covered in white stubble and his thin white arms jutting out of the standard-issue blue and white hospital gown. He asked me to get him a book called *Last Exit*. He mentioned it casually, as though requesting the latest bestseller, but when I went to a bookstore, I discovered that it was a suicide manual published by the Hemlock Society. I was furious that he had put me in such a compromising position. I returned to the hospital and told him that I would not get it for him. He sulked like a child denied a new toy. As I was leaving that day, he pleaded with me to bring him another bottle of champagne, and though I knew this was almost as detrimental to his health as the Hemlock Society book, I agreed. Anything to avoid another argument.

Although my father claimed he did not want to live, he was angry about dying. On bad days, he railed about the incompetence of the doctors and the nurses and the injustices of his situation. "If I can't live the way I want to live, what's the point of living?"

I didn't know what to say. These were impossible questions with impossible answers. "If I can't go to a restaurant, eat the food I want to eat, and drink the wines I like, what's the point?" he demanded. The fact that he was more concerned about being deprived of food and wine than being without his loved ones did not surprise me.

Visiting him in the hospital became increasingly difficult. I was aware that time was running out and he did not have long to live. I knew that if I did not attempt some kind of resolution with him, I would always regret it.

Behind the drama, the peculiar sexual appetites, and the obsessive socializing, I occasionally saw the compassionate man I knew he was. I saw it when he mentored young writers and aspiring playwrights. I saw it when he expressed sympathy with Jim over the frustrations of the film business. I saw it when he "loaned" money, knowing he would probably never get it back, to friends who were going through tough times.

I wanted to acknowledge that compassionate man, and I wanted to tell him how I felt about him before it was too late.

So one day, emboldened by a few swigs of the champagne I had dutifully brought him, I tentatively broached the subject. "You know, Daddy, I've never told you this"—I took a huge gulp of air, and the rest came out in a rush—"but I . . . I . . . I . . . love you."

He reached out and held my hand briefly. Then he let go and said, "Now let's talk about something else," and poured himself another glass of champagne. "This is beginning to sound like a bad hospital movie."

This was not the scenario I had planned. As he drained the bottle, I sat there, devastated. He thought I was being maudlin and sentimental; I realized I had said the wrong thing. Overwhelmed by feelings of failure, I invented an appointment and ran out of the hospital into the blazing Santa Monica sun. I sat in my sauna-like car and broke down in tears.

After that visit, I stayed away for a while. I did not have the strength to be around him. I felt both angry with him and guilty about my anger. Then, just when I was ready to give up on him, he sucked me back in.

One day he was back in the hospital for tests and called to say he had something very important to talk to me about. Kathleen was away on a business trip. When I arrived, he surprised me by announcing that he had decided to bequeath his diaries to me. He said that they contained, among other things, an explicit account of the sadomasochistic affair he had been carrying on with Nicole. He knew that this was controversial material but felt it was among the best things he had ever written—his justification of sadomasochism. Eventually, he wanted it to be published, he told me, and he was concerned that Kathleen might try to destroy it. (There was evidence that she had already made an attempt; he had recently discovered that some pages of his diary had been ripped out.)

I was stunned and secretly pleased by this sign that my father loved me. Why else would he entrust me with such a valuable document? But the sensation of elation was quickly followed by fear. If and when the material was published, it would be sensational, explosive, and potentially embarrassing. I knew Kathleen would be furious and would consider my agreeing to take the diaries an insult and a betrayal.

As I left that day, he handed me an envelope containing a typed codicil to his will leaving the diaries to me and my half siblings and recommending that they be donated to a university. If they were published, the proceeds were to be split equally among my half brother and sister and me.

The next time I visited him at the hospital—as we surreptitiously drank champagne from the hospital's paper cups—he anxiously asked if I had signed the codicil. I told him I had not.

"Well, you'd better hurry up," he said. "Kathleen's back." He paused. "She's found out that I'm giving you the diaries, and she's furious."

"How did she find out?" I wondered.

"I told her," he said proudly, pouring himself some more champagne. I could feel yet another family drama unfolding, and as usual, I felt powerless to do anything about it. That afternoon at home, I signed the document and had Jim sign as a witness.

A few weeks later, Kathleen gave a luncheon that included only family and Jim. My father was back at home—the hospital could do nothing more for him. He looked pale and thin, more like seventy-three than fifty-three, but he seemed in good spirits. He was wearing a white *guayabera* that seemed about four sizes too big. With his pale skin and white trousers, he looked ghostly.

A record was playing, and I asked my father what the music was. He told me it was the Mozart Clarinet Quintet. He said he was planning the music for his funeral, but there was so much to choose from, he was having a hard time making a selection: Miles Davis, Bing Crosby, the Beatles, show tunes—all the eclectic music he loved, along with his recent discovery, opera.

The whole lunch had a surreal quality, as if we all were acknowledging his impending demise without directly talking about death itself.

At one point his internist, Dr. Giorgi, stopped by, and she and my father joked about his champagne intake, both of them knowing full well that he was not adhering to the prescribed regime. He complained about being lethargic—not unusual for a dying man—and tried to convince her to prescribe some "pep pills," but she refused. Kathleen had to leave before the luncheon was finished—she had work to do—and he launched into a witty monologue about feeling like a character out of a bad Tennessee Williams play. "I'm the doddering old man that everybody's waiting to snuff it." He pointed to Kathleen. "That's my glamorous wife, going off gallivanting with God knows who."

Actually, I did know who: I had introduced her to a French director, Barbet Schroeder, a friend of Jim's, with whom she was having an affair. Kathleen had asked me to put them together: She was considering writing an article about him. I couldn't really think of a good excuse not to help her out, although I did have a sense that she had something else in mind—Barbet was (and is) a very charming and attractive man. Knowing what I knew about my father's affairs, I couldn't blame her for wanting a love life of her own. Ironically, Barbet was reported to have an interest in sadomasochism—he had made the notorious film *Maitresse*—and I thought it was interesting that despite her disapproval of my father's behavior, Kathleen had picked another man with similar tastes.

Then my father turned his attention to me. "And here's my opinionated daughter come to pay her last respects."

To me, the scene felt more like Noël Coward than Tennessee Williams, light and gay and sad.

When the luncheon was winding down and we were ready to leave, I leaned down to kiss him goodbye—he didn't have the energy to stand. The image I retain of him from that afternoon is of a frail, elderly man with plastic tubes up his nose, attached to an oxygen tank, engulfed in an oversize white *guayabera*. It was the last time I saw my father alive.

CHAPTER 20

Black Is Black:
Memorials 1, 2, and 3

On an overcast July day a few weeks later, I was talking to a friend on the phone, and she asked me how my father was. I told her that he was out of the hospital and back at home. I didn't mention that essentially, he had been sent home to die. I was being casual and glib—my current mode of denial—when suddenly there was an emergency break-in on the line. (This was before call waiting.) The operator announced that Dr. Giorgi needed to talk to me urgently. I quickly hung up, and when Dr. Giorgi called back, I learned that my father had had another crisis and had been admitted to St. John's Health Center in Santa Monica. Things were not looking good, she said, and I should get over there as soon as possible.

I drove my VW Rabbit as fast as I could, but by the time I got to the hospital, it was too late: My father was dead. I stood there, trying to grasp the finality of the situation. He and I had been through so many medical crises together, but he had always managed to come back, like a phoenix arising from the ashes of his disease.

I insisted on seeing him. At first the nurses were reluctant, but eventually, they agreed and told me to wait while they "cleaned up." I sat in the hallway on a plastic chair, trying not to let my imagination run rampant about what they might be cleaning up—blood, vomit, feces? The possibilities were endless. I knew so little about death, I had no idea what to expect.

"Are you sure you want to see him?" the nurse asked as she showed me into a room.

"Yes," I replied.

I was twenty-nine years old and I had never seen a dead person, but some basic instinct in me knew it was important that I see my father. I walked into the small pale green room. It had a vaguely acrid smell, some combination of disinfectant and death. My father lay on a gurney, his body covered by a sheet except for his face and one elegantly tapered hand, the hand that had so lovingly held the cigarettes that had killed him. His face was gray and ashen. It already looked like a death mask.

As I began to absorb this new reality, a part of me was relieved that he would no longer suffer pain. Finally, he had gotten his wish and left this world, the place he had come to hate and resent. But I also felt his loss selfishly, focused on the many aspects of my life that I would never be able to share with him now—he would never witness my marriage, if I ever did get married, or know his grandchildren, if I ever had children. Though these were conventional rites of passage, even my determinedly unconventional father might have enjoyed them. He would have been a different sort of grandfather, not exactly cuddly or doting, but he would have entertained his grandchildren with good stories—a retelling of a play, a movie, or a book. And he would have enjoyed initiating them, as he had me, into the pleasures of travel, fine food, and wine. "The good life," as he always called it.

I was glad he had, at least, seen my completed documentary, *A Great Bunch of Girls*. Afterward, he had even told a friend that he was very proud of me, and although it was indirect, the praise meant a lot to me. I thought about all this as I stood in that hospital room. In spite of our rocky relationship, he was the one parent with whom I felt a real bond. Now I felt very alone.

When I returned to the waiting room, Kathleen, who had gone to pick up my twelve-year-old half sister, Roxana, and my eight-year-old half brother, Matthew, from school, had arrived. We all looked stunned and dazed; no one was crying. For such a vocal, articulate group, no one had much to say—we were spent, exhausted. The moment we all had anticipated and dreaded had arrived, and we were at a loss as to how to proceed. The person who had run the show, dictated our lives, angered and infuriated us, was gone. For the moment there was nothing to fill up the huge void he had left behind.

I drove home to Jim and Jesse. Jim hugged me and held me tight. His physical comfort meant more to me than words, so finally, I could relax and cry.

This brief lull was soon broken by a flurry of decisions and arrangements that had to be made about the funeral. Kathleen quickly assumed her new role of bereaved widow, and she played it well, firmly and swiftly sweeping me aside. To be honest, I was relieved.

On a swelteringly hot, smoggy day in August, we gathered outside a crematorium in Hollywood. The grounds looked parched and run-down. The graves with flowers were either wilted or brown. Kathleen had decided that my father was to be buried in England, preferably at Oxford if she could swing it, but as the cost of flying a casket to England was exorbitant, the expedient thing was to have him cremated in Los Angeles, thus reduced to a more convenient travel size.

I had been uneasy about what to wear for this occasion, which was not a funeral but was . . . something. Black was not the staple of my wardrobe that it is now. I had to scrounge around in my closet to find a pair of Mary Kay Stolz–designed black silk pants that I had bought at a sample sale. I paired them with a dark blue collarless silk Harriet Selwyn shirt. Entombed in all this silk, I was sweating profusely. I clamped my elbows by my sides in an attempt to disguise the wet patches that I could feel spreading under my armpits. Kathleen, who always dressed well, was somber but almost casual. She hadn't brought the kids; in fact, there was hardly anyone else there except for my father's secretary, Judy.

Eventually, the hearse pulled up, and I was surprised to see what appeared to be a large cardboard box being unloaded. Kathleen, sensing my discomfort, quickly pulled me aside. "It seemed pointless to spend a lot of money on a wooden casket that was going to be burned," she whispered.

I couldn't argue with her logic, but the image of that box remains seared into my brain like the sun that was beating down on my head. The idea that his large life could be contained in a giant shoe box perplexed and saddened me. I wondered if they had dressed him in one of his leisure suits. Or if they had dressed him at all.

As we sat inside the chapel and watched the box being sent to its fiery destination, my mind flashbacked to an experience a few years earlier. A friend's husband had died from a heroin overdose. I had gone over to her house for tea and to offer my condolences. We had barely finished our tea when she asked me if I wanted to see Michael, her husband. Thinking she was referring to a photograph, I agreed. She walked to the mantelpiece and took down an urn, brought it over to the coffee table, and pulled off the lid. After I recovered from the shock, I was riveted. She poured some of the contents of the urn into her palm, and I stared at what looked like tiny granules of bone. "Do you want to touch it?" she asked.

Feeling it might be rude to say no, and being curious, I did. As I rubbed the gritty substance between my fingers, I thought how strange it was that this is how we all wind up—literally ashes to ashes, dust to dust. The sight of the ashes made everything seem so incredibly mundane and impersonal. What would distinguish my father's dust from Michael's? I wondered. In some ways it was comforting to know that in the end, we're all indistinguishable and equal. In other ways, the banality of the concept troubled me.

The aftermath of my father's death was turning out to be as exhausting as the lead-up. After the cremation came one of two memorial services, the first held in a small church in Beverly Hills. It was supposed to be an "intimate" event for family and close friends, but when Kathleen gave me a list of people to call, I realized that notion was absurd. It read like the Who's Who of Hollywood and included everyone from Johnny Carson to Orson Welles.

Kathleen kept calling me to check on my progress. "Don't just leave messages," she insisted, "make sure you speak to them personally." Right, I thought: Gene Kelly, whom I had met once when I was five years old, was going to answer my call. Not likely. Most of the people on the list—or rather, their secretaries and assistants—were courteous and genuinely saddened by my father's death. The outpouring of letters and tributes both overwhelmed and moved me.

The day of the memorial was another hot day. A friend had loaned me a black sleeveless shift. It wasn't particularly elegant, but I was beyond caring what I looked like; I just wanted to be cool and comfortable. Poor Jim was stuffed into a dark suit that he had borrowed from a friend—suits weren't part of his wardrobe; he was more of a jeans-and-T-shirt kind of guy—and an open-collared shirt and no tie. (The only one he had was a brightly colored orange and green '40s tie that we decided was unsuitable.)

Kathleen greeted us at the church, looking cool and elegant in a black skirt and a cream silk shirt with a ruffled collar. As always, her honey-blond shoulder-length hair was impeccably coiffed. She gave Jim the task of making sure everyone signed the guest book. He nervously agreed, having come to understand that Kathleen never missed an opportunity to put family members to work. As they say in the theater, the service was well "attended." I think even my father would have been pleased at the celebrity turnout; everyone from Joan Didion to Warren Beatty was there. Shirley MacLaine spoke and ended her speech by saying, "I have something else to say to you, Ken, but I guess it'll have to wait until I see you." Then she paused dramatically and lifted her head toward the heavens. I tried not to look at Jim, fearing I would burst into uncontrollable giggles.

George Axelrod, not surprisingly, gave a brilliant tribute. "There are, in one's life, if one is extremely lucky, certain people who, when you see them across a room—no matter how dreary the place, how awful the party—cause your heart to leap up. Such people are called 'Life Enhancers.' These Life Enhancers have several things in common: boundless energy, tremendous wit, and wild, if frequently eccentric, enthusiasms. In addition, they are all crazy."

He proceeded to tell a story about a visit to the Hamburg zoo with my father and Kathleen. My father, having done "slightly too much research," was so immersed in his numerous guidebooks and maps (and making witty ad libs about the Latin names of the animals) that he failed to notice most of the animals had been removed for the winter.

As I listened, I had to smile, remembering how my friends refer to me as the "Nazi Tour Guide," and realizing that my love for guidebooks and travel came directly from my father.

Roxana read Psalm 6 from the Bible. Listening to this young girl reading the fierce piece about a "soul in torment" was powerful. She appeared so self-assured, and when she finished, the Mozart Clarinet Quintet reduced everyone to floods of tears.

Then we all dutifully filed outside into the blistering summer sunshine. There was an eclectic mix of writers, artists, and actors. Many of the women were wearing floppy hats, flowing skirts, and soft tops in muted colors. The men were mostly in jackets and pants, with some in suits. There was a relaxed garden-party atmosphere. The style was Hollywood casual, and everybody was wearing sunglasses.

I had barely collected myself when I saw Swifty Lazar, the superagent, walking quickly toward me.

"Have you been getting the roses?" he demanded.

I looked down at this gnomelike creature encased in an immaculate pin-striped suit, his bug eyes peering at me from behind large black-framed glasses. For a moment I didn't grasp what he was talking about.

"I don't know. I'm not sure. I don't live with Kathleen," I mumbled.

"Does she still live in Bel Air?" Swifty insisted.

"They moved to Brentwood months ago," I said.

"Shit, we've been sending the flowers to the wrong address," Swifty barked, momentarily perturbed. "There must be five or six arrangements . . ." Swifty turned his head and looked at Jim, who was trying to corral people into signing the guest book. "Couldn't he pick them up and bring them to the house?" he said.

"No!" I said firmly, insulted that he would even ask. Swifty seemed momentarily at a loss for words but was quickly distracted by a gaggle of celebrities across the lawn and rushed off to greet them. The flowers were lost to some anonymous posterity.

Afterward, the party at Kathleen's house was a blur of familiar and unfamiliar faces, all offering condolences and regretting my father's premature death. Half the time I was in a panic about not remembering names, and the other half I felt distanced, as though I were only an observer rather than my father's daughter. This was Kathleen's scene. Many of the people were her friends, people I barely knew.

I was relieved to see some old friends like Penelope Gilliatt, the writer and *New Yorker* film critic, who had flown in especially from New York and was becoming increasingly drunk and outrageous. Penelope had not spoken at the memorial service but was determined to speak at the service in London planned for later in the fall. All evening she pulled me aside to try out lines of her speech on me.

Sandy Mackendrick, the Scottish director of brilliant Ealing comedies like *The Lavender Hill Mob* and *The Man in the White Suit,* was there. (The latter film starred Alec Guinness, who claimed to have based his performance on my father, particularly the way he held his cigarette between his third and fourth fingers.) Sandy was an old family friend and a witty raconteur. Well lubricated by generous amounts of whiskey, he launched into a story about a friend of his who had died during World War II and had requested that his ashes be scattered over the sea. Unfortunately, when they flung open the door of the plane to throw out the ashes, the wind blew them right back in. When they returned to the airbase, the commanding officer insisted they clean up the mess. "So after all that"—Sandy delivered the punch line with great relish—"most of poor old Johnny wound up in the vacuum bag!" He roared with laughter, and I laughed, too, knowing it was the kind of story my father would have appreciated. Feeling slightly woozy from too much champagne (my father's favorite, Chandon Blanc de Noirs, of course) and too little food, Jim and I left before the gathering was over. I felt sad and numb.

The day before, I had spoken briefly to my mother, who wanted to know how I was doing. I felt uncomfortable talking to her about my father, since she was always so negative about him, but she mentioned that they had communicated during one of his hospital stays. She had sent him her latest book, a biography of Peter Finch, and he had written to tell her how much he admired it. I was relieved that there had been at least some kind of rapprochement before he died.

By the following month, September, Kathleen had managed to twist some arms and get permission to bury my father in a small cemetery near his old Oxford college, Magdalen. It seemed fitting that he should be buried at the place where he had begun his literary life, where he had lost his Birmingham accent and severed his ties with family and friends. And reinvented himself.

On an overcast, chilly autumn day, Kathleen, Penelope—still working on her tribute—Roxana, Matthew, and I drove down to Oxford in my father's old XK Jaguar, a car that had spent most of its life out of commission in a garage but seemed to miraculously revive itself for this final jaunt. Kathleen looked very chic in a three-quarter-length dark gray wrap coat and boots. (She often wore boots, as she was self-conscious about her thick ankles, which my father insisted came from her years of studying ballet. I was secretly relieved that this great beauty had at least one flaw.) Rox wore a dark sweater and skirt. Matthew looked adorable in a navy jacket with brass buttons and a tie. I was wearing a short black jacket with padded shoulders (part of a '50s suit that I had found in a thrift store, which had the label of Adrian, a famous Hollywood designer), a white shirt, and khaki pants. Despite our somber attire, everybody was surprisingly jolly. We started singing Beatles songs, songs that effortlessly stretched over the generations, so that everyone was able to contribute at least one verse. Roxana won the prize for remembering the most words.

At the St. Cross cemetery in Oxford, poet and playwright Adrian Mitchell and his wife, Celia, Christopher Logue (another poet and old friend), and the dean of divinity from Magdalen College joined us. A small rectangular hole had been dug. Standing beside it was a black box—this time wooden—containing my father's ashes.

Adrian read a stanza of his poem "Calypso's Song to Ulysses":

What is sweeter than the human body?
Two human bodies as they rise and fall.
What is sweeter than two loving bodies?
There is nothing sweeter at all.

I noticed the dean shifting uncomfortably as Adrian read. I supposed poems about copulating bodies were not standard fare at Oxford burials, but I thought it was a great choice, and I was grateful to Adrian for reading it.

Christopher Logue, in a gruff staccato voice, read a short poem he had written. The last line was "uttersome child," which I thought might be some reference to my father, but I wasn't sure and was too embarrassed to ask him afterward. Roxana then read a section from C. S. Lewis's "Screwtape Proposes a Toast." Lewis had been my father's favorite don at Oxford. Then the small wooden box was "committed" to the earth.

I felt resentful that Kathleen had not asked me to contribute to any of these services, though if I had been asked, I don't know what I would have said. My feelings toward my father were still so confused and complicated. Maybe I would have said something like "I loved you, Dad, but you were more like a friend than a father. You were too wrapped up in your own dramas to see who I really am, but I'll miss you." And I knew I would, despite the fact that I had been preparing for his death for months, even years.

As we were driving back to London, my frustration was exacerbated when we stopped off to place the order for my father's gravestone. To everyone's surprise, Penelope knew a great deal about stone, and everyone was pleased with her final selection: pale gray granite with dark veins running through it. I wanted to make sure that my father's middle name, Peacock—actually, his father's name—was included on the stone. To me, the fact that my father was a bastard and had, in effect, two surnames, was an important part of who he was. Also, he was proud of the name and had given it to both Matthew and me as a middle name. Kathleen was vehemently against this, insisting that professionally, my father had been known as Kenneth Tynan, and that was how he should be remembered. Penelope, who was usually vocal in matters of this sort, said nothing, and when I realized mine was a losing battle, I gave up. To this day, I regret that I did. Kathleen's refusal to put Peacock on the gravestone seemed to me in some way a denial of part of his heritage and, by extension, a denial of mine.

A photo taken that day shows me standing apart from the family group with my arms folded firmly across my stomach, staring straight at the camera and looking uncomfortable. It sums up my feelings about that afternoon.

A whirlwind of activities surrounding the upcoming memorial service began the moment we arrived back in London. Kathleen and I had already disagreed about the music selection. I wanted to include some more of my father's offbeat choices, like the Beatles, Miles Davis, and Bix Beiderbecke, from his admittedly overlong funeral selection. Kathleen was adamant that we include only classical music: the Mozart Clarinet Quintet and the Viviani Trumpet Sonata No. 2, music that I felt didn't capture the breadth of my father's bold and playful eclecticism.

This argument took place while we were visiting the Axelrods. George finally pulled me aside and whispered, "Tracy, this is Kathleen's party, and you have to let her do what she wants." I knew he was right, and I backed off, though the irony of George referring to my father's memorial service as a party was not lost on me.

For the final memorial, I had run out of black clothing options. The prospect of shopping for a special outfit did not appeal. I don't think there was a moment in my life when I was less interested in clothes. Viv, a friend I was staying with, offered to lend me a black wool skirt, which I gratefully accepted, and somehow I managed to cobble together an outfit with a black jacket—the same one I had worn at the graveside—and a white shirt. Just as I was unprepared for the heat in L.A., I was unprepared for the cold and rain in London.

The next day I arrived, slightly sodden and damp, at St. Paul's in Covent Garden for the service. Kathleen gave me a seating plan. (George had gotten it right: This was like a dinner party after all.) She wanted to make sure I sat in the right spot with her mother and brother and Roxana and Matthew. I would have rather sat with my friends, as I did not feel much of a part of Kathleen's family. I looked around: Everybody was wearing black; some of the women were even wearing black hats. The London memorial felt much more formal compared to the one in Los Angeles.

To Kathleen's credit, the memorial service was a triumph, a star-studded event that included even royalty. Princess Margaret arrived and joined the service like a member of the family. Following protocol, all the speakers had to nod to the princess before they acknowledged the rest of us and began to speak.

Albert Finney, Alan Brien, George Axelrod, Penelope Gilliatt, and

Tom Stoppard read tributes. They were witty and moving, though ultimately, I think my father remained a mystery even to those who knew
him well. Still, I'm sure he would have felt that he'd received a suitable
send-off, or as George Axelrod so succinctly put it, "We're enjoying
it—we enjoyed you."

Afterward, I was relieved that this part of my father's death was over.
I looked forward to returning to my life in Los Angeles.

CHAPTER 21

The Diaries and the Gold Watch

Kathleen and I were in her bedroom of the Tynan flat in Thurloe Square, getting ready for the post-memorial party, still wearing the same outfits that we had worn in the church. The room was small, filled with beiges and neutrals, a bed and a dressing table and a mirror. The anti-burglar bars on the windows made me feel like I was in a prison. I was dabbing makeup on my post-adolescent acne when Kathleen unexpectedly asked, "Have you told anyone about the diaries?" "No," I lied. In fact, I had mentioned them to a family friend, producer Michael White, who said, "The only way you'll get those diaries is if you steal them." I looked into the mirror to avoid Kathleen's eyes.

"They belong to me," she continued. "How could you do this?" she rebuked as she rubbed powder on her perfect English-rose complexion, having concluded that it was somehow my fault that my father had left the diaries to me.

"I think Dad was afraid that something might happen to them," I replied quietly.

She knew what I was talking about. "I was angry," she said. "I tore out some pages, but I put them back." Kathleen snapped her compact shut. "Besides, I need them for the biography I'm writing on your father."

This news stunned me; I wasn't sure where to look. I knew he had signed a contract to write a memoir sometime before he died, but a biography written by his widow, so soon after he was buried, seemed grotesque. I wasn't sure how to phrase it, but I felt she was capitalizing on his death.

With some trepidation, I ventured in. "Don't you think you should wait a while? You might have a better perspective in a few years."

"I can't wait," she said as she stood up and turned from the mirror. "I need the money now. We'll have to give back the advance if I don't write it." She walked to the bed and picked up her black Chanel bag with the gold chain. "The publisher is going to be at the party. Promise me you won't say anything about the diaries?"

Still reeling from this cascade of new information, I silently nodded, turned back to the mirror to give myself a final once-over, and thought how typical it was of my father to bequeath me something that would cause such family dissension. He must be having a good chuckle up in heaven, or wherever he wound up. Kathleen and I walked out of the room, barely speaking, and made our way together to the party.

After I returned to L.A., I showed a lawyer friend my father's codicil. He explained that I could not claim the diaries as my inheritance because the document had been typed and, as a result, was required by California law to have four witnessing signatures. There were my father's, Jim's, and mine; I was one signature short. We looked into pursuing it in a British court, since my father was a British citizen, but after some investigation, it became clear that a legal wrangle would be prolonged and would offer an uncertain outcome. I did not have the money or the stomach for it, so I stepped aside and let Kathleen keep the diaries for the moment. But her behavior in the matter deeply angered and hurt me. We didn't speak for over a year. And when we did speak again, it was very perfunctory.

Without those diaries, my sole inheritance from my father comprised a gold watch and a pen, both of which Kathleen had turned over to me in Los Angeles. The elegant gold Patek Philippe watch was a gift to him from my mother's father when they married. Miraculously, he had kept it—and worn it—for over twenty-five years. I was very happy to have it. I had always worn men's watches. I liked the way their big faces looked on my thin wrist, and it was a good deal nicer than the Timex I was currently sporting. It made me feel tough, and it reminded me daily of my dad. Sadly, not long after I got the watch, it was stolen from our apartment in L.A. and never recovered.

The pen was a faux gold Dunhill ballpoint. Somehow it has survived all these years and sits in a cup on my desk, out of ink, as Dunhill no longer makes the refills. Still, it is the pen my father used to write with. I'll keep it forever.

Five years after my father's death, Kathleen's biography of him was published. It came out with considerable fanfare, excerpted in *Vanity Fair* and widely reviewed. For the most part, it was very well received. Kathleen sent me a copy: I read only up until the pages just after my parents' divorce. I couldn't go on. Her pictures of my parents' marriage and of my mother were not flattering, though I didn't find them precisely wrong. It was, rather, as though someone had taken a painting I was very familiar with and painted over it: Although the original was not obliterated, it was disturbingly distorted.

The last time I saw Kathleen was ten years after my father's death, at a large party at director Tony Richardson's house in the Hollywood Hills. She had been living in London but came back to Los Angeles from time to time. Tony was looking frail and was soon to die of AIDS. Kathleen, as always, looked glamorous, dressed in white pants and a pale gray silk shirt. She had a new beau, a wily young producer. Roxana was also there, now in her early twenties, grown into a beautiful young woman. We all were cordial and civilized; we had become so expert at presenting the facade of the happy family that I almost believed we were.

Roxana was now living in Los Angeles, and she and I had started to spend time together, getting to know and like each other. She was working for City Councilwoman Jackie Goldberg and embarking on a life of politics and community service. Matthew was at Oxford University. They both had been making frequent trips to London, but I didn't know why until a friend of Roxana's pulled me aside at a party and told me that Kathleen was dying of cancer.

Kathleen had so wanted to be in control at all times. Taking an approach like the one she had taken with my father's illness, she had sworn a small circle of friends to secrecy and insisted that no one reveal how serious her disease was. She did not want pity or even sympathy. That November an interview with her appeared in *Vogue*, the accompanying photo showing her smiling, beautiful, and poised. Casually dressed in an unstructured jacket and slacks, with no sign of the cancer that was ravaging her body. She knew she did not have much time to live, yet in the interview she talked as though she would go on forever. She had just finished editing my father's letters and had bought a small flat in Notting Hill Gate.

The last time I spoke to Kathleen was on Christmas Day in 1994.

Knowing that she didn't have very long, I called from California to wish her a happy holiday and try to make amends. As with my father, I wanted there to be some resolution to our relationship. I had a little speech planned that went something like "I know we've had our difficulties, but I just want you to know that I'll always be there for the kids." The conversation was awkward, and I never found a moment to give the speech, but I was scheduled to go to London in a couple of weeks and thought I'd make it to her there. I never got the chance. The day before I was meant to leave for London to see her, as I was typing the words "The End" on a screenplay I had written, I got the call that she had died. She was fifty-seven years old, only four years older than my father had been when he died. Her ending, although not surprising, was still shocking.

I arrived in London just in time for her cremation. There was a small but loyal gathering, including Jeremy Irons and architect Richard Rodgers and his wife, Ruthie Rodgers. A larger memorial service was planned later. As I sat with Roxana and Matthew—both in black and looking very punk with their newly bleached-blond hair—and watched Kathleen's casket (wood and brass) lowered beneath the red velvet curtains to its final destination, I felt strangely dislocated and sad. An era had come to an end. Kathleen had devoted the fifteen years since my father's death to organizing his life and work. *The Letters*, which had been published in England the previous November, was scrupulously researched and annotated and well received. There were plans for a "Tynan Omnibus" and a "Best of Tynan." My father couldn't have asked for a more diligent guardian of the flame. By keeping his writings alive, Kathleen had sacrificed her own work—laid aside plans for novels and screenplays. My father's life and work became both her yoke and her ticket to freedom. I began to understand that her love for him was stronger than I had imagined or fully understood.

I was grateful that Roxana, Matthew, and I had finally managed to forge a real relationship. I had always longed for siblings, and all these years later, I felt my dream was being fulfilled. My brother is physically similar to my father—tall, with an oblong face and a high forehead—and has many of my father's mannerisms. And his wit. Watching Matthew, I am sometimes struck by their uncanny similarities. Roxana has inherited Kathleen's striking beauty and my father's passionate dedication to left-wing causes. They both have inherited an interest in clothing, too. Roxana is more muted and classic, like her mother; Matthew is bolder, and if he had the money, he would probably be a Paul Smith fashion plate or wear bespoke suits of billiard-table baize. Whenever we get together, we always check out one another's attire. We can't help ourselves. They're also ailurophiles.

One day out of the blue, Roxana and Matthew called to say they wanted to give me the diaries. A friend had told them about the saga between Kathleen and me. I was very moved by their generosity. It seemed nothing short of a miracle that, after all the twists and turns of the last fifteen years, the diaries had landed where my father had meant them to go. When I hung up the phone, I wept.

Not long after, Roxana arrived at my house with a small black canvas bag containing the twelve slim volumes my father had written from 1969 to just before his death in 1980. It was the first time I had seen them, and I was struck by how small they looked. They were barely four-by-six-inch loose-leaf leather binders. Not stylish or practical but unmistakably his, filled with page after page of his elegant, tiny, barely legible handwriting. There were also typewritten transcripts, which amazed me: Had Kathleen been planning to publish them after all?

But I couldn't bear to open them up and see what they said. After all the waiting, I didn't feel like being thrust into the inner world of my father's musings, which I imagined would be soiled and sordid. That is, until Matthew, who'd had fewer qualms, let me know that our father had written some nice things about me. That did it. Since it is never too late for parental approval, I opened the diaries again, hoping for some insight and maybe even resolution.

As it turned out, during the ten-year period the diaries cover, I was mentioned eight times. It was more than I had anticipated. He did write about feeling close to me, which surprised and touched me. He also mentioned going to parties with me and people mistaking us for "brother and sister," which he found "very flattering." And made me feel slightly queasy.

Nonetheless, the language, as always, was brilliant, sparkling, and very moving. The diaries chronicle a man fighting the demons of writer's block and encroaching death from an incurable disease. They also offer detail, as he had warned me, about his long sadomasochistic affair with Nicole. The descriptions of his activities are well written and graphic and gave me some understanding as to what made those encounters so pleasurable and necessary to him. They were not shocking or upsetting, but I couldn't help wondering: If my father had satisfied his need to perform in other arenas—directing movies or plays—perhaps his sexual hijinks would not have become so compulsory.

In spite of his assertion that he was not ashamed of his behavior, that he was almost proud of it, I came to believe that his need for sadomasochism spoke to some deep-rooted sadness and insecurity within him. He was the one who liked to be humiliated and hurt in his trysts, but his behavior hurt others, too—particularly his wives, lovers, and children. I don't imagine all that hurt could have felt that good, whatever the sexual taboos he thought he was conquering.

Twenty years after my father's death, I managed to find an agent and editor for the diaries. In 2001 they were published by Bloomsbury Press, edited by John Lahr. Unfortunately, they came out right after 9/11, and in spite of good reviews, there was little public interest in the musings of a long-dead theater critic in the midst of the world's efforts to come to terms with a frightening new landscape. Still, I was glad that despite all the obstacles, I had carried out my father's wishes to preserve and publish his final work. The cover photo, taken by Lord Snowden—Princess Margaret's ex—shows my father lovingly inhaling a cigarette held, in his trademark style, between his third and fourth fingers.

CHAPTER 22

The Chitenge

After I got back to L.A. from England and the memorial, Jim and I decided to take a trip to Montana. Jim loved "Big Sky Country," and he was eager to show it off to me. Jesse was staying with Clarissa in New York, and it seemed like a good time to take a vacation, so we flew to Bozeman, where we rented a car and drove across a landscape like none I had ever seen. Vast open vistas punctuated by spectacular mountain ranges. Rivers and lakes surrounded by lush forests of pine and fir trees.

Driving through the sparsely populated prairies was a welcome contrast to the claustrophobia of London and all the accompanying dramas.

Ever since attending boarding school in bucolic Devon, I'd found that being in nature had a healing effect on my psyche. This trip with Jim was the perfect antidote to the stressful previous months.

We stayed on a working ranch in a rustic cabin. We rode horses. We befriended a Vietnam veteran who worked for an oil company. He took us up in his helicopter, and from above, the views of the mountains and open vistas were still more stunning.

One day we were swimming nude in an icy cold stream near the ranch, and I foolishly mentioned the subject of our future. Jim categorically stated yet again that he wasn't interested in marriage or more kids. He insisted his resistance wasn't about me; it just wasn't part of his plan. He didn't want a long-term commitment; he wanted to focus on his work. For the first time, it seemed, I heard what he was saying, and I felt suddenly cold. I started to shiver and climbed out of the water. "Why can't you accept things the way they are?" he asked as I struggled to pull my jeans up over my wet legs. "We have a good life together, we have shared interests, shared friends, why is marriage so important to you?"

I couldn't explain, because in many ways I knew he was right. Maybe my disappointment and sorrow weren't about marriage but about the fact that he made such a big deal about not wanting to get married. This seemed like a slap in the face no matter how many times he told me it wasn't about me. His decision signified his fundamental lack of commitment to me.

Jim tried to comfort me, but the exchange cast a pall over the rest of our trip. I knew I couldn't tolerate the imbalance in our relationship much longer.

Soon after we returned to L.A., my godfather, Dick Watts, who had been the theater critic for the *New York Post*, died. Dick had been an inveterate traveler, and since he had no family, whenever he traveled to exotic lands like Outer Mongolia, he listed me as his next of kin. He had left me a small inheritance, and I decided I would use the money to travel to Africa, something I had always wanted to do. It seemed like the perfect way to honor his life.

An old boarding school friend, Susanna, was working for Oxfam in Malawi and proposed that I visit her. We would travel together and spend Christmas on the tiny island of Likoma in the middle of Lake Malawi. I jumped at the chance to get out of L.A. and especially to leave Jim and my growing resentments.

My trip to Africa was a revelation—an entirely new world. Having lived such a Eurocentric life, I found everything about this continent exotic: the sights, the sounds, the smells, and of course, the people. We started our journey in Lusaka, the capital of Zambia. During my first night, there was a cricket invasion. People were literally plucking them out of the air to eat. Susanna explained that crickets were considered a great delicacy and very nutritious and that, when cooked, they had a nutty texture. I was tempted but not quite brave enough to try this unusual treat.

We drove to Malawi and took a small boat to Likoma. On the way, we passed women dressed in brightly colored patterned cloth with the image of the dictator, President Banda, emblazoned on them. We attended a rally where everyone wore Banda cloth in different colors—green, blue, or maroon, depending on their stature in the party. Everywhere women were draped in beautiful fabric pieces known as *chitenge* in Malawi (pareo in Tahiti and sarong in Southeast Asia), inventively wrapped around them as skirts, tops, dresses, and turbans. They used the cloth to carry their children and their possessions. Susanna and I haggled with Indian vendors at outdoor markets and bought yards of cloth—ironically, most of it made in Holland. We picked up a book that showed us 101 ways to wrap the *chitenge* into various items of clothing and bags. With a couple of *chitenge*, you could create an entire wardrobe. They reminded me of the Fragment Bag components.

Likoma was a small lush paradise. The weather was warm and balmy, and we stayed in a thatched grass hut, minutes from the lake. We wore nothing but our *chitenges* wrapped around us and spent Christmas Eve listening to the locals singing hymns in St. Peter's Cathedral, one of the largest Anglican churches in Africa.

While traveling, I had time to think about Jim. I decided I had to end our relationship once and for all. Living with someone who I didn't feel was as committed to me as I was to him was too painful. So I wrote to him, explaining my feelings. When I didn't hear back, I was forced to accept that he agreed. I was disappointed: I suppose I still held out hope that he might change his mind. But in many ways, I was relieved that it was finally over. Now I could get on with my life.

After a month, I returned to L.A. and discovered that he had in fact responded to my letter, but I had never received it. We were standing in his kitchen, and I was telling him that I had decided to leave.

"Didn't you get my letter?" he asked.

"No. What did it say?" I asked, feeling the stirring of hope.

"Well, what does it matter? You have decided to move out."

"But have you changed your mind?"

"Not really. I just don't want you to leave."

I knew I had to leave now or I would get sucked back in and feel endlessly frustrated and unhappy. I packed up my belongings and moved out. This was the second time we had broken up. This time I was convinced it was final.

Using the remains of the inheritance, I found a small apartment on Fountain Avenue in a building that had turrets and looked like a castle. I draped my African cloth over tables and chairs. I worked as an assistant to film director Gary Weis, and I wrote a script called "Daddy's Little Girl," about a woman who, having been abandoned by her father as a child, rediscovers him when she's in her twenties. The script told the story of their growing relationship, and as I wrote, I realized I was still working through the loss of my father.

CHAPTER 23

The T-shirt Wedding Dress

Four months later, just as I was starting to date yet another film director, I went to see an Italian film at the Los Angeles Film Festival, an
epic about three generations of Italian farmers. A friend, Bernardo
Bertolucci, had organized the screening and had cordoned off a row of
seats for his people. I arrived early and sat in the middle. But as the
film began, Jim arrived—with another woman, Susan, a woman I knew.
They settled in just a few seats away from me. I was freaked. Since I was
in the middle of the row and the other seats were taken, I was trapped.
With the first shot of the stunning southern Italian countryside, I began
to cry and didn't stop until the last credits rolled. I have no memory
of what the film was about, but I am pretty sure the subject matter and

performances didn't warrant my outpouring of tears. At the end of the movie, before the theater lights came up, I dashed out of the row, stumbling over Jim and his date, ducking my head to avoid being seen with my tear-stained, puffy face before the lights went on.

The next day Clarissa called me and said she had spoken to Jim. "He's depressed and upset," she said.

"Upset!" I said in disbelief. "But he's with Susan!"

"First off, he's not dating Susan, they're just good friends. And second, he misses you."

"Well, he never calls me," I said defensively, swallowing down tears that threatened again, though this time maybe they were tears of relief.

"He thinks you don't want to talk to him," Clarissa said.

The truth was, I didn't want to talk to him because of the pain I felt over his unwillingness to change. I couldn't explain that to Clarissa, so I changed the subject.

A few hours later, Jim called. I struggled to sound nonchalant and cool, and for a few minutes we chitchatted. Then he said, "Tracy, I miss you."

The tears threatened again. "I miss you, too," I said softly. "But—"

"I'll even marry you if you want me to," he interrupted.

You could have knocked me over with a feather. "What kind of offer is that?" I laughed. Joy was beginning to replace tears. But I was angry, too, not ready to capitulate.

"Well?" he asked.

Drawing on every ounce of willpower and self-preservation I could muster, I said, "I'll let you know," and hung up.

The next day I called my friend Anne and told her about my predicament—now that Jim wanted me, I wasn't so sure I wanted him. "Maybe we should just live together again or something," I said.

Anne is very French and very practical. "*Non,*" she said emphatically in her heavily accented English. "What's the matter with you? It's what you want, *non?*"

As much as I had tried to forget Jim, he was the person I most wanted to be with. Rejecting him after all I had been through was tempting; some part of me wanted to see him suffer, too. But my desire to be with him overrode that corrosive urge. Yes, there were obstacles: He was ten years older than I was, his career was not secure, he had the responsibility of a child, and even as he had proposed, he hadn't sounded perfectly committed. As I listed these concerns for Anne, she reminded me of Joe E. Brown's line in the final scene of *Some Like It Hot*: "Well, nobody's perfect!"

I called Jim and told him I was in.

For a man who had been so noncommittal for so many years, his enthusiasm was surprising. Twenty minutes later, he was standing at my front door with a single long-stemmed red rose. We kissed passionately. His familiar smell and his familiar taste suffused me. After a long, lonely journey, I felt as if I had at long last come home.

We told Jesse that afternoon when he came home from school. He was eleven years old. After Jim and I had split, I would take him out for the occasional meal, and he would always ask if his dad and I were going to get back together. He was thrilled by the news. "After you marry Dad, can I call you Mom?" he asked.

The question touched me, though I knew that Clarissa would be hurt if I agreed. I tactfully suggested that he already had a mom. "You can just keep calling me Tracy, okay?" This seemed to satisfy him. I think all he wanted was the assurance that we were going to live together like a "normal" two-parent family.

Now that we had finally made the decision to tie the knot, we didn't see any point in delaying the wedding. We decided to get married in Las Vegas in a month. The year before, on our way to Montana, we had visited Vegas. Ever since I had read Hunter Thompson's famous book *Fear and Loathing in Las Vegas,* I had been curious to visit this mythic town. At Jim's recommendation, I had also read architect Robert Venturi's iconic book, *Learning from Las Vegas.* I fell in love with the tacky neon and kitschy decor. It was so uniquely American. In 1981 the city was still run-down and funky. But we thoroughly enjoyed ourselves, visiting the Liberace Museum—filled with displays of his glitzy costumes and ornate grand pianos—and indulging in some minor gambling. Las Vegas seemed the perfect place for us to get married; it would take away from the solemnity of the wedding ritual, something with which neither of us was particularly comfortable. Plus, we wanted to get married at midnight, between May 11 (Jesse's birthday) and May 12 (my birthday). Where else but Vegas could we get married at midnight?

All I needed was a wedding dress. I had a pretty good idea of what I wanted: something short, cheap, and white. Something I could wear after the wedding. The idea of a dress that you wore for only one day had always struck me as wasteful.

On a warm spring afternoon, I wandered into a clothing store in West Hollywood, more famous for its macho-studded leather items than its clothing for women. I was perusing the merchandise when I discovered, hanging on a rack in the back, the perfect dress. It was short and white and made out of T-shirt material with a cowl neck and a drawstring waist. And it cost just thirty bucks. I tried it on. It fit me perfectly. It was soft, lightweight, and flattering. As I looked at myself in the mirror from different angles, I wondered if, for such a momentous occasion, I should look for something more elaborate, something more like a traditional wedding gown, but I liked what I saw. The gay salesperson, trained to chat, asked if the dress was for a special occasion. "It's for my wedding," I answered.

"Really?" he huffed disapprovingly. "You know all sales are final, don't you?"

"I know," I said, grabbing the bag and practically skipping out of the place.

A couple of weeks later, Jim and I were an hour out of L.A., driving at ninety miles per hour on our way to Vegas, when I suddenly realized that I had forgotten my wedding dress. After all the ups and downs on the road to marriage, how could I have forgotten my dress? Leaning against the window, I silently wondered if maybe I didn't want to get married as much as I'd thought I did.

I realized, too, that I had never actually been to a wedding. My friends my age were unmarried, and my older friends had married before I knew them. I was nervous. I didn't know what to expect. The nearest I had gotten to attending a wedding was when I was six years old. I was meant to be a flower girl at a friend of my parents' nuptials, but on the day of the ceremony, I had come down with measles. Despite my insistence that I really didn't feel sick at all, I was forced to miss the event.

I was roused from my marriage reverie by the sight of a gas station. I made Jim pull over (this was long before cell phones) so I could call my friend Linda. She was coming later that day to join us for the wedding. I asked her to stop at our apartment to pick up the dress, since she was already picking up Jesse from school.

As I climbed back in the car, relieved at having averted one wedding disaster, I had no idea another was brewing.

We drove in silence for a while, and then Jim said, "So, I guess you'll be becoming Mrs. McBride soon?"

"What?" I asked, sitting up straighter, staring at him.

"Well, we *are* getting married," he said.

"But I'm not going to change my name," I told him.

"I don't get it. I thought you wanted to get married."

"I do," I said. "But I want to keep my name."

"It's because of your father? You prefer his name to mine?" Jim pouted. He didn't turn to look at me; he steadfastly kept his gaze on the highway ahead. But I felt the accusation in his tone.

"It has nothing to do with my father. It's my name, and I want to keep it. Do you want my name?"

"That's different," Jim said.

"No, it's not," I retorted.

He reached over to turn up the volume on the radio, which was, ironically, playing Roy Orbison's "Love Hurts."

"Let's not discuss this anymore," he said over the loud, beautiful baritone.

"Fine," I yelled above the music. We drove the next four hours in silence.

A few weeks earlier, when I had called Caesar's Palace to make reservations, the perky operator asked me about the purpose of our visit. I had told her we were getting married. "Would you like Caesar's to arrange your wedding?" she asked.

"Why not?" I replied, and went on to explain our particular need for a midnight ceremony.

"No problem," said the operator. "Just leave everything to us."

That afternoon, when Jim and I checked in to Caesar's, there was a message informing us that a limo was coming at eleven-thirty to take us to City Hall to pick up our marriage license, then on to the Candlelight Wedding Chapel, the very same chapel where Elvis had married Priscilla. How great was that, I thought, though I was concerned that there might not be enough time for us to get the license.

"Plenty of time," the receptionist assured me. "City Hall is only a few blocks from the wedding chapel."

Some of the gloom from the car washed away as we began to feel well taken care of. Our room was perfect Las Vegas kitsch, gold-flocked wallpaper and a turquoise shag carpet; the centerpiece was a circular bed with mirrors on the ceiling and a gauze curtain we could pull around us. The bathroom had a Jacuzzi. Jim was cheerier, and he rolled a joint and flipped through the TV channels that instructed viewers how to play poker and blackjack and how to bet on the mysterious jai alai. Vegas made me feel as if I had dropped into an alternate universe, and that evening, as I shared Jim's joint, I felt like I was embarking on a fun Disney ride.

Gradually, the few friends who were joining us arrived: Jack, one of Jim's oldest friends, and his girlfriend, Linda, who brought my wedding dress and Jesse, who had carefully selected his outfit—a black tuxedo jacket, a white shirt, and black pants. He looked adorable. Jim, who never bought new clothes—partly due to lack of funds, partly to some sort of principle—wore a white-and-gray-flecked '50s sport jacket that I had found in a thrift shop, with a black shirt and black scarf. The three of us together were an eclectic ensemble that perfectly fit the circumstances.

Jim's stepson, Joe (Clarissa's son from a previous liaison), and his girlfriend, Chalayne, who were attending college in New Mexico, arrived. An old English friend of mine, Teo, unexpectedly showed up to complete our motley group. They all planned to leave right after the wedding—they either had to get back for work or couldn't afford a room. After the wedding, Jesse was going to travel back to L.A. with Jack and Linda and stay with them until we returned from our honeymoon. We had a casual dinner together and arranged to meet up at the Candlelight Wedding Chapel at midnight.

The limo arrived late, at 11:45, and by the time we got to City Hall, the registrar's office was closed. When we showed up at the chapel, the Filipina judge was adamant: Without a wedding license, there could be no wedding. Two girlfriends, Mary Ann and Ellen, an old friend from New York, surprised me by showing up dressed in lime-green and Pepto-Bismol-pink bridesmaids' outfits that they had purchased on

Fourteenth Street in New York. "They only cost fourteen bucks apiece," Ellen proudly announced. "And the salesguy said we could return them after the wedding!"

Even better than their dresses! Ellen's father was a judge on Long Island, and she was convinced that he could help us solve the license problem. Not surprisingly, he wasn't happy about being woken up at three in the morning. Besides, he told Ellen, there was absolutely nothing he could do.

Others made other phone calls. I called the so-called wedding planners at Caesar's, who were totally indifferent. We pleaded, we begged, we cajoled, all to no avail. The judge remained firm: no license, no wedding.

Finally, we convinced the wedding chapel and the judge that since most of our friends had to leave early the next day, they could at least allow us to have a fake wedding ceremony that we could videotape. We promised to return the following day with the license so they could officially marry us.

By this time it was two in the morning and I think we had worn them down, so they reluctantly agreed; they just wanted to get rid of us so they could go home to bed.

Apart from being slightly stoned, I had started drinking champagne in the limo and then moved on to swigs of vodka that Teo had sneaked into the chapel. That plus the combination of nerves, fatigue, and lack of food made me feel giddy, and when at long last the judge started to read the vows, I was seized by an uncontrollable urge to giggle. By the final vow, I could no longer contain myself and burst into hysterical laughter. I was unable to utter the final vow until Jim grabbed me by the shoulders and lightly shook me, and I sputtered, "I do."

Exhausted, clutching our wedding video, we trooped back to Caesar's. Though it was three A.M., Jack and Linda decided to take Jesse and head back to L.A. We hugged and kissed goodbye, and then Mary Ann,

Ellen, and Teo piled into our room and draped themselves over chairs or curled up with blankets on the shag-carpeted floor. I collapsed on the bed in my white T-shirt wedding dress, Jim drew the "privacy" curtains around the bed, and we fell fast asleep. So much for an intimate, romantic wedding night. That night we slept as if we were in a dorm room.

The next day, fighting severe hangovers, Jim and I dressed in matching T-shirts covered in colorful photos of Prince Charles and Princess Di, respectively. A few months earlier, my friend Herky had sent these tacky royal wedding souvenirs from England. I'd been saving them to wear on the right occasion, and now they seemed completely appropriate. Teo, Mary Ann, and Ellen had to return to L.A., but Joe and Chalayne had remained in Vegas (in their own motel room), and they volunteered to be our witnesses. The four of us returned to City Hall and got the elusive license.

We traipsed back to the wedding chapel, where the clerks seemed surprised to see us. I don't think they were counting on our returning. The Filipina judge from the previous night was there to officiate. She looked me in the eyes and said sternly, "Marriage is a very serious thing."

"I know," I said, desperately fighting the giggles again. This time I managed to control myself, and the ceremony went off without a hitch.

The judge, barely able to hide her skepticism that the marriage would last past the weekend, wished us good luck. Jim and I said goodbye to Joe and Chalayne, got into his car, and drove off to our honeymoon. A couple of hours later, we arrived in Death Valley, where the temperature was unseasonably high: It was well over a hundred degrees. We could endure only a few minutes out of the car to survey the amazing desert lunarscape, which, Jim informed me, had provided the setting for the fictional planet Tatooine in *Star Wars*. Or to gasp at the mineral-rich salt pans and the miles of sand dunes immortalized in *Zabriskie Point*, before returning to the welcome coolness of the air-conditioned car. We read the guidebook, trying to understand the geology of the exotic-sounding alluvial fans, but outside, the ground was so hot we could feel it burning through the soles of our shoes.

When we got to the hotel, there was an urgent message for Jim to call his agent. I heard only Jim's side of the conversation, but then he put his hand over the receiver and whispered excitedly, "Richard Gere has agreed to do *Breathless*!" I whooped with joy.

"Keith wants me to return to L.A. immediately," Jim added.

I defiantly shook my head. After all this effort to get married, I wasn't going to be denied a honeymoon, even if it was 120 degrees in the shade. "Tell him we're on our honeymoon," I pleaded.

"We're on our honeymoon," Jim repeated obediently. There was a long, silent pause. "We'll be back after the weekend, on Monday," he finally said.

When he hung up, we both screamed in celebration.

This was truly a miracle. Jim hadn't directed a film in ten years and had been struggling for the last five years to get *Breathless* made. Now, after only four hours of marriage, another dream was coming true. Things were definitely looking up.

We had to agree that marriage might not have been such a bad idea after all.

CHAPTER 24

Breathless Beginnings: The Shirt-jac

Six weeks after the wedding, Jim started pre-production on a remake of *Breathless*, the classic new wave film by Jean-Luc Godard. For his version, Jim wanted the protagonist—who had been played by the dashing French actor Jean-Paul Belmondo—to be an American and the girl—originally played by the previously little-known American actress Jean Seberg—to be a French student living in L.A. With Richard Gere slated as the lead, Jim still had not cast the role of the girl. Gere had only a few months before he had another film commitment, so pressure mounted to find just the right girl. The producer, Marty Erlichman, and Richard and Jim all wanted to cast an unknown.

The four of us flew to Paris on a mission to find her. We stayed at the deluxe Bristol Hotel. As a way to rationalize my presence on this trip (and assuage my half-joking fears that he was going to run off with a starlet), Jim suggested I operate the video camera for the casting sessions. I was happy that those long-ago video classes with my aunt Shirley were paying off; fortunately, the camera was on a tripod and did not require much more than setting the frame and turning it on and off. Still, as I filmed one candidate after another, I nervously worried that I might do something wrong and we would lose the audition tape of the next Brigitte Bardot.

The two casting women diligently presented Jim, Richard, and Marty with hundreds of photos and tapes of young actresses. As I watched them scour the photos, I thought this must be one of the ultimate male fantasies: an endless supply of gorgeous young actresses to scrutinize and discuss. I had never experienced firsthand the infamous "cattle call." It really was like a market, with discussions of the actresses' physical pros and cons (nice tits, terrible legs) as though they were pieces of meat. When I lived in New York, I was briefly with the Zoli modeling agency and did some performing in children's theater. Now, I was glad that I had never seriously considered a career in this line of work; I could never have developed a thick enough skin to survive the constant rejection.

After seeing many girls—including Isabelle Huppert, who got my vote (though she was famous in France, American audiences didn't know her), the guys decided on newcomer Valérie Kaprisky. Marty was particularly excited about discovering an unknown actress whom he could mold into a star. He had been Barbra Streisand's manager since the beginning of her career and so had some experience with doing just that. Jim and Richard were pleased that Valérie spoke English well, had enough acting experience, and most important, was willing to shed her clothing and bare her lovely breasts, as required by the script.

Richard Gere was at the beginning of his ascent from famous actor to big-time movie star. *An Officer and a Gentleman* had just been released and had become a huge hit. Wherever we went, clusters of fans awaited him. One night when we came back to the hotel late, the very proper uniformed doorman greeted Richard with humble apologies: "I'm so sorry, monsieur, but your admirers have left for the night." I think the poor man felt that he had failed in his duty to keep the fans waiting.

Jim and I stayed in Paris for a week. We were mainly ensconced in the hotel, but during the brief forays we made outside, what I had always noticed in French films was confirmed: French women have a distinctive chic. Whether it's a scarf casually tossed around the shoulders, or a well-cut jacket paired with jeans, or an oversize men's shirt worn belted over a narrow skirt, there's always flair to what they wear.

When we returned to L.A., Jim plunged headlong into pre-production, interviewing key crew positions—cameraman, production designer, and costume designer. Each night, back home over dinner, he discussed the myriad of problems that he faced, the many locations they needed, and his desire to make the city of Los Angeles an integral part of the film rather than merely a backdrop. As he talked about his problems, I became more and more interested in the process of filmmaking and the decisions that constantly had to be made, each one bearing on the next, like a domino effect. Jim was open to suggestions that I might make about a possible location or about Valérie's character—after all, I had been a college student more recently than he had.

One night he came home particularly excited. It turned out that Dick Sylbert, a well-known production designer who had done *Chinatown*, among many other wonderful films, had agreed to work on *Breathless*. I shared Jim's enthusiasm and mentioned that I had met Dick and thought highly of him, too. (Coincidentally, one of his early films had been my aunt Shirley's *The Connection*.) Dick was quite the man about town and hung out with the likes of Warren (Beatty) and Jack (Nicholson). He was charming, always dressed in the same uniform—a safari jacket and khaki pants. He liked to smoke a pipe and had a professorial air about him.

"Never shoot from the point of view of furniture," Dick would pronounce. "Stay away from blue; it pops too much with the new Kodak film stock." This was the first time Jim had worked with such worldly professionals. He was regularly bombarded with such sage advice from every corner, much of which he was very pleased to embrace.

The one person giving him difficulty was the costume designer, Allen Highfill, who had designed many terrific and/or artful films, including *3 Women* and *Heaven's Gate*. Jim was having problems communicating with Allen. Jim had a penchant for the tacky and garish— that "good bad taste," a combination always tricky to pull off—and he felt that Richard's character, Jesse, ought to dress that way. For instance, Clarissa had given Jim a jacket that was black on one side and gray on the other, made of polyester with a frizzed surface: outrageous, yet so unique it was stylish. Allen tried several times to copy it, but his taste tended toward well-tailored clothing, subtle colors, nothing too loud, and so the result was always way too classy for a hooligan like Richard's character.

Allen and Jim were often at cross purposes, and most nights Jim came home talking about his frustrations. I offered suggestions: a sliplike dress that would allow Valérie free movement, since they were constantly running in the film, and for Richard, a funky combination of thrift-shop and contemporary clothing that would reaffirm his outsider status. Finally, after a particularly frustrating meeting with Allen, Jim came up with the idea of putting me on the film as Allen's assistant. I nervously agreed to the idea. I wanted to help Jim, but asking the acclaimed costume designer to work with the director's wife had the potential to become a disaster. Still, the job seemed perfect for me. I could at last combine my two obsessions—clothing and film—and I began to envision Richard dressed in a red tuxedo shirt and turquoise suit and Valérie in a skimpy frock that showed off her curvaceous figure.

Fortunately, Allen was professional and secure, and from the moment I started to work with him, I was careful to let him know that he was in charge and my role was merely that of facilitator. Later, when we became friends, Allen confessed to me that he was relieved to have someone helping to interpret Jim's often contradictory desires.

Working on *Breathless* was a crash course in film costume design for me. I had good taste and a sense of style but absolutely no idea about the day-to-day requirements for costuming a film. Luckily, because I had worked on films as a still photographer, an editing assistant, and even once as an assistant director on an AFI short, I did know something about the process. For instance, I knew that films and even scenes within them were shot out of sequence—one part of a scene might be shot one day, and another days or weeks later. This made the job of costume designer—keeping a clear continuity over a whole shoot—more complex than it might seem.

With only a few weeks to go before we started shooting, Allen and I started putting together "closets" for Richard and Valérie—or, to be more accurate, for Jesse and Monica, the names of the characters they played. Due to the way the plot evolved, Jesse and Monica were on the lam from the police and therefore had to wear the same outfits for a big chunk of the movie. This meant they had to wear clothing that looked good on the actors and that the audience wouldn't tire of looking at. At the same time, it meant we'd have to provide multiple copies of each costume as backups, for use by stunt doubles, and to track changes, as when an outfit got dirty or torn in a scene. I also thought it vital that the outfits be realistic—a student wouldn't wear Prada, for instance, and a petty thief wouldn't dress in Armani. Both Richard and Valérie had great bodies and looked good in almost anything, and they both were open to suggestions and eager to offer ideas. Since it was my first foray into costuming, I didn't appreciate how unusual it was to have such collaborative actors until much later, on other, less joyful films.

In the case of Jesse, he early on finds himself without money and having to exchange the fancy-ish clothes he's wearing for whatever he can find in a Salvation Army store. This gave us a chance for the character to reinvent himself with a patchwork of other people's cast-offs. One day at a thrift shop, Allen had found two pairs of identical green polyester plaid pants, a kind of cool golf pant. They were perfect. Jim loved them, and they looked good on Richard. The only problem was that one pair was smaller than the other. Allen imaginatively concocted the idea of inserting a strip of black fabric down the side of each pant leg, making them look like a tuxedo pant. Thus we were able to make the tighter pair of pants looser. Even so, we had only two pairs, and on any normal set we'd have had at least six. Still, the pants were so right that Allen decided to take a chance. At the time I had no idea how risky this decision was, but once we started shooting and I saw Richard's dresser carefully taking the pants home each night to hand-wash, I began to understand: These pants were our treasure, and they needed to be closely guarded.

I had always liked the '50s shirt-jacs: short-sleeved shirts with tabs at the waist. I found one at a vintage store that was white with beige and black stripes that looked terrific on Richard and went well with the green plaid pants without looking too designed. Although the shirt was old and one of a kind, we were able to find a store in Beverly Hills that had a stash of vintage fabrics. We hired seamstresses to reproduce the shirt and provide us with the six that we needed for the shoot.

For Valérie, Jim wanted a dress that would show off her great body. I found a Betsey Johnson dress with spaghetti straps that was made out of T-shirt fabric and clung sexily to her top half; the gathered skirt gave the dress a flirty, flouncy look whenever Valérie walked or ran. The only problem was that the dress was white—not the best color on-screen and a color that cameramen often hate, as it can appear too bright under the lights. Allen came up with the idea to dye it ballet-slipper pink, and it looked very pretty. Unfortunately, after we had purchased several of these dresses at various department stores and boutiques, we discovered that some of them had different fabric content, so when we dyed them, they came out in varying shades. We saved the less pretty ones for the stunt doubles.

Once we had solved the major issues of our stars, we continued to design the wardrobes for the many other characters. One of the most important things I learned from Allen was to think of the actors not only as individuals but also as people who would appear in scenes with other actors. You never wanted to discover on the set that you had created a scene in which everyone was wearing the same color or the same type of clothing. This variety is hard to achieve. Secondary characters are cast much later than the stars, and the costume designer has less time and less money to select those outfits. Choices are limited, but the puzzle must work as a whole.

I also learned to always be aware of the background. If an actor was to be sitting in an apartment on a blue sofa, you didn't want him to be dressed in blue, or he would look like a floating head in a sea of blue. This meant keeping in constant contact with the production designer and with the set decorator to find out what they were up to and what color palettes they were using. If you maintained a good relationship, you could help each other out. For example, I could ask the set decorator to put a different-color throw rug over the blue sofa to break up the mass of that color if I'd dressed the character in blue; or he could ask to borrow some items of clothing to give the set a more lived-in feel.

Another reason the production designer, the set decorator, and the costume designer must work together is to ensure continuity of taste.

The character who chooses his clothes also chooses his furnishings. We decided that a foreign exchange student like Monica would have limited funds, so her apartment could not be fancy. At the same time, she was an architecture student, so she probably would have a certain level of taste: Her place ought to have some interesting objects and lots of books.

Breathless is about a passionate but doomed love affair; consequently, the film called for a lot of nudity. As a feminist, and also an appreciator of masculine beauty, I had always felt it unfair that there was such an imbalance between male and female nudity on-screen. I made Jim promise that whenever he showed Valérie's breasts, we would at least catch a glimpse of Richard's extremely sexy ass. Jim told Richard about my concerns; he found them amusing and was happy to oblige. In the shower scene, if you look very closely, you can see that we managed to get away with some blurry, steamy frontal nudity, which Richard and Valérie were good-natured about. Both were comfortable in their own bodies. They understood that it wasn't an exploitative decision but, rather, an integral part of the characters they were portraying.

The three months working on *Breathless* were a giddy time for Jim and me. We were newly married. This was Jim's first film in over ten years and his first Hollywood film. And I had discovered the elusive career I had been seeking, a career that utilized all my disparate talents—a sense of style, a sense of color, a love of film, an ability to interpret characters and portray them visually, and perhaps most important, an obsession with clothes.

After the film wrapped, we broke apart the characters' closets and sent most of the clothing to storage, in case of a need for reshoots. After a year or so, the clothing is often folded back into the studio's costume department or sold to resale clothing stores like It's a Wrap. Occasionally, actors will ask to keep certain pieces of a wardrobe, but after having worn the same clothing day after day after day, neither Valérie nor Richard wanted to see any of it again.

I felt differently. I asked Allen if I could keep one of Richard's shirt-jacs as a memento of the film. That shirt still hangs in my closet with Richard's name sewn on a label inside the collar—a touch that costume houses don't do anymore. I used to wear it as a jacket over a T-shirt or a tank top, and I always loved its softness and the way it drapes so nicely. It looks just like a regular vintage shirt, but I know it's a fake and has lived many lifetimes, and that a movie star wore it on a movie directed by my husband.

CHAPTER 25

Freebies, '50s Glamour, and Funky Smells

After we wrapped *Breathless* in early fall, my old boyfriend Hercules (Herky) Bellville called with a proposition: "How would you like to design a period film for free?" He and his fellow producers didn't use the word "free"; they used the euphemism "deferred payment," which meant I would not receive a dime until they had sold the film and started to make money. In the '80s, when a lot of independent movies were being made, this sounded like a good idea. It had the feel of one of those Mickey Rooney/Judy Garland films: Come on, everybody, let's put on a show! For people like me, who were just starting out, it offered an additional perk: experience. I eagerly signed up.

The film, *Strangers Kiss*, was about a Hollywood director trying to finance a B movie. It was set in L.A. in the '50s and loosely based on Stanley Kubrick's *Killer's Kiss*. It starred Peter Coyote and Victoria Tennant.

Vintage clothing had always fascinated me. Who wore it? And why? And where? I was a great frequenter of thrift shops in those days and purchased a good deal of my wardrobe—not to mention Jim's and Jesse's—from them. Now I had the chance to put my penchant for nostalgia to professional use. I loved doing the research, going to the library and bringing back stacks of '50s photography books. I pored over them, xeroxing particular photos for inspiration. I would show them to Matthew Chapman, the director, and Victoria, and we'd discuss what look would suit the role of the gangster moll she was playing. We had no budget, but we did have access to a seamstress on the lot who could alter the old clothing for a nominal fee.

The fabrics and cuts of the '50s were superior to anything at any of the local department stores and a lot cheaper. Oversize jackets with padded shoulders had recently come back in style, and there were plenty of finds to be had in the thrift shops on Melrose Avenue. I found men's jackets made out of great wool fabrics flecked with pink, blue, or green. I also liked the tightly cinched dresses made out of satin and taffeta, or '40s dresses of crepe de chine. Those dresses were fun to wear for a party; they made everyone feel stylish and glamorous.

Matthew Chapman and I decided it would be cool if Peter always wore black (his character being so Machiavellian), but finding a '50s suit that fit Peter's long, slender legs seemed well nigh impossible. First, there were few complete suits to be found, as most of the jackets and trousers had been split up; second, the suits that were intact seemed to have been made for rotund men with short legs. Eventually, we had to go to a costume house.

This was a new stage in my education in cinema couture. Costume houses have everything, from every time and everywhere, in every style and every size, but finding what you need when you need it is another story entirely. The minute I walked into this large warehouse, filled to the rafters with rails of tightly packed clothing, I was overwhelmed. There was so much choice, I didn't know where to turn first. Each costume house has a different layout, and it takes a while to figure out where everything is located. To complicate matters further, clothing from one era can get put in the wrong section, so a pair of pants from the '70s winds up in the '50s and vice versa.

In the twenty-five years that I have worked in the business, costume houses have remained virtually unchanged, which is amazing, given the many advances in other areas of film. They are still as badly ventilated; they all have that same dank, musty smell. Also, due to an antiquated bar-code system, it takes hours for clothing to be written up, and it takes hours for it to be returned. Shoes are housed in large cardboard boxes that you have to dig through, trying not to think about all the sweaty feet that have lived in them. A costume house is a designer's Mecca— the place, I quickly discovered, where all the goodies are hidden. But it resembles hell.

After what felt like days but was probably only a couple of hours, I found Peter a black jacket and separate pants that looked like a suit. Still, we had to take down the hem of the pants right to the edge to make them long enough. Victoria was the opposite—she had the perfect '50s body. With her tiny waist, she looked great in everything. In fact, we had too many choices and struggled to pare down the number of outfits she might wear. Sometimes, as in real life, it's good for an actor to repeat an outfit and not be constantly wearing something different in every scene. It makes the character seem more authentic and less like a fashion plate.

Because our budget was so limited, we couldn't afford doubles of any of the clothing, so cleaning posed problems. If something had gotten lost or damaged in the cleaning, we would have been screwed. To avoid cleaning, my assistant, Sandra, and I sewed underarm shields into every shirt and blouse to help absorb the sweat. Since we were the entire costume department, we also had the unenviable job of changing out the shields every day, spraying Lysol around the area, and replacing them with clean shields. The men's cotton shirts we could take home and wash, but many of the period shirts were rayon, and we couldn't risk shrinking them. So those poor actors wore the same clothing for the entire shoot. To make matters worse, it was hot that summer. Needless to say, our small wardrobe room looked and smelled funky. Finally, the shoot ended in July. As there was no money for dry cleaning, we stuffed the rank clothing into plastic bags and prayed there wouldn't ever be a need to do reshoots.

Despite all the pressure and long hours, I felt I had done a good job. I had learned a tremendous amount about costume design and particularly about designing a period film. I enjoyed being part of the creative process, and I began to feel more confident that this might be the right career path for me.

CHAPTER 26

The Maroon Plaid Dress

Soon after *Strangers Kiss,* the producer Carolyn Pfeiffer called me about working on Alan Rudolph's new film, *Choose Me.* Alan had started out as a protégé of Robert Altman's and subsequently written and directed quirky, unique films like *Welcome to L.A.* and *Roadie.* I met him for a drink; we discussed the project and got on well. Alan claimed he didn't know anything about clothing and hired me on the spot. Although it was a low-budget project (of course, or why would they be hiring a neophyte like me?), it had an interesting cast: Keith Carradine, Lesley Ann Warren, Geneviève Bujold, and John Laroquette.

Geneviève Bujold had not acted in a film in over five years. Alan was very excited about working with her and a bit nervous. I was dispatched

217

to her house in Malibu to meet and discuss her wardrobe. Geneviève's character was called Dr. Love; she hosted a radio talk show in which she gave advice about relationships. I had come up with the idea that Dr. Love's clothing should feature a lot of pink as a nod to her obsession with romance. Also, the color looked good with Geneviève's brown hair and golden coloring. Geneviève was intrigued. I proceeded to find various items of clothing—shirts, skirts, and dresses—and bring them to her house for fittings. She looked great; it was a very different look from her normal casual Malibu style, and she loved it. Alan was relieved that things seemed to be going so smoothly.

The next actress I met was Lesley Ann Warren. I have to say that she has one of the most perfectly proportioned bodies I have ever worked with. Everything looks terrific on her, and she knows how to work it. Since the budget was so low (under a million dollars for the entire film!), we started by looking in her closet, where I found, to my delight, a few '40s dresses. One was red crepe with padded shoulders and folded in a V across the front that gathered at the waist and draped in folds over her hips; the other was a similar style made of beautiful gray-on-gray patterned silk, and we used it as a basis for her look.

Keith Carradine was playing an eccentric hustler. He was a real pro and willing to try anything. As his character had a noir-ish feel, '50s-styled suits seemed appropriate. They also happened to look terrific on his tall, lean body. I had a friend who owned a very popular clothing store called Clacton and Frinton, which specialized in custom-made suits. My friend agreed to make the suits—in midnight-blue and dark-olive-green linen—at cost in return for a credit on the film. Alan was delighted that all the actors were happy, and the producer was happy that I was spending so little money.

The first day of shooting arrived, and I felt well prepared. All the main cast members were called to the set. As often happens on first days, nothing went quite as planned. By the time we finished shooting, Geneviève still hadn't been used. It was the first time she had been separated from her young son, and she was upset.

The next day we were shooting at a different location. Geneviève was scheduled to work after lunch, but she never showed up. Frantic calls were made. Nobody could find her. She had gone AWOL. Alan reluctantly filmed around her.

That night I received a call from the producer. They had found Geneviève: Alan was in Malibu talking with her. She promised she would show up at the set the following day. To guarantee it, they were sending a driver to pick her up.

Optimistic, I arrived at the set the next day bright and early. My assistant and I were prepping Geneviève's clothes when Alan came running into our makeshift wardrobe room, looking haggard and sleep-deprived.

"She's here," he said, as if announcing the queen.

"Great," I said.

"But she's a bit nervous," he continued. "She says she wants to talk to you."

Now I was nervous. "Please come with me," I begged.

"No," he said. "It's better if you go alone." He ran off before I could stop him.

I went into the bedroom that we were using as a dressing room. Geneviève was sitting on the bed. She seemed calm enough. "I've been thinking . . ." she said.

My stomach fell. It's never good when an actor says "I've been thinking." It's usually code for "I've changed my mind."

"I don't like the pink idea," she continued.

I gulped. My mind flashed on her entire film closet filled with pink items.

"I don't think it's right."

"Oh," I said. It was all I could come up with. We were due to start filming in an hour. I took a deep breath. "Is there anything that we've selected that you like?" I stressed the "we." She and I had spent hours picking out those pink clothes.

"No," she said, shaking her head, "it's just not right."

"What would be right?" I asked, trying hard to stay calm.

"I don't know," she said. "Something like the dress you were wearing the other day."

I knew exactly what she was talking about. I had been wearing a simple cotton shift in a purple and maroon plaid with a yellow leather belt, both of which I had purchased in Paris when Jim was promoting *Breathless*. Before I could explain to Genevieve that there was no way we could get our hands on a dress like that, she said, "I have to go to hair and makeup," and left the room.

My first instinct was to flee. What was I to do? It was seven in the morning. Most stores didn't open until ten. We were meant to start shooting at eight. One of the great unwritten rules of film is that shooting can never, ever be held up for wardrobe. It's as if the clothing magically attaches itself to an actor's body without any effort or tweaking. A favorite costumer's expression (said under the breath) when asked to accomplish one more impossible feat is "No problem, I'll just pull that [shoe, shirt, skirt, tie, etc.] right out of my ass!"

I ran to look for Alan and Carolyn. I explained what had just happened.

Alan clutched his forehead. "You've got to do something," he said.

"We can't lose another day without her," added Carolyn. "It'll shut us down."

"Do what you can. I'll try and shoot around her . . . again," Alan said, sighing.

I left my assistant on the set to deal with the other actors and did the only thing I could think of doing: I drove to my house—which was fortunately nearby—ran upstairs past my bewildered husband, grabbed virtually every item of clothing in my closet, including the maroon plaid dress, stuffed it all in my car, and drove back to the set at top speed.

When I arrived, they were almost ready to shoot. The first assistant director was giving me dirty looks, as though the entire situation were my fault. Alan was pacing. The cameraman was making final adjustments with the lights. My assistant and I unloaded my car, brought all the clothes to Geneviève's dressing room, and laid everything out for her inspection. Although I am about four inches taller than she is, we are of similar build. With a little luck and the help of a belt and hemming tape, we could make almost any of my frocks fit her—I hoped.

I held my breath as she looked through the clothing. Please, please pick something quickly, I prayed. She chose the Paris dress, which was short on me. She tried it on. With a belt, it looked good and, more important, right for her character.

I dashed back to Alan and Carolyn and told them that Geneviève would be ready momentarily. They were thrilled. And I was able to breathe freely.

After this hair-raising first day, as Geneviève gained more confidence in me, I was able to gently guide her back toward our original concept. Slowly, we incorporated some of the pink clothing I had originally purchased, along with pieces of my own clothing. Halfway through the shoot, Geneviève called and apologized for her behavior. She admitted to having been nervous and not knowing if she could trust me. From this fraught beginning, we formed a friendship, and the next year, she requested me to do her clothing on a Clint Eastwood film, *Tightrope*. I even dressed her for the Oscars in 1985, when she was a presenter. Worried that she would be swamped in a long gown, she opted for a simple short black taffeta dress cinched at the waist. It remains the first and last time an actor ever apologized to me for difficult behavior, and I've always treasured it.

Alan and Carolyn were so pleased with the results of *Choose Me* that they invited me to do Alan's next film, *Trouble in Mind*, which they were planning to shoot in Seattle. The cast included some of the same actors—Keith and Geneviève—with the addition of Kris Kristofferson, Joe Morton, Lori Singer, and Divine.

In the '80s, Seattle was an emerging hot spot and a fun place to explore. It was filled with interesting places to eat and shop (including well-stocked vintage stores) and a supply of talented people eager to work on films (unlike L.A., where the general public was burned out from working with movie people). It was virgin territory, if you will.

Alan wanted the film to have the look and feel of sometime in the future. He wanted all the exteriors to be peopled with extras in uniform, to give the sense of a police state. I had the challenge of inventing a uniform. I found bits and pieces at local army-surplus stores. I decorated jackets with a stash of red ensigns and medals that I found hidden at the back of a store, which I later discovered were Russian.

Gradually, the actors came to Seattle to rehearse. Joe Morton was the first to arrive. He is a charming man and a dedicated actor. Alan wanted him in a kind of ersatz uniform. So I found dark navy pants and a short navy jacket with epaulets. He looked pretty dashing, but we felt there was something missing. A scarf? A hat? Lying on a table nearby was one of those odd '40s items, a pair of real foxtails, including their actual heads. As we started to play around with them, winding them through his epaulets, we came up with a unique look that completely worked for Joe's character.

Keith was also willing to take risks with his look. In collaboration with the makeup artist and the hairstylist, we came up with a cross between glamour rock and punk. Keith's hair was done in a pompadour, and he wore sparkling eye makeup. Before leaving L.A., I'd been to a clothing store called Parachute (famous for supplying rock musicians with edgy clothing) that was going out of business. They had very extreme, over-the-top, drapey, brightly colored clothing that, clearly, nobody wanted to wear in real life, but I scooped some of it up for Keith. My instinct was right: He carried it off with great aplomb.

Alan wanted Kris Kristofferson to look like a detective in a '40s film noir, and to wear a fedora, trench coat, and suit. Everything went well until we got to the suit. Kris never wore suits. He only wore western shirts and jeans.

I kept saying, "I understand, Kris, but Alan"—invoking the director's name to try and make my point—"feels that your character would wear a suit."

Each time we put a suit on him, Kris would grab the crotch and say, "I'm not wearing this; this is old man's clothing." One of the women working for me—Rudy—had a great suggestion: "Why don't we make a suit for you that has pants cut like jeans?" After an endless moment of deliberation, Kris grudgingly agreed. But the look on his face told me the story wasn't over.

Well, the day dawned when Kris's suits were ready. We had made them out of beautiful dark gray and navy blue wool with a nubby texture. I had prepped Alan to stop by the fitting, unannounced, and shower Kris with praise. Kris tried on the whole ensemble—the black hat, the black trench coat, the suit, a black shirt, and a red tie. He looked very suave. He inspected himself in the mirror and liked what he saw. He rakishly pulled the hat over to one side. Then he took off the coat. I glared at Alan to make appropriate sounds. He did. Kris peered in the mirror with those ultra-blue eyes and grudgingly conceded that the suit was okay. "But . . ." he said, and my heart froze, ". . . the pants are still too baggy."

I heaved a sigh of relief: no problem. The seamstress took in the pants, which made them skintight. I prayed that he didn't gain an ounce and that they wouldn't rip when he sat down.

Halfway through the shoot, there was a fight sequence between Kris and Keith. A stunt coordinator and stunt doubles had flown up from Los Angeles to prepare the sequence. The idea was to use a combination of actors and stunt doubles. The day we started shooting the scene, Kris decided he didn't want a stunt double; he wanted to do the whole thing himself. The coordinator begged him to reconsider: Though it wasn't a very complicated scene, if something went wrong, it could endanger the whole production. But Kris was in full macho mode and determined to do his own stunts.

Keith and Kris rehearsed. Keith was very athletic and seemed able to weave and dodge Kris's punches. Everybody was encouraged. Kris's stunt double, dressed in Kris's clothing, looked a little forlorn, watching from the sidelines, but he would get paid whether he was used or not. They started filming. The first take went well but not perfectly. Keith had moved his head a little too quickly, so the punch looked fake.

The camera was reset and they started over. This time it looked real. Too real. There was blood spurting from Keith's nose. Alan yelled "cut" and the set medic rushed over to Keith. Everybody was frozen to their spots, not knowing what to do. Had Kris broken Keith's nose? Busted his teeth? After some ice had been applied and the bleeding stanched, it turned out it was just a nosebleed. Everyone heaved a sigh of relief. Meanwhile, Kris was clutching his fist. It was bleeding. It turned out that Kris had landed his punch on Keith's mouth and been gashed by Keith's teeth. Kris was whisked away in an ambulance.

If you want to injure someone, just give him a good hard bite. Apparently, the germs in one's mouth can be extremely dangerous if they enter another person's bloodstream; they can cause a serious, even life-threatening infection. The entire production had to shut down for a week while a special antidote was found to fight the infection that had lodged in Kris's hand. There was even a rumor that he might lose the hand if they couldn't find a cure. A guitar player with one hand would not have been a good outcome.

The good news was that most of the crew got the week off. I welcomed the break and flew back to L.A. to see Jim and Jesse. One of the hardest things about being on location is being separated from your family for weeks and sometimes months at a time.

The rest of filming went off without a hitch. One of my favorite cast members was Divine, aka Harris Glenn Milstead. He was best known from his roles in John Waters's films, in which he appeared as a bizarrely made-up overweight woman. Memorably, he ate dog shit in *Pink Flamingos*. In *Trouble*, he was making his screen debut as a Mob boss with elegant taste. Knowing his generous dimensions, I was sweating over how to clothe him properly on our meager budget. When we talked on the phone, he told me that he'd recently had two suits made by the famous British tailor Tommy Nutter—who, coincidentally, had made shirts for my father in the '60s—and he would be happy to wear them in the film. I was thrilled. Bespoke suits for Divine would have cost us a great deal of money. (The yardage alone on someone his size would have been formidable.) When he showed up in Seattle, I was delighted to see that his suits were even more beautiful than I had imagined. The quality of the fabrics—exquisite pin-striped Italian wools, pink and lavender shirts made out of the finest cotton—and the way they fit Divine was far beyond anything I could have had done in Seattle.

Divine was the sweetest, funniest person. Inside that oversize, extravagant frame was a lonely man with a heart of gold. Even when he wasn't working, he liked to hang out on the set—often in the wardrobe truck, where we had a small heater—gossiping and telling stories in his high-pitched voice. He was so entertaining, it was often hard to focus on the work. Unfortunately, our truck was rather small, and when things got busy, we had to tactfully ask him to leave, as there wasn't room enough for someone of his size.

About six months after we finished filming, Divine was found dead in his hotel room in Los Angeles. He had died in his sleep of a heart attack. He was only forty-two years old. I was sad that he never got to see his debut as a man, wearing his exquisite double-breasted bespoke suits.

Despite my complaints about tight budgets, difficult working conditions, and on- and off-set dramas, I was having a ball, growing with each film and, with each film, being recognized more and more as a professional. Each film led to another and another. The culmination of this early ascent was the chance to work with the great Blake Edwards (*Breakfast at Tiffany's*, the Pink Panther movies, *10*, *S.O.B.*). I was so in awe of him that I have no memory of what I said when I met him, but the next thing I knew, I was hired.

The film was called *That's Life!*, and it was going to be a sort of independent, elegant home movie, starring Jack Lemmon and Blake's wife, Julie Andrews, and her two daughters, and Jack Lemmon's wife and son. Almost the entire film was to be shot at Blake and Julie's house in Malibu. I was handed a four-page outline. There was no script, and the entire piece would be ad-libbed. The only parameters I had were that the film took place over a single weekend, and it was going to include a big party.

Working with Blake was like working with a well-oiled machine. He knew exactly what he wanted, and he trusted the people he hired to give it to him. God knows why he trusted me, but the company's collegiality and sense of common purpose made it easy for me to fit right in. Like the dialogue, a great deal of the wardrobe came from the actors. It was great fun for me—and for them, too, sometimes—to raid their closets and then finish off their outfits with items that brought the look into general coherence with the rest of the cast.

I called in my old boss Harriet Selwyn to help with Julie Andrews. For the party scenes, I selected a shimmery gold chiffon skirt, a black camisole, and a sexy see-through black jacket with a sprinkling of gold, silver, and bronze sequins. Julie looked stunning. The rest of the movie, she was more casually dressed in jeans and shirts, which she liked to wear with the collars turned up. Julie is just as she appears—a delight with a wonderful sense of humor. She also had the greatest legs I'd ever seen on a woman over fifty. I insisted she wear shorts in a beach scene to show them off.

CHAPTER 27

It Helps to Be Married to the Costume Designer: The Crepe de Chine Wedding Dress

One of the best things about working on those films was gaining experience and skills, so when Jim was hired to direct *The Big Easy*, starring Dennis Quaid and Ellen Barkin, he could legitimately request his wife as the costume designer.

There were a lot of firsts for me on the *The Big Easy*. It was the first time I worked with Jim as the official costume designer; it was the first time we were on location together; and it was the first time I had a decent budget and crew. The whole experience was very positive. We really were like one big family: the cinematographer, Affonso Beato; the production designer, Jeannine Oppewall; and the set decorator, Lisa Fischer, became lifelong friends of mine, and we worked together on

229

many future projects. We had the added bonus of living and working in New Orleans, one of the great American cities. When we weren't too exhausted from our busy schedule, there was always delicious food and fantastic music to be experienced.

Dennis Quaid was portraying a homicide cop. For research, he hung out with a group of detectives in the New Orleans Police Department who were nicknamed "The Hollywood Squad" because of their flashy attire. Without taking too much liberty, I was able to design (with the help of my friend Mary Kay Stolz) suits made out of dark blue and dark gray lightweight wool and custom-made shirts in blue plaid and gray stripes. When Dennis donned one of our snazzy ensembles for the first time, he looked at himself in the mirror and broke into one of his trademark grins. Dennis had given some memorable performances, but he had never played a romantic leading man. Now he felt equipped for the task.

Despite the good atmosphere on the set, Jim was having major fights off the set with the producer, Steve Friedman, about the ending of the film. Jim wanted the final scene to be Dennis Quaid in a tuxedo carrying Ellen Barkin in a wedding dress over the threshold of her apartment, the idea being that they had just gotten married. As usual, this was a last-minute decision. Renting a tuxedo for Dennis was no problem, but finding the right wedding dress for Ellen in twenty-four hours was a little more difficult.

After scouring New Orleans, I found what I was looking for in a small boutique in the Garden District: a long white dress made of crepe de chine with a cowl neckline. It wasn't a wedding dress, but it worked. Simple and sexy. Ellen looked stunning and everyone was happy. Well, almost everyone. When the producer saw what we had shot, he decided he wanted to add another scene (with them in the same wardrobe) and some sappy dialogue. Jim was vehemently against this.

We had only one day left to shoot, and among other things, there was the all-important love scene to be done. Jim was apoplectic. There was no time, it would be bad for the actors, bad for the film; he couldn't do it, he *wouldn't* do it.

Mort, the line producer, said, "You have to."

I piped up: "You need the wedding clothes, right? I'm not sure the dress is available."

"What?" cried Jim and Mort in unison, for different reasons.

"Tell Steve to call me," I said. "I'll explain the situation."

Puzzled but relieved, they agreed. Minutes later, in my office, I had a very angry producer on the phone.

"What do you mean, the dress isn't available?"

"Well, in order to save money, I rented the dress and—"

"Well, rent it again!" yelled Steve.

"I can't; they sold it," I replied.

"Find out who they sold it to!"

"I tried, but it's a small boutique, and they have no record."

"This is the most ridiculous thing I've ever heard!" he yelled, and he hung up on me.

So we never shot that scene, and we spent the final day filming a very intimate and sexy lovemaking scene. When it was over, Jim asked me, "Were you telling the truth?"

I smiled. "Don't ask, don't tell."

After the film was released, I received many requests from people wanting to know where they could find a wedding dress like Ellen's. I tried to refer them to the little shop on Magazine Street, but it had gone out of business. Too bad. I liked the idea of these Ellen clones walking down the aisle and tying the knot in a dress inspired by *The Big Easy*.

CHAPTER 28

Great Balls of Fire!
The Faux-Leopard-Trim Suit

One of the reasons I had been so eager to marry Jim was that I wanted us to have children together. Fortunately, Jim had also come around to the idea. But neither of us was prepared for the five-year struggle, including a miscarriage, that it took for me to get pregnant. The process of taking my temperature, calculating the optimum moment to have sex (which never seemed to coincide with when we actually wanted to do it), and the disappointment and sense of failure when another month went by and I discovered I wasn't with child, all conspired to create a lot of stress within our marriage. There were moments when I felt utter despair and frustration as I looked around me and saw friends who were able to get pregnant in the blink of an eye. Nonetheless, I was deter-

233

mined—probably in the same slightly crazed way that I was determined to be with Jim—to have a child and create my own family. Just when we had almost given up and were considering adoption, a miracle happened and I became pregnant.

On September 2, 1987, we welcomed Matthew (after Jim's father) Peacock (after my father) Midtown (suggested by a friend after we told him about Peacock, whereupon he insisted that Matthew would need an alternative middle name later in life) McBride. Jesse was sixteen and as welcoming to Matthew as his half brother, Joe, had been toward him when he was born. It was very touching to see Jesse hold Matthew with such love and tenderness.

When Matthew was fourteen months old, Jim had the opportunity to direct *Great Balls of Fire!*, based on the life of the singer/piano player Jerry Lee Lewis. I was both excited by and nervous at the prospect of designing this epic film, which took place in the '40s and '50s, my favorite clothing eras. The only snag was that it would be shot in Memphis, which would require our whole family moving there for at least three months. Jesse was in his last year of high school, so he could not come with us, but we had a close family friend who agreed to stay with him. A housekeeper who had been helping me since Matthew was born was able to join us for the duration of the film. With all the domestic issues sorted out, we decamped to a high-rise in Memphis overlooking the Mississippi River.

Jim and I were working long hours, under a lot of pressure, particularly because Lewis, a bitter methadone addict with a tendency toward psychotic outbursts, was unhappy. He was being paid large sums to be a consultant on the film and for his music, but the movie was based on his ex-wife's memoir and not his own book—he didn't have one, and there were rumors that he could barely read. He proudly showed Jim a copy of the script, on which he had scribbled over every page the word "LIES." Yet when Jim asked, he could never explain what he wanted or even what he didn't like about what we were doing. What he did like to repeat over and over was "Elvis never had a movie made about him while he was alive."

Meanwhile, the lead actor, Dennis Quaid, felt that in order to portray a hard-living, pill-popping, drunken musician, he had to become a hard-living, pill-popping, drunken musician. He often came to the set late, hungover, and grouchy, so all of us had to work late to make up the time. With our budget escalating, the studio and the producers were constantly fighting.

Designing *Great Balls of Fire!* was one of my greatest challenges as a costume designer, because it was a biopic based on a real person, and I felt committed to making it as accurate as possible. It was also a musical and therefore subject to stylization, exaggeration, and flights of fancy, as was the performance aspect of Jerry Lee's career. I had a good research resource in the Sears and JCPenney catalogs of the period, which really gave one a sense of how ordinary folk dressed, but they were hard to come by. So if either the art department or I found one, we would rip it in half; I would take the clothing section, and they would take the furniture section.

There were many crowd scenes involving hundreds of extras, and as we were shooting in Memphis, far away from costume houses that we could rely on to supply period clothing at the last moment, we had to be extra-organized. We scheduled pre-fits for the background people to make sure we had enough clothing and accessories. Then everything was tagged and photographed. On the day of the shoot, we instituted an elaborate voucher system so that extras wouldn't be paid each day until they had returned their outfits, some of which were very stealworthy.

All of Dennis's performance suits had to be custom-made. I discovered that Jerry Lee's original outfits had been made by Lansky Brothers, a Jewish clothier in Memphis that specialized in flamboyant suits for many famous musicians, including Count Basie, Elvis Presley, and Roy Orbison. (It was unusual at that time to find a store that catered to both black and white musicians.) There were plenty of photos of Jerry Lee in his stage outfits, but most of them were in black and white, so we had to find further documentation to figure out the exact colors. (Jerry Lee's memory was not reliable; too many years of drug abuse had done some serious damage.) Again I worked with designer Mary Kay Stolz, who scoured flea markets to find the perfect faux-leopard trim for one of his famous suits.

Re-creating Myra, Jerry Lee's wife, posed a different kind of problem. She was only thirteen years old when she first met Jerry Lee, and I wanted her clothing to capture her youth and vulnerability. Fortunately, she was to be played by seventeen-year-old Winona Ryder, who perfectly exemplified those qualities. There was an iconic picture of Myra wearing a skirt with a little black and white sailor top. I looked in all the costume houses and couldn't find anything similar. And then one day I was browsing in a tiny vintage store in Long Beach and found it in mint condition. Sometimes I felt like I was on a prolonged treasure hunt: I had the clues, but finding the hidden treasure was another matter.

Every now and then Jim and I somehow managed to save enough energy to have sex; it was probably a necessary release from all the off-screen drama. Since it had taken us five years and so much effort to produce Matthew, I didn't bother with birth control. In the third week of filming, when I began to feel faintly nauseated and even more tired than usual, I thought the problem was simply stress.

The nausea should have been the first clue, but it wasn't until my period was six weeks late that I made an appointment with a Memphis gynecologist I found in the Yellow Pages. On a dreary, rainy day, I left the set to go see him.

When the doctor confirmed that I was pregnant, I was stunned. I was sure it had been a cyst or something else interfering with my periods. I couldn't believe that after all the previous difficulties, it could happen with no effort. I kept asking the doctor if he was absolutely sure.

He asked, "Are you . . . are you not happy about this?"

"Oh yes, very happy. It's just so unexpected."

As I put on my jeans and sweater, I felt a surge of joy: This truly was a gift. Having been an only child for most of my life, and lonely, I was thrilled that my son would not suffer the same fate. I was secretly hoping for a daughter.

I drove back slowly in the pouring rain—after all, I was pregnant and had to be careful. As I stepped out of the car, the wardrobe supervisor, John, waylaid me. "You've got to come quickly," he said, "Bernie's had a heart attack." Bernie was a tailor we had brought with us from L.A. Just that morning I had yelled at him because he'd mistakenly altered a jacket that didn't need altering. I rarely yelled at anyone, and all the way back I'd been planning to apologize to him. Filled with guilt, I rushed to the set: a '50s re-creation of Myra's teenage bedroom, where poor Bernie lay on top of a pink chenille bedspread, looking pale and in pain and breathing with difficulty. Desperate as I was to tell Jim my good news, I couldn't abandon Bernie, so I sat there and held his hand, begging his forgiveness, and waited for the ambulance to come. After the EMTs came to pick him up—and after they reassured us that he would be fine—I went to look for Jim, only to discover that he had gone off on a location scout. When he finally came home, I had just put Matthew to sleep. As Jim and I stood over the bed, staring at this innocent cherub, I said softly, "I'm pregnant."

Jim turned and looked at me. "You're kidding," he said.

"I'm not," I assured him.

"I hope it's a girl," he said.

"Me, too," I said as he hugged me tightly, and I silently said a prayer of gratitude for Bernie and for my unborn child.

CHAPTER 29

The Pink Knitted Cap

Two months later, after Jim and I had wrapped the film and were back in L.A., my gynecologist called to give me the results of the amniocentesis.

"Everything's fine," he said. "No Down's syndrome, no spina bifida—"

Impatient, I interrupted him: "What sex?"

When he told me it was a girl, I whooped with joy. A normal, healthy girl. I was ecstatic. Ever since I'd wanted to have children, I had wanted a girl, maybe because Jim already had Jesse and I wanted something different. I have to confess that I was the tiniest bit disappointed when I found out Matthew would be a boy. Girls seemed much easier than boys, more familiar, although my friend who had a thirteen-year-old daughter had warned me not to romanticize. "Girls may be easier when they're little," she said, "but wait till they hit the teenage years. You'll beg for a boy."

As soon as I hung up, I called Jim at the editing room to tell him the news. "A girl, a girl," he kept repeating, as in the old Beatles song.

I couldn't resist thinking about the fun I would have dressing a girl. And the corny girlie things we would do together, like going shopping, having manicures, and reading one of my favorite children's books, *Eloise*.

But our joy was brief. A few weeks later, I was four and a half months pregnant, and I started to spot. My doctor tried to reassure me that it was nothing serious: I had spotted during my pregnancy with Matthew, and he was healthy and strong from birth. "Try not to worry, just take it easy," he advised.

Unfortunately, I had just read about premature births in one of those *What to Expect When You're Expecting* books, and I couldn't get the image of a premature baby out of my head. I envisioned a creature more like an alien than a soft, cuddly baby. Finally, to distract myself, I stopped reading pregnancy books and poured my energy and attention into house hunting.

We had lived for six years in a three-bedroom duplex in Carthay Circle, and now we needed more room for the new baby. Jim was busy editing *Great Balls of Fire!*, so he was happy to let me do the hunting, and I quickly became obsessed. I drove up and down streets, writing down the phone numbers I saw on "For Sale" signs. I wanted to stay close to the mid-Wilshire neighborhood because the public schools were good and it was convenient to studios and costume houses. I scoured the newspapers for houses that my real estate agent might have missed. I explored far-flung neighborhoods like West Adams, with large Craftsman houses, and I seriously entertained fantasies about grand but fading houses way beyond our budget that would require huge amounts of remodeling.

Eventually, I found a house that I liked, an odd-looking Mediterranean—possibly built by the semi-famous architect Irving Gill—with Doric columns and a pool. It was close to where we lived and close to what we could afford. Our celebrations, however, were short-lived, because my bleeding was increasing steadily. Early one morning I was woken up by painful contractions. I was barely five months pregnant. I panicked. Jim rushed me to the doctor, who told me to go back home and stay in bed. He put me on a medication to help stop the contractions.

Terrified, I lay in bed listening to relaxation tapes, soothing music, anything that might help stop my body from trying to have this baby too soon. But by evening the contractions had worsened, so Jim and I left Matthew with a neighbor and drove to Cedars-Sinai, where the doctor met us and gave me magnesium sulfate in a drip; I had been taking it orally. He hoped a higher dose would end the contractions.

The baby needed three more months inside of me, and as I lay in the hospital bed, I kept imagining giving birth. It was inconceivable. Jim tried to be positive, but I couldn't listen. I felt responsible for what was happening, sure that I had done something to harm this baby, that my body had some weakness that I should've been able to control. I replayed events of the last few months and blamed myself: If only I hadn't looked for a house, if only we hadn't overpaid for the house, if only I had gone to bed the minute I had started spotting, if only, if only. Eventually, I told Jim to go home. There was nothing he could do but stand there and watch me worry, and he wasn't helping me feel better, anyway.

After he left, I tried to watch TV to divert myself from the dire scenarios in my head, but the monitor attached to my belly was uncomfortable, and exhausted as I was, I couldn't sleep. Just as I would doze off, a nurse would come to check my vital signs and wake me. At last, around seven A.M., the contractions stopped and I fell asleep. When my doctor

241

came to check on me a few hours later, he was optimistic. The crisis had been averted. He told me I would be able to go home soon. A little while later, Jim and Matthew came for a brief visit. Seeing Matthew's smiling, cheerful face, so happy to see me, so excited about having a sibling, I felt buoyed and immensely glad I wouldn't have to disappoint him.

As I was preparing to leave, I went to the bathroom and noticed a yellowish discharge. I reported it to the nurse, who told me they would give me a sonogram and check it out. Twenty minutes later, as a technician rubbed a gel-covered instrument across my belly, I felt the contractions starting up again, stronger than before. Then, suddenly, I felt a warm trickle of water seeping between my legs. My water had broken.

"Code blue!" yelled the technician.

"What's the matter?" I asked, my panic rising.

"I think you're going into labor," he told me.

"No!" I screamed. I started to cry, and the nurse hurried into the room and tried to comfort me, assuring me the doctor was on his way. "You'd better call your husband," she said.

I called Jim and burst into tears.

"Pediatrics is sending a doctor to talk to you," the nurse said. "Tell him what you want."

What I wanted? I wanted this not to be happening. I wanted to be somewhere else. I wanted my little girl to be all right. I wanted this nightmare to end. But all I could do was worry and cry until the doctor, a soft-spoken Indian man, walked into the room. He looked sympathetically at me and said gently, "I have to tell you that your baby has only a ten to fifteen percent chance of survival."

I couldn't absorb his words. It was as though he were speaking in a foreign language.

And then these words started coming out of my mouth: "I don't want any extraordinary measures taken!"

"I am not sure I understand you," he said. "We will do our best to keep the baby alive." Without another word, he turned and left the room.

I lay in the bed, crying. I knew what I had meant. If my baby were born a vegetable, I didn't want her kept alive. If my baby wasn't perfect, I didn't want her. I felt like a terrible coward, but I was awash in terror. It was not my finest moment.

When Jim arrived, I told him what the doctor had told me, and now he started to cry. Before we could say much to each other, the doctor was there, and he and the nurses were preparing me for surgery.

When I realized he was preparing me for a C-section, I asked why, and he explained that the baby couldn't survive a vaginal birth. I realized I had no choice in any of this, that I was merely a cog in a medical, governmental wheel, and my baby would be born and kept alive at any cost.

This movie, my life, which I seemed to be watching in slow motion, sped up as I was rushed to the operating room. Meanwhile, Jim was directed into a closet where he could quickly change into a sterile gown and be present for the operation.

A clumsy anesthesiologist kept jabbing at my spine in an attempt to insert the epidural. My doctor lost his cool and yelled, "If this doesn't happen soon, it won't be worth doing." At last the anesthesiologist hit the right spot and the lower part of my body went numb, but I felt like the wrong half was numb. It was my brain that needed shutting down, stopped from thinking these endless horrible thoughts. Was this day going to end with a dead baby and a sliced stomach?

I looked up at the clock: one P.M. It was only lunchtime. Twenty minutes later, my daughter was pulled from my abdomen.

"She's breathing," one of the doctors announced. A nurse placed her in an incubator. I barely saw her before they whisked her away to the neonatal intensive care unit. Then they injected me with morphine, and after all those hours of terror and misery, I felt strangely exhilarated.

Two hours later, I was wheeled out of the recovery room and brought to my own room. I was grateful my doctor had thoughtfully put me on the gynecological floor, so I wouldn't be on the maternity floor, surrounded by happy mothers and healthy babies. As I started to come down from the morphine, my high gave way to high anxiety.

Jim brought me a Polaroid picture of our daughter. Just as the book had warned, she seemed barely human; rather, she looked like a small bird, with skin so transparent I could see her veins. She was completely naked. Beneath the photo, Jim had written the name Ruby, and when I saw that, I once again burst into tears. We had not committed to a name, although we had discussed Ruby as a possibility. We thought we still had three months to make a final decision, but he had gone ahead and named her. I think he hoped that if she had a name, she would survive.

When I was in my early twenties, a friend had a daughter named Ruby. I loved the name the minute I heard it. I loved the sound of it and the connotation of jewels and beautiful reds. Ruby red. I decided that if I ever had a daughter, I would name her Ruby, and because our daughter was due in late July, when her birthstone would have been a ruby, the name had seemed perfect. But here she was in April, and it was all so imperfect.

That evening Jim wheeled me to the NICU. I was still in a haze from all the drugs. The nurse showed me how to scrub down so that I would be germ-free to meet my daughter. When I saw her for the first time, she looked even smaller than she did in the photo, her head barely the size of a tennis ball. She weighed a mere one and a half pounds and seemed so vulnerable, surrounded by the armory of equipment that was keeping her alive. My heart nearly stopped.

I watched her closely, listening to the eerie swishing sounds of the ventilator that was helping her breathe, thinking, This isn't right. She's not ready, she's not done. I wanted to pick her up, rip out all the wires and tubes, and stuff her back inside my belly. It was, after all, only stapled shut.

A doctor walked toward us. "She's doing remarkably well, considering. You're lucky that she's a girl," he continued. "At birth they're much stronger than boys." I nodded weakly, the feminist in me briefly rising. He told us that the first twenty-four hours were critical. If our daughter survived this period without any traumas, brain bleeds, or infections, her prognosis was good. We waited, anxiously hoping our presence would make a difference. At seven in the evening, the nurse told us to go get some sleep. There was nothing we could do, she said.

We returned to my room, and as I crawled into bed, a nurse appeared with two beautiful flower arrangements, one from my friend Mary Ann and the other from my agent. We even received a surreal call from Richard Gere, with whom I hadn't spoken in years, not since *Breathless*. I was very touched by his concern, but I didn't know what to say to him. I didn't know what to say to anyone. After I hung up, I started to cry, and my husband asked, "What's wrong?"

"I don't know if I'm waiting for a funeral or a celebration," I sobbed.

But Ruby made it through the first twenty-four hours. The doctors performed numerous tests and reported, "As far as we can tell, she's suffered no brain damage." Jim and I looked at each other. As far as they could tell. What did that mean?

I knew only that Ruby had arrived too soon, that just as my belly had begun to swell with this gift, this girl child who had happened so effortlessly, she was taken from me. "I guess she just wanted to be in the world," well-meaning friends would say, not knowing how to explain the unexplainable.

"But I don't want her to be here," I wanted to scream. "She's not ready to be here."

The words of the neonatologist kept ringing in my ears: "We will do our best to keep her alive." But at what cost? Was it right, this new technology that made the impossible possible? If Ruby had been born in a third-world country or even in remote rural America, she would have died. Thanks to advanced medicine, she was being kept alive. I was deeply grateful, of course, but also deeply confused. I wanted her to live, but not like this, not strapped to a little pad in the neonatal intensive care unit, enveloped in wires and tubes, covered by something that resembled a plastic cake dome. I didn't want my daughter to endure the endless poking and prodding, the relentless search for tiny new veins to stick with the lifesaving IVs. How could all this interference fail to negatively affect her development? I felt powerless, unable to protect her, and when I asked the nurses if the prodding hurt her and they tried to reassure me—"her nervous system isn't yet fully developed"—I was not reassured. How did they know? Had they asked these preverbal infants what it was like to be poked and prodded, to live under bright lights twenty-four hours a day?

"Isn't the light bad for their eyes?" I pestered the nurses. Those tiny eyes that, only a few days prior to Ruby's birth, were fused together.

"We need the light so we can see them," the nurses rationalized. "We have to monitor changes in skin color. It's one of the best ways to judge oxygen intake."

"Aren't the monitors checking the gases?" I argued.

They argued back, "The monitors are unreliable. They malfunction. We need to *see* the babies."

I knew they had a point. Sometimes, while I was watching Ruby, I'd see a monitor go off for no reason, and I'd feel my own heart nearly stop.

The nurses told me Ruby had to weigh at least four pounds before they would allow me to take her home. I'd read a study reporting that babies grew faster when they were touched, and I longed to hold her. But we couldn't hold Ruby for at least two months—the cold air outside the isolette would be too much for her fragile system; in the cold she would burn too many calories to sustain her tiny body. We were allowed to reach inside and touch her. The doctors encouraged us to touch her firmly. "They don't like gentle touching," they told me. "It irritates them." When they told me that, I froze; I was afraid to touch my fragile daughter, terrified I would break a bone or puncture her skin. But I suppressed my fears and did what the doctors told me to do; I had no choice. The first time I held her, I was overcome with emotion: To be able to feel her tiny swaddled body in my arms, to touch and smell her, were basic maternal instincts that I had been denied. I was so grateful to be making some kind of physical contact with my tiny daughter. I began to have hope that she might survive.

One day when she was two months old, I went to the hospital to visit Ruby and found her sporting a knitted cap made of pale pink cotton yarn with a folded ribbed brim. The nurses told me that the mother of another premature baby had knitted it, and I imagined her in a rocking chair, holding tiny needles and knitting this tiny hat, so small and perfect, keeping Ruby warm, helping her to grow. The gift touched me deeply.

I learned so much about premature babies in those days. Conventional baby clothes do not fit them; sometimes parents buy their babies dolls' clothing. Our son had a teddy bear with a yellow T-shirt and blue shorts, and I found myself wondering if one day Ruby would be able to wear them. But for now I was grateful that she had this pink knitted cap. I loved it. And when another parent took a photo of little Ruby in her pink watch cap, held in a nurse's palm, I stared in wonder. One of Ruby's minuscule hands was up by her open mouth, and she looked as if she were saying, "Oh! Oh my gosh! What am I doing here?" I smiled. That hat made Ruby look like a normal baby. Well, almost.

As Ruby was three and a half months premature, the doctors predicted that it would be at least three and a half months before she could leave the hospital. During those weeks, all I could do was sit and stare, trying to watch out for her, being her advocate. Was she getting too much oxygen? Was there brain damage? Were they turning her frequently enough? That was important for her physical development. After I had exhausted all the questions I had, there was nothing left to do but wait. The doctors kept repeating, "Every baby is different," and no one promised anything.

My husband was working long hours each day, editing *Great Balls of Fire!*, and I envied him his absorption in work. My job was to be a milk machine. Every three hours I attached plastic cups to my breasts and pumped milk, a minimum of six times a day to keep the flow of milk going. Nurses froze the milk and gradually were able to feed it to Ruby. I hoped the antibodies in my milk would protect my baby from infections, would help her immature digestive tract to develop.

The swishing sound of the breast pump—eerily resembling the sound of the respirator that was keeping Ruby alive (and the respirator that had kept my father alive when he was in the hospital)—became part of my daily rhythm. When Ruby was doing well, I pumped more milk. When she was sick, I pumped less. I resented those women who left the hospital carrying their normal, healthy babies wrapped in pink or blue blankets after only a few days or a few weeks.

As the weeks wore on, my paranoia grew—I was Howard Hughes in disguise. Whenever I saw a parent sneeze or cough, I wanted to roar. How dare they visit the NICU and spread their diseases to these poor helpless babies? When I saw a nurse blow her nose, I'd pray she wasn't taking care of Ruby that day. I was on high alert; everywhere around, I sensed disease and contamination.

One day everything seemed fine, but the next, Ruby was in the throes of a near-fatal infection, and I felt as if it were my life that was ending. Whenever the phone rang, Jim and I steeled ourselves for the request to come to the hospital immediately. One day, after we had rushed to the hospital, where we anxiously awaited the results of tests, I noticed a screen being put up around the baby in the next isolette. I asked the nurse what was going on, and she looked at me and said softly, "We don't think he's going to make it. We wanted the parents and baby to have some privacy."

I knew some babies didn't make it. But not the little boy lying right next to Ruby, not the little boy whose parents we said hi to every day. After that night I lived in dread of the screen—that pale blue fabric with the innocuous childish print, the NICU's symbol of death.

After six weeks, exhausted and despairing, I joined a support group. Jim refused to come. In the midst of our pain, we grew apart. He was the optimist who daily said things like, "Ruby is doing great. She's going to be fine. It's just a matter of time." He quietly read all the literature and guidelines the hospital gave us. I was the pessimist. I viewed every setback as the end. I couldn't see how any good would ever come of the experience. I feared Ruby would be permanently scarred if she survived. I couldn't read the literature. It sent my mind spinning into the worst possible scenarios.

Every day I threw on the same jeans and T-shirt, barely bothering to change, and drove the familiar three-mile route to the hospital. I struggled to find a space in the overcrowded parking lot, and carried my cooler with my daily supply of breast milk to the NICU. This was the same hospital where my father had fought his final battle with emphysema, and his birthday, April 2, was only a few days before Ruby's, April

5. Here I was in the same place I had been eight years earlier, watching my father struggling to breathe, now watching my daughter struggling to breathe.

At long last Ruby's lungs improved, but as they did, her eyes became a concern. The blood vessels surrounding the retinas of premature babies can grow in the wrong direction and cause the retina to detach. (According to one of the doctors, this was what had caused Stevie Wonder's blindness.) They called in a specialist for a second opinion. As Jim and I sat nervously awaiting his verdict, we barely spoke.

Finally, the doctor emerged from the NICU, but the news wasn't good. "I'm afraid there has been a deterioration," he said. "If it continues, we'll have to operate."

"What happens if you don't?" asked Jim.

"She'll go blind," said the doctor simply.

I stopped listening. I had heard too much. I leaned against a window for support and secretly hoped that it would split open and I would be hurled into oblivion.

"And if you do operate?" continued Jim in his calm, rational voice.

"Well, it's a new operation. But we've had about a twenty to thirty percent success rate."

I was concentrating so hard on breathing, in, out, in, out, that I almost didn't hear what he said next: "We may not have to operate; some cases resolve themselves spontaneously."

A shard of hope, something I could cling to. I held my breath, afraid to alter the atmosphere.

"What do you think will happen with Ruby?" Jim asked.

"My gut feeling is that we'll have to operate."

I let the air out in a gush. We were back to ground zero.

"We'll watch her closely," the doctor added. "The deterioration can be very rapid. We'd want to operate before it's too late."

I remained silent. I had lost the power of speech. My mouth was open, but words didn't seem to be forming. I had so many questions, but I only wanted impossible answers: Everything is going to be fine, your baby won't go blind.

"Blindness isn't the end of the world, you know," he continued.

Right at that moment I thought it was.

"Well," he said at last, "I have to be going. Call me if you have any questions."

"Thank you," Jim said as the white coat of this well-meaning harbinger of doom disappeared down the corridor.

Jim held me, and we both wept. "There's nothing we can do," he said, tightly gripping my shoulders. "We'll just have to wait and see what happens." I knew he was right. Exhausted, we held on to each other.

Now the truly bad times began, the roller coaster we had been warned about, waiting for the doctor to check on Ruby's eyes, never knowing exactly when that would be. Doctors are busy people with many patients, many emergencies, and a holiday or a weekend might delay a checkup. We worried that she might be blind by the time he returned. Would he have to operate? Would the operation be successful?

Under the stress, my milk supply rapidly diminished, but when she was two months old, I finally was able to hold Ruby in my arms. Though it was brief, holding her felt so good, almost normal. But unlike her brother, Matthew, who had so greedily latched on to my nipple the first time he was introduced to my breast, Ruby had been started on my milk in a bottle and was reluctant to take to the breast.

One day seven weeks after Ruby's birth, Jim fell off his bike on the way to the hospital and he broke his arm. Instead of feeling relieved that he hadn't killed himself, I was angry that he could no longer drive a car to pick up Matthew from preschool. I couldn't cope with one more unexpected event.

Two and a half months after Ruby was born, Jim and I traveled to New York for the opening of *Great Balls of Fire!* It was the first break we'd had in months, and it promised to be a gala event. But we were damaged goods—Jim had his arm in a sling and was twenty pounds overweight. I was a zombie. I had lost weight and started taking tranquilizers. Determined to keep pumping milk while I was away, I brought along my apparatus. And when we checked into the fancy hotel, I embarrassedly gave it to the eager bellboy to carry to our room, hoping he wouldn't know what it was. Halfway through the weekend, I realized I just couldn't go on pumping anymore. I was hardly getting any milk. With a combination of guilt and relief, I stopped. The sad truth was that Ruby would gain weight more rapidly on formula, which had more calories than my breast milk. And the sooner she reached that magic four-pound mark, the sooner she could come home.

For the premiere of *Great Balls of Fire!*, I was dressed from head to toe in black. My clothing matched my somber mood. Everyone else was bright and colorful.

Gradually, miraculously, Ruby's eyes seemed to heal themselves. The doctor told us this was unusual and warned that they might deteriorate again. "Nothing is certain, anything is possible" became our family mantra. When someone told me that green was soothing to the eyes, I painted every room in our new house a different shade of green.

Three and a half months after Ruby's birth, on the exact day she'd been scheduled to be born, we finally took her home. The doctors, using their favorite phrase, "As far as we can tell," claimed she had no permanent brain damage, but we wouldn't know for sure until she was four or five years old and started school. She weighed just four and a half pounds, and she was attached to an apnea monitor to warn us if she stopped breathing at night. Nurses gave us CPR instructions so important I immediately forgot them. "Don't worry," they said. "Everyone does, just remember to call 911."

I waited in the reception area for Jim to bring the car around. I was holding Ruby, who was sleeping peacefully, wearing a tiny blue and white cotton onesie, which, despite the many times I had washed it in hot water to try to shrink it, still swamped her. I remembered watching other women taking their babies home, and being so afraid this day would never come. Finally it had arrived, against all odds, but I felt strangely detached, unable to completely believe it, terrified that a nurse would swoop down from the NICU and take her out of my arms, insisting that there had been a mistake and Ruby wasn't ready. Much as I wanted her home, I was scared of taking her away from this protected environment.

As children are not allowed to visit the NICU, Matthew had never met his sister. A few times when her crib was by a window, we had lifted him up to see, and with his nose pressed against the glass, he had caught a glimpse. We had shown him photos and told him that eventually she would come home. He would eagerly point at the pictures, mispronouncing her name, saying, "Wuby, Wuby." But nothing could have prepared me for seeing the smile spreading across his face the moment we walked through the door with Ruby. My heart melted. Here we were, together as a family, a perfect nuclear family: mom, dad, boy, girl.

Twenty-six years later, Ruby has a master's degree in library and information science. She lives in New York, and after working for various nonprofits, she is now working at the Gap clothing archive, where she organizes and catalogs clothing and helps designers find items from past collections. Growing up, she mostly resisted my clothing suggestions—refusing to wear skirts and dresses and girlie stuff that her other friends liked—much to my chagrin. She even rejected a great black boyfriend jacket from the Kate Moss collection at Topshop that I bought her. She's always had an independent spirit (I think it helped her survive those first difficult months). Like me, she knows what she wants and won't compromise. I guess mothers and daughters are doomed to tussle over clothing. But we do share a love of *Eloise*, mani-pedis, and cats.

Ruby loves to tell the story of her precocious birth. To this day, she likes to show off the photograph of her tiny self, lying in a nurse's hand, wearing that pale pink knitted cap.

CHAPTER 30

The Striped Silk Socks

"You know," said my producer friend Carol, "your father's diaries would make a great play." She had been listening to the audio version of the diaries, read by Simon Callow, the witty British actor and writer. My initial reaction was to say no. After all, who would want to see it? My father had been dead for twenty-five years, his cachet long past, and his work, though brilliant and rich and vividly of its time, didn't have the same currency it once had. Anybody can say "fuck" on TV these days. And there were other concerns: How could *The Diaries*—one man's internal dialogue with himself—be transformed into a dynamic theater production? When they were published, just after 9/11, despite good reviews, no one read the book. Why would anything be different three years later?

But over time I began to think a play wasn't such a bad idea. For six years I had fought for the publication of *The Diaries* because of my father's conviction that it contained some of his best writing. I hoped a play would revive interest in him.

After a few missteps, Carol and I found a New York theater director and writer, Richard Nelson, who wanted to adapt the diaries as a one-man show. He had done a play based on the life of Oscar Wilde—whom my father both admired and somewhat emulated—so they seemed like an ideal match. (In the late 1940s, during his student days, my father had lived in Oscar Wilde's old rooms at Magdalen College in Oxford. He claimed a bullet remained lodged in the mantelpiece after an angry father took a shot at Wilde for having compromised his daughter.)

Over the next few months, Richard crafted a beautiful adaptation and arranged for it to be mounted at the Royal Shakespeare Company's "New Work" series at Stratford-upon-Avon in 2006. Richard had worked with Corin Redgrave and was determined to have him portray my father. This choice came as a surprise to me. I had always imagined Jeremy Irons or some other angular British actor in the role. Corin, who was blond, blue-eyed, and thickset, seemed an odd choice. But Richard was insistent and eventually managed to convince the RSC and us.

When the question came up of who should design the costume for Corin, Richard offered me the job. Though I'd seldom worked in theater, I jumped at the chance to dress my father—or, more accurately, an actor who was pretending to be him—something my father never would have allowed of me in life. Although he had a great sense of style, the era during which *The Diaries* takes place—the '70s and '80s—was not one of his best fashion phases. Neither the leisure suits nor the *guayaberas*, which my father managed to carry off on his lean physique, were a great look for the more solid Corin. So we decided to take an artistic leap and dress Corin in a dark navy version of one of the exquisite bespoke

Tommy Nutter suits my father wore in the late '60s. We would jazz it up with a floral shirt and solid tie, in the spirit of how my father would have dressed himself.

When I arrived in Stratford in the fall, leaving Matthew and Ruby with Jim, rehearsals had already begun. Corin had had an excellent brown wig made to cover his own grayish-blond hair, and he had lost quite a lot of weight. The RSC tailor had made a beautiful navy blue double-breasted suit of Italian wool with a silk lining. Now all I had to do was find the shirt, tie, and socks. I felt the socks were important, not only because Corin spent the entire show sitting down—so the audience would see them—but also because my father always wore distinctive, garish hose. There was probably one person in the entire audience who would have known that fact, but this style tic was important to me.

As always, the budget was tight, so custom-made shirts were out of the question. Luckily, fashion was going through a retro '60s period, so I had a plethora of floral shirts to choose from. In the Selfridges men's department, I found the perfect blue and lavender item and a dark purple tie to go with it. Corin looked handsome in both, and they complemented the smart navy blue suit. I had just about given up on the socks when I found a couple of pairs with a bright yellow striped pattern that didn't exactly match anything else. That was the point. They were expensive and silk, just like the ones my father used to flash.

When I first saw Corin dressed for the part, I was shocked and unnerved: He did resemble my father. Sitting through many rehearsals, I heard him picking up the tones and rhythms of my father's speech and ultimately becoming an uncanny simulacrum of the man I grew up with. Listening to Corin repeating over and over my father's descriptions of his infidelities and his perverse sexual predilections aroused hundreds of memories and some discomfort. Friends kept asking, "How can you stand it?" I had to admit that though the experience wasn't a pleasure, it wasn't unbearable, either. The most disturbing aspect was the vivid description of his sadomasochistic obsession, one of the main reasons Kathleen had tried to suppress the diaries.

When they were published, I gave them to a therapist who told me that my father's explanation of his sadomasochist pleasures was the most comprehensive, clarifying, and moving that he'd ever read on the subject. While I had never been drawn to the behavior, this interpretation helped me to become less judgmental of my father and others who lean that way.

As I listened to Corin's rendering of my father's text, I appreciated more and more my father's amazing facility with words. His ability to write perfect sentences, to create elegant aphorisms and clever metaphors, was truly impressive, especially given my knowledge that the original manuscript contains few cross-outs or alterations. And then there was the humor, so uniquely his, perhaps the most personal aspect of the diaries. His rapturous review of an acrobatic singer, Frank Ifield, who he mistakenly thought was blind, or his effort to escape a tryst with a hooker by jumping off a balcony into a row of garbage cans—these were stories that once again made me laugh and revel in his humor and his outrageousness. Even his description of giving himself a vodka enema as part of some ill-conceived sadomasochistic activity was explosively entertaining.

Corin and the play both received rave reviews. One critic even commented on the garish socks, remarking that they reminded him of my father's style, although he hadn't remembered them as yellow.

A year after Stratford, *The Diaries* had a brief run in London, to be followed by a stint in New York. Just before the play went up, Corin confessed that he had lost one of the striped yellow socks. I searched all over London to try to replace them, but another fashion cycle had gone around, and I found nothing quite as delightfully loud. I had to settle for a more somber pair—gray with purple chevrons up the side—but still unusual. Just before the play was due to start rehearsals in New York, Corin suffered a major aneurysm from which he never completely recovered. By this time we had all become so attached to him in the role that the Broadway version had to be postponed and then abandoned when, a year later, Corin died.

I've always wondered what happened to the original outfit. I hope it found its way into the Royal Shakespeare's wardrobe department and has maybe been recycled for another play.

Thirty-five years after my father's death, not a month goes by when I don't see him quoted in a magazine or newspaper. He may be dead, but his words live on.

CHAPTER 31

The Pink Quartz Heart

It's hot. It's L.A. It's May 1, the first day of spring. I am on my way to a ten-day silent meditation retreat at the Institute of Mentalphysics in Yucca Valley. I am wearing comfy sweatpants and a T-shirt. Meditation gear. Around my neck on a leather strap, I am wearing a small pink quartz heart. A friend gave it to me when Ruby was in the hospital, and I put it in her crib. Pink quartz is meant to have healing properties, and I felt she needed all the healing she could get. Since then I had kept it as a lucky talisman. I liked rubbing its cool, smooth surface.

There is backed-up traffic on the I-10 freeway as far as the eye can see. Despite the heat and the delay, I'm in a good mood. I am softly singing along to Zooey Deschanel singing an old, forgotten Beatles tune. Life is good.

My cell phone rings. I fumble around in my bag and barely manage to retrieve the phone without rear-ending the car in front of me.

"Is this Tracy Tynan, the daughter of Elaine Dundy?" a male voice inquires.

"Yes," I reply, immediately on the alert.

"This is Officer Richardson, and I am at your mother's apartment at Park La Brea."

What is a cop doing at my mother's apartment? My mind starts racing: a robbery, a—

"Your mother's had a heart attack," the cop continues. "Where are you?"

"I'm in my car," I reply.

"You might want to pull over," he says gently. I do.

"Is she okay?" I ask, my throat tightening.

"I'm afraid she's dead," the cop answers.

I gasp, and tears start to roll down my cheeks. The cop asks when I will be arriving at my mother's apartment. I look out the window of the car and check all the mirrors. I am surrounded by gridlock on all sides. It will take me at least two hours to get back to L.A.

My mother's caretaker, a sweet Filipino girl who has taken care of her since she developed macular degeneration, gets on the phone. "When you coming back? Who get the body?" she demands tearfully. Not knowing any answers, I say I will call back.

What should I do? What I *want* to do is go to the retreat. I feel like a child who is being denied a treat she has been looking forward to. What kind of a daughter doesn't immediately turn around and race back to be at her mother's—albeit dead—side? The terrible truth, which I can barely admit to myself, is that over the course of our fifty-six-year relationship, I have often wished my mother dead. Now that she is, it's almost as if I willed it so.

I call Jim and tell him what has happened. He encourages me to keep driving toward the retreat. I am my mother's only child, no siblings or blood relatives to wonder where I am or to judge me. First I have to figure out what to do with the body. A few years ago my mother gave me an envelope containing explicit instructions in the event of her death. She told me that she had booked a spot at the same cemetery in Westwood where Marilyn Monroe was buried. A celebrity hound to the last. I call them and they tell me not to worry, that they will "take care of everything," including collecting the body. I heave a deep sigh of relief.

Finally, I arrive at the Institute of Mentalphysics. I check in at the Caravansary, a striking seven-hundred-foot-long structure made out of beige-brown sandstone, designed by Frank Lloyd Wright. As part of the program, the participants are required to do daily chores. I stand there and mumble that my mother has just died and I am not even sure if I will be staying. They are very kind and tell me to talk to one of the leaders of the retreat after the first meeting.

After a nutritious but tasteless vegan dinner, a hundred and fifty people pile into the meditation hall. I can't help noticing the amazing number of accoutrements that are required for the simple act of meditation: blankets, cushions, back supports, knee supports, water bottles, notebooks, and writing implements. We are given an overview of the schedule for the retreat. But the most important element is "Noble Silence." There will be absolutely no talking, 24/7, including meals. I have been on daylong and even two-day retreats. But nine days of silence, two hours after my mother has died, is a tall order.

After the talk, I approach Trudy, a teacher whom I know from previous retreats. In a whisper—I am already self-conscious about talking—I tell her my situation. She is very sympathetic. She says there is no reason to have a funeral immediately, I might want to wait a week or two. Obviously, I need to return to L.A. to make arrangements, but if I want to, I can return to the retreat, which may be very beneficial. I am surprised and reassured by her suggestions. I figured that leaving would be the only option.

Back in L.A. the next morning, I open the letter my mother gave me. It contains a long list of people to call announcing her death. There are even categories of friends: very important and less important. Some people might have resented being told so precisely what to do, but I am grateful. She has planned the aftermath of her death meticulously, even down to what is to be written on her gravestone.

Jim and I go to Westwood Cemetery to meet with the "funeral adviser." In between movie theaters and high-rise office buildings in Westwood lies this little jewel of a walled garden filled with graves. As we walk through the cemetery, I can't help noticing the witty inscriptions on the celebrity graves. Rodney Dangerfield: "There goes the neighborhood." Merv Griffin: "After a short pause, I won't be back." My mother's proposed inscription: "Elaine Dundy, author, *The Dud Avocado—Elvis & Gladys*."

The people at the funeral parlor are soft-spoken and sympathetic. They inform us that everything has been paid for. It appears that in her death, my mother has been much more thoughtful than she was in life. Still in a daze, I decide to postpone the memorial service for a couple of weeks and return to the retreat. I feel so discombobulated that being back there and staring out at the wide-open desert vistas seems the only solution. Trudy calls, and I tell her that I am returning. Then I get back on the infernal highway. Three times in two days. I feel every shopping mall is etched in my brain.

When I arrive at the Institute of Mentalphysics, I get a schedule and sign up for my chore. Franz, a nice Swiss man who also teaches tai chi, informs me that I don't have to do a chore; all the duties are filled up. "Unless," he says, peering at me with his pale blue eyes, "you want to?" I shake my head. I explain that I may have to break silence to notify my mother's friends and make final arrangements. This will not be a problem. I am beginning to feel that my mother's death has given me a get-out-of-jail-free card.

Finally, I do what I have been avoiding: I start calling, as my mother requested, the "important" people. I reach one of my mother's oldest friends, Gore Vidal. He immediately launches into a tirade against my long-deceased father, delivered with snarky asides like "I learned all about wife beating from your father" and ending with "Well, at least Elaine had two books in print when she died; your father had nothing." Stunned at his vitriol, I have nothing to say. I am just amazed that this man, who was friends with my father for many years, who attended countless parties at my father's house, and who is my half sister's godfather, feels the need to be so mean about him thirty years after his death. Clearly, he was well indoctrinated by my mother. Repressing the desire to say something nasty, I ask him to speak at my mother's memorial, as I know it is what she would have wanted. He agrees. I move on to her next "important" friend, Gloria Vanderbilt. Gloria is awash in tears. "So hard to bear. We had been such great friends. Long lunches where we talked about everything. Your mother was so smart and witty." Another old friend, Judy Feiffer, responds, "Oh, shit, shit, shit. She was impossible, but I loved her."

I make calls to London, where she still had many friends. Writer Jilly Cooper asks, "How did she die?"

"A heart attack," I reply.

"Ah well, she gave so much of her heart," says Jilly, "she didn't have any left."

Over the next few days, in between meditation and dharma talks, I sit in the dusty parking lot of the Institute of Mentalphysics, huddled in my car, talking to my mother's friends. Without exception, they seem to be devastated by her death. It's a curious process, as I seem to be the one comforting them instead of vice versa. This person whom they are talking about is not the person I experienced.

Is there some flaw in me? Why did I not see that Elaine? I saw only the Elaine who struggled with alcohol and drug addiction for over fifty years. The Elaine who was in and out of rehab so many times that I lost count. She was always Elaine, never Mother. She never took care of me. I took care of her, albeit reluctantly. All I saw was the Elaine who was so nervous that she couldn't stop talking. So self-absorbed that there was nothing to talk about except herself or her obsession with Elvis. No matter how many times I described to her my work as a costume designer, she would always ask me, "What exactly is it that you do?"

I know she moved to L.A. to be near me. But I couldn't be near her. It was as though I were allergic to her. I kept trying, but each time the reaction got worse, until I literally couldn't tolerate her presence for more than twenty minutes. I saw how she behaved with other people, the doctors and nurses in the hospital, waiters, salespeople, the so-called unimportant people in life. She was mean. She frightened them. She frightened me. I felt when I was with her that I no longer existed. She sucked up all the oxygen in the room, and there was none left for me to breathe. I know she loved me and she didn't want it to be that way. But that's how it was and I couldn't change it, no matter how guilty it made me feel.

I try to focus more on the retreat and deepening my meditation practice. It is hard, as I have the attention span of a gnat and am constantly distracted. I request a meeting with one of the top advisers at the retreat, Jack Kornfield, a man who is very knowledgeable and has written many books about Buddhism. He greets me at one of the small bungalows where the teachers reside.

"Listen," I blurt out, "I don't know if I believe in reincarnation or whatever, but please reassure me that my mother's not coming back."

He asks how old my mother was when she died.

"Eighty-six," I answer.

"Well, she had a good long life," he replies matter-of-factly. "To be honest," he continues, "I really don't see what all the fuss is about when someone dies at a ripe old age. Of course it's sad, but it's just the nature of things. Old people die." He mentions Buddha's First Noble Truth, the existence of impermanence. The only thing we know for sure is that we will die.

I talk about generation after generation of bad mother-daughter relationships: my mother's terrible relationship with her mother, my bad relationship with mine.

"How's your relationship with your kids?" Jack asks.

"Good," I reply.

"Obviously, you were sent here so you could break the cycle."

Even though it sounds kind of goofy, it feels good. Because I do feel that whatever I may or may not have achieved in my life, I have achieved good relations with my kids.

On the property, I discover a primitive, dusty labyrinth delineated by rocks. I find the process of walking the labyrinth soothing. I like that there is only one way in and one way out. No decisions required, just follow the path.

As an offer to my mother, I decide to bury the small rose-quartz heart that I have been wearing around my neck. Out loud, I wish peace and understanding to all the other daughters who have bad relations with their mothers.

As I walk down the hill in silence, the sun is setting. There is a golden glow suffusing this odd, rocky lunar landscape. The Joshua trees cast shadows; a jackrabbit flits across the terrain and hides behind a creosote bush. I feel peaceful for the first time in a long time. Now I am an orphan, without mother or father. But I have my own family. A family who has survived despite all the dysfunctions. A family who has beaten the odds and stayed together. A family I love who loves me. What more can I possibly ask for?

CHAPTER 32

The Muji T-shirt

The death I cared about—the one that felt like the final goodbye to my life in England and my life as the daughter of my parents—was not my mother's. It was my friend Herky's, a year later, in 2009.

I could hear from the sound of his girlfriend Ilana's voice when she phoned me in L.A. on an early February morning that things were not going well. "He's really bad, I don't know if he'll . . ." Her voice faltered.

"Shall I get on a plane?" I asked.

"Yes, yes," she replied, "I think you should."

Faster than I thought possible, I managed to buy a ticket, pack a suitcase, and get on a plane to London to say goodbye to my ex-boyfriend, my dear old friend Hercules Bellville.

How to explain Herky, a tall, rail-thin man with the extraordinarily inappropriate name of Hercules. He had never told me why his parents had chosen this unusual name, but I knew he had suffered terrible teasing at the Catholic all-boys' boarding school where he spent most of his childhood. By the time I knew him, he had developed a sense of humor about it and would stand with one foot perched on the coffee table and roll up his sleeve, flex his arm, and challenge you to feel his nonexistent muscle.

I first met him when I was seven and with my parents in Spain. He was in his late teens, spending the summer caretaking his father, Rupert, an inveterate alcoholic, gambler, and bullfight aficionado. All of us were staying with an American couple, Bill and Annie Davis, who owned a large ranch in Málaga called La Cónsula, that catered to bullfight aficionados like Hemingway, Rupert, and my father. Although I was too young to remember Herky from that visit, I do remember a unique feature about La Cónsula: In certain parts of the main house, the doorknobs were too high for small children to reach, a none too subtle way of keeping the kids separated from the mysteries of adulthood.

Nine years later, when I was sixteen, I met Herky again at my parents' house in London, and it was there I fell in love. He was elegant and dashing, and we shared an interest in music—the Beatles and Buddy Holly. At the time he was living with a woman, but that didn't stop me from accepting an invitation for tea at his house, which developed into an intense snogging session, only to be interrupted by the unexpected return of said girlfriend. That ended our little dalliance, but we stayed in touch.

Two years later, during my gap year, while I was teaching pottery in Sicily, Herky and I started a flirtatious correspondence. He wrote witty letters in the style of e. e. cummings, without punctuation or capital letters. He wrote offering to pick me up from the airport when I returned to London, and hoping for a romance, I accepted. (By this time his girl-friend had departed.) Lugging my knapsack filled with vast quantities of beads (I was a full-on hippie, making necklaces, bracelets, and anklets), wearing an embroidered Indian top and faded frayed jeans, I shortly moved into his house just off the trendy Kings Road.

He was in the thick of the cultural scene in London and endlessly curious. He was a wonderful mentor, and I learned a great deal from him, including quirky things like how to navigate a large museum show: You go through it fast and then return to the particular pieces you like and spend time contemplating them, a habit I've maintained to this day.

Our romance lasted under a year (our thirteen-year age difference was one issue and our unsatisfactory sexual relationship, due to my vaginismus, another), but after we split up, we remained good friends for life.

When I arrived at the hospital, the hallway outside his room was jammed with many of Herky's nearest and dearest—somewhat to my chagrin, I realized that I was only one of many—all jostling to get in to see him. For the moment, at least, Ilana had barred the door.

I peeked in through the small window and caught a glimpse of him, eyes closed, pale and wan, frailer than ever, breathing fitfully. I noticed he was wearing one of his beloved Muji T-shirts. No backless hospital gown for Herk. Right to the end, he was going to make a fashion statement.

When we met, and throughout the early '70s, he was in his dandy period, always dressed in elegant suits made by top-notch British tailors, with colorful silk linings that he proudly displayed. Instead of ties, he wore decorative art nouveau silk scarves from Liberty's. In the '80s his wardrobe became more casual and mundane, though he always liked to add a colorful scarf or an arresting pin.

After a major breakup with an actress in the '90s, he seemed to lose interest in his appearance, wearing baggy corduroy jackets and jeans.

Eventually, prompted by ex-girlfriends and friends, he perked up, but this time the clothes were all about economy. He derided anything that cost more than twenty dollars. Despite his considerable wealth, he took pleasure in finding a bargain. He started wearing curious canvas shoes with rubber soles made in China; he bought them by the case and wore them until they had no sole left.

Every Christmas he would visit L.A., partially for business—he was a film producer—but also to escape the gloomy British winter and visit his friends. During one of these visits, he noticed that I was wearing a Muji T-shirt. He immediately launched into a catalog of their virtues: They were green in the environmental sense (made from reused yarn), they were unique (no two were alike), they were soft and comfortable, and due to their multistriped colors, they went with everything. Plus— and this was probably their biggest selling point—they were cheap. He was slightly miffed that I had discovered them for myself. He always liked to be the first kid on the block with something new.

Eventually, Ilana emerged from Herky's hospital room. Making her way through the well-wishers, she greeted me with a hug. She reported that he was hanging on, barely. He had a perforated bowel, and due to the weakened state of his body from the cancer, it was inoperable. She said that after the doctor had delivered this grim verdict, Herky had turned to her and quipped, "Well, he's a bit of a downer!" I laughed—this was vintage Herky, one of the many reasons he was so loved. I asked when I could see him, but she put me off, saying he needed his rest because they were to be married in the morning.

I was surprised. Although Ilana and Herky had been together on and off for almost three years, their relationship seemed to have cooled in recent months. Herky had come to L.A. without her, and he'd told me she was in the process of moving into her own apartment. Yet when he had returned to London and started another series of treatments, she had been by his side. She was one of the few people who knew how ill he really was. During his fifty years of dating and romance—including glamorous actresses like Rachel Ward and Greta Scacchi—Herky had assiduously avoided marriage, yet on his deathbed, he had decided to do the right thing and marry the woman who had been there for him in his hour of need.

The next morning, when I arrived at the hospital with Clare Peploe (another old friend from way back), Ilana reported that in the early hours, Herky had requested a priest for last rites. Clare and I were flabbergasted. We knew that Herky had attended a Catholic boarding school and both his parents were Catholic, but his attitude toward religion had always seemed lukewarm at best. As the ultimate tourist—his collection of guides and maps was legendary—he loved visiting churches, though more as architectural attractions than as religious centers. But if Herky wanted a priest, we would find him one.

The hospital chaplain wasn't Catholic. The matron said the priest they normally used was out of town, but she had left a message for someone else. This was far too vague for us. I whipped out my iPhone and Googled "Catholic Church, Fulham Road UK." A few choices came up, but when we called around, it turned out that no one was within the parish of the Royal Marsden Hospital. Who knew that priests couldn't cross parish lines? The idea astonished me. "Even when someone is dying?" I asked, and they assured me they could not. We were about to give up when Clare found a priest from the Brompton Oratory (a rather grand Catholic church in Knightsbridge), which was within the Marsden parish.

Half an hour later, Father Ignatius showed up. He appeared to be in his fifties, but it was hard to tell, since priests and nuns always seem to have those smooth, unlined faces that appear ageless. (Maybe all that praying acts as a wrinkle deterrent?)

Father Ignatius walked into Herky's room while we waited outside. Still unsure that our man had indeed wanted a priest, we gathered around when he emerged, eager to hear what had transpired. Father Ignatius reported that Herky seemed "very alert and"—he paused—"quite feisty, in fact." It turned out that the priest had studied French and Spanish at Cambridge, and Herky had studied French and Spanish at Oxford. They had even conversed a bit in Spanish. Naturally, Herky had corrected the priest's pronunciation. And when Father Ignatius mentioned he had heard that Herky was in the film business, Herky corrected him again: "Was in the business? Still am!"

That afternoon there was a very private wedding ceremony at Herky's bedside. After most of the others had gone away, I still hadn't had a moment alone with Herky. When I insisted, Ilana granted me a brief visit. I was nervous. There was so much I wanted to say—how important he'd been in my life, how much he meant to my family and me—yet I knew it was imperative that I not become sentimental. Herky would despise that. On another night, one of his friends had shown up at midnight, slightly drunk and looking like Batman in a voluminous black coat. He sat by Herky's bed and, according to Ilana, for half an hour wept and spoke of his everlasting love. This had greatly upset Herk. Knowing that, I wanted to be careful. I sat in the plastic chair beside his bed and told him that I loved him and I kissed his hand.

Close up, he looked gaunt and old but still elegant. His hair was almost white, and he had a scraggly beard. He was propped up on pillows and his breathing was labored, yet there was still something formal and slightly intimidating about him. I hardly dared say much else for fear of sounding maudlin. He smiled at me and said, "Thank you, dearie."

I told him that everyone in L.A. sent love. I mentioned a few names—Jim, Lyndall, and Adelle. Jeremy Thomas, Herky's business partner, who was sitting in the corner of the room, interrupted. "He doesn't need to hear that," he said.

I suddenly thought, What am I doing here? Maybe I am not really wanted, maybe this whole trip was a mistake. Fighting back tears, I stood up and walked out of the room.

Seeking refuge in a nearby restroom, I tried to gather myself. I was angry for being so intimidated by Jeremy. It made me feel like a child again. It reminded me of the deathbed scene with my father and my awkward final conversation with Kathleen. At these critical moments I seemed unable to stand up for myself. I was fifty-seven years old, when was I going to grow up? I wish I could say that I marched back into Herky's room and demanded to spend time with him. I didn't.

Instead I realized that I had to get over my disappointment. After all, this was about Herky, not me and my insecurities, and despite the brevity of the visit, I had accomplished what I had set out to do by coming to London. I had seen Herky and expressed my love for him. That was all that mattered in the end.

Soon after I saw Herky, he asked to be allowed to "slip-slide away." He was always a fan of what he called "sweet sounds." It seemed completely appropriate that he would quote Paul Simon in his final request.

Half an hour later, doctors unhooked all his life support tubes and put him on a special cocktail of meds called the Liverpool Care Pathway. This combination is said to allow a patient to die with a minimum amount of pain and a maximum amount of dignity. I noticed the whiteboard on his door had "Nil by Mouth" ominously written on it.

As Herky drifted into unconsciousness and toward death, I was allowed into his room more frequently. I took turns with Ruby Baker, his goddaughter, staying with Ilana as she kept vigil. I sat on a chair and meditated, focusing on my breath and simultaneously listening to Herky's rasping, uneven breathing. Witnessing the process of his death was a profound reminder of all the deaths that had gone before—my father, my mother, various friends—and of the inevitability of deaths to come. I felt both sad and privileged to be part of this intimate experience. On the second night, I slept on the floor of the room on a bed of pillows and blankets. Herky probably had no clue I was there, but it felt important to be sharing these last days with him.

Outside the room, in our makeshift corridor waiting room, we took turns monitoring Herky's phone. Friends were calling from around the world to check on his status. Herky's great forte in life was creating and maintaining friendships. He made an art of it, and they all wanted to wish him adieu.

The third day, Saturday, dawned, an unexpectedly sunny day in London. The nurses changed Herky into yet another Muji T-shirt. As the day wore on, his breathing began to get erratic. After a few stops and starts, it stopped altogether at 7:50 P.M. "A tease right up to the end," Ruby observed. We tried to call some people, but all our phones were out of juice. The only one still working was Herky's, but using it seemed too macabre.

After Herky's funeral, I met the daughter of another ex-girlfriend, Natalie. She told me that a few weeks before, they had visited him in hospital. At that point he was still hopeful that he would be able to return to his flat, and they had offered to come cook for him. He said, "Thank you, but my dear friend Tracy is coming to take care of me." This amazed me: Even though I had offered, I never imagined he'd taken me seriously. It also reassured me that my decision to come to London and pay my final respects had been the right one.

Before I left London, Ilana invited me to Herky's apartment. He was an inveterate collector of ephemera and never threw anything away. I wandered around his rather posh flat, filled with orange-crate labels, rubber ducks, plastic rabbit lights, miniature Eiffel Towers, art nouveau posters, movie-star head shots—all the collections that he'd had in his previous house when I lived with him over thirty years earlier—and the tears started to flow. This was stuff that everybody had presumed he would throw out when he'd moved into this new place a few years earlier. But he had kept it all and continued adding to it: his own private art installation that he took such delight in assembling and showing off to all his friends.

Ilana had wanted to let each of Herky's closest friends pick something to take home and remember him by, but she had been informed by lawyers that nothing could leave the house until the estate was settled. She told me to pick something that she'd send to me later.

On a small table I noticed a framed photo of the famous bullfighter Antonio Ordóñez doing a pass with his *muleta*. It was inscribed *"para Hercules."* Ordóñez was one of Spain's greatest *toreros,* the main reason my father, Herky's father, and Hemingway used to gather in the '50s to watch the *corridas.* Looking at the photo of this dashing bullfighter brought full circle my connection to Herky. Bullfighting, once considered exciting and glamorous, had been deemed barbaric. The glamorous writers and aficionados who had gathered at La Cónsula were all dead. And now Herky was gone, too.

On the way to the bathroom, I passed Herky's closet and noticed a neat pile of stacked Muji T-shirts. I grabbed one and stuffed it in my purse. That was all I'd need to remember him by.

CHAPTER 33

The Ultimate Blended Family:
More Wedding Attire

In 2002 Jesse, who had gone to college in New York and stayed to work in the restaurant business, decided to return to L.A. Around the same time, Roxana, who was living in L.A., had just ended a relationship. Jesse and Rox had known each other intermittently throughout their childhoods. I remember a time when Jesse was six years old and I took him and Jim to my parents' place in Santa Monica. Splashing around in the pool was gorgeous ten-year-old Roxana, bossing around Matthew. Jesse shyly stood at the edge of the pool, watching this mini-goddess in action.

Twenty years later, they started to hang out together. When Matthew visited, they all took a trip to Mexico. It made me feel good that these disparate members of my family were getting on so well together. After a family brunch during which Jesse and Rox were both looking particularly attractive, Jim and I turned to each other and said, "God, wouldn't it be amazing if they got together. Imagine the incredible kids they would produce." It would never happen, we agreed.

It turned out that the trip to Mexico had ignited something more than platonic friendship between them. Soon after, they started dating and then living together. A year later, Rox confided to me that Jesse wanted to get married, but she wasn't sure. I was very touched that she had confided in me, though I was hesitant to advise. On many levels, it seemed like a wonderful idea—they certainly had a lot in common, not to mention relatives—but on another level, it was scary: What if something went wrong? It could make family life very complicated. Indifferent to my concerns, they decided to trust their instincts, throw caution to the wind, and go for it.

Jim and I both grew up as only children and always longed for siblings. Coincidentally, we also were raised with mothers descended from Russian Jews and fathers descended from Irish Catholics. So we were mongrels, in the best sense of the word, but unattached to either tribe, wishing we belonged to something bigger than ourselves. The wedding of two of the people we loved most in the world was an unexpected culmination of all that striving for connection.

Who could possibly object to such a union? Who but our offspring? Matthew and Ruby McBride, being the only members of the family who are related by blood to both Rox and Jesse, responded with an unequivocal "Eeeeuuew." Followed by "That's disgusting!" They soon recovered from their initial distaste and embraced the wider world of ersatz clan identity.

Rox asked me to help her select a wedding dress. Like me, she wanted something more casual than the full-on traditional wedding gown. We went on a couple of shopping expeditions, but nothing seemed quite right. Ultimately, she borrowed an elegant white skirt from an old family friend and bought a beautiful white silk shirt to go with it. (Strangely enough, I had sketched a shirt with long gathered sleeves that looked almost identical to the one she ended up buying.) She looked stunning. Jesse wore a nontraditional white suit with a white shirt and black tie; he looked very handsome, as always. I wore a sleeveless green-and-orange-plaid silk shantung '60s dress, with matching stole, that I had picked up at a vintage store in Palm Springs. It felt very mother-of-the-bride, with a twist. Jim wore a pale gray seersucker suit and looked dashing. (Seersucker is one of my favorite fabrics, such a quintessential American item. In every film I have ever done, I have never missed an opportunity to slip in a character wearing seersucker.)

In my life as a costume designer, I tried not to impose my personal tastes on the people I dressed, but instead to have their clothing grow out of the characters they were portraying. So it is with my truculently independent family members—they dress as they choose, though they often check with me first.

It was clear from his snappy wedding outfit—turquoise shirt, black tie, and white patent-leather shoes—that my son, Matthew, had inherited the fashion gene from me and the flamboyant gene from my father. Ever since he was little, he has been obsessed with clothing, meticulously laying out what he would wear for school each day, actually appreciating any clothing that I might buy for him, particularly shoes. He has always coveted fancy sneakers, the latest Air Jordans, the newest Nikes, keeping them pristine in their original boxes and bemoaning the least bit of scuffing. Ruby, on the other hand, refused all of my entreaties to doll herself up for the occasion and dressed down in a turquoise tank top, layered skirt, and sandals. She still looked pretty cute.

People arrived from all over. On Rox's side, our brother, Matthew, came from New York with his girlfriend and soon-to-be wife, Dalia; a few of their mother's relatives, the Haltons, descended from Canada. On Jesse's side, there was his mom, Clarissa, also coming from New York. She had two other sons, each from a different father: the first being Joe Ainley, who was ten when Jesse was born and grew up with him on and off over the years in Jim's and Clarissa's separate households. He drove down from Santa Rosa with his wife, Chalayne, and their three kids, Henry, Lucy, and Chloe. Then there was Bo Allingham, who Clarissa had given up for adoption when he was born, but who, at the age of twenty-five, had sought her out and reunited with her and his previously unknown half brothers, thus becoming indirectly related to us as well. He flew over from England with his wife, Tessa, and their brood, Rose, Polly, and William.

Although the wedding was done on a shoestring in our backyard, it was a very festive and touching affair. Rox's old boss and mentor Jackie Goldberg, now a California state assemblywoman, drove down from Sacramento to marry them in a most nondenominational and ecumenical way. Alexander Ruas, Jesse's best friend from childhood summers in New York, flew in from Sweden to be best man and official photographer. Jack Baran, the man who effectively introduced Jim and me; father of Cody Baran, Jim's goddaughter; and godfather to both Jesse and Matthew McBride, led the toasts. There were about a hundred people, and I felt connected to each and every one of them, part of a far-flung, complicated, wonderfully messy network of people who, by blood or by choice, had come together to comprise . . . a family. My family.

Nowadays, Jesse and Rox have two gorgeous (just as predicted) kids: Isobel (Izzy), eight, and Jack, six. Because I'm their aunt on their mother's side and their (step)grandmother on their father's side, they call me "Grauntie."

And they wear everything I buy for them. For now.

CHAPTER 34

The Black Trench Coat

My costume career was stalling. Part of it was that directors like Jim and Blake Edwards, with whom I used to work, were no longer active, and a great deal of the lower- and medium-budget films that were my specialty were now being filmed in places like Canada and South Africa, where local hiring was mandatory. But the main reason was that, like many women, I had put my work on the back burner while child rearing. I kept my hand in, to be sure, but I had to decline films that were shot on distant locations, except for the couple that Jim did, where the whole family could travel together. In effect, I had taken myself out of the loop, and now that I was trying to get back in, I found a changed world in which I was an un- or lesser-known quantity.

I had some near misses with films I was asked to do that fell apart at the last minute, like so many low-budget independent films do. Yet I kept hoping that I still had the potential to be hired. Most important, my agent, despite my diminishing track record, had not entirely given up on me.

One morning my friend Lyndall called. "Meet me at eight thirty at H and M on Sunset."

"Eight thirty in the morning?" I asked. Usually, at that time I like to be drinking my cup of tea and perusing the obituaries.

"Yup," said Lyndall.

"Why?"

"Comme des Garçons has designed a line of clothing for H and M, and it hits the stores tomorrow."

"So?"

"It'll be sold out by the end of the day. It's really cute. And cheap. I might be a little late . . ." I smiled. Lyndall is pathologically late. "Just get on line," she continued, "and I'll bring the Starbucks."

I didn't need any clothes. My closets, testament to twenty-five years of costume designing, were well stocked. Actually overstocked. But old habits die hard, and a famous brand designing for a low-end label was irresistible, so I said yes. Besides, I wanted to be more aggressive about looking for costume jobs. I'd had just two interviews in two years of unemployment, though during that time, there'd been a writers' strike that put a dent in almost everyone's employment record. I reasoned that if a job interview came up, having something cute, hip, young, and by Comme des Garçons would be helpful. As usual for me, the clothing came first and the job opportunity later.

The next morning I stood waiting in the cold on the corner of Sunset and Alta Loma with a hundred other folks outside H&M. A store representative passed out fliers informing us that we were allowed to purchase only two of the same style. The edict puzzled me until a fellow shopper explained: "Otherwise people buy a ton of one thing and sell it on eBay."

At nine Lyndall arrived with one half-finished double nonfat, one-pump-mocha Venti. When I reminded her of her promise to bring me a coffee, she offered me her leftovers. Desperate for caffeine, I accepted.

"At the Beverly Center H and M, the line stretches for half a mile," she announced, and I realized this was something bigger than a clothing sale. This was a clothing event.

At nine thirty the doors opened, and there was a mad rush into the store. I swung into action, grabbing everything off the racks, regardless of size, style, or color, just making sure it had the ubiquitous "Comme des Garçons made for H&M" label. I waited in a long line for the dressing rooms. Once inside, pressured by the impatient crowd outside, I hurriedly tried on clothes, forming an instant bond with the other occupants.

"Anyone got a size eight in a cardigan?"

"No, but I got a six in a black shirt."

"Trade you for the black shirt."

Goodies in hand, I emerged from the dressing room with a substantially smaller pile than the one I carried in, including a few things for Ruby, knowing full well that she would reject them, just on the principle that I had selected them. Naturally, I'd chosen several items for myself, none strictly necessary, but I was happy, and clutching my environmentally correct Envirosax bag, I waited on another long line to pay.

Two weeks later, I was sitting in an office in Pasadena, dressed in my H&M black trench coat over a maroon polka-dot wool cardigan over a maroon cotton polka-dot shirt and jeans. I felt chic and youthful, especially for a fifty-seven-year-old. As I waited, I flipped through *People* magazine and spotted a picture of fashionista Katie Holmes wearing a similar ensemble—though I suspected she didn't wait in line for hers.

I was waiting to be interviewed by a young director for a costume design job. In the twenty-four hours since my producer friend had called to bring me in, I'd read the script, which I liked (a comedy about a guy trying to date a girl whose son keeps trying to keep them apart), I'd seen the director's previous film (made for a mere fifteen thousand dollars), and I'd spent fifty dollars on fashion magazines and put together a folder of tear sheets showing examples of what the different characters in the film might wear. In short, I was prepared. And genuinely enthusiastic, which was unusual.

In the past I'd gone to many interviews for jobs I needed on projects I didn't admire. In those interviews I'd given what I considered Oscar-worthy performances, pretending that I thought the script was a work of genius. Even so, I often lost the job because the director didn't find me "enthusiastic" enough.

This time the director liked my ideas and was impressed with my résumé. After the interview, my friend the producer walked me to the elevator and said, "You done good."

I drove home, nurturing high hopes.

Two days later, my agent called to tell me they'd hired someone younger. I was devastated. I'd begun to dream about resurrecting my career, about hiring all my unemployed friends. All the stars had seemed aligned in my favor, and hearing that the director considered me too old crushed me. When I called another friend to tell her what had happened, she was outraged. "That's illegal. You could sue them for ageism."

That wasn't an option: My friend was producing the film. Besides, she'd just been honest; she'd wanted me to know the problem wasn't lack of talent. The director was thirty-four. How could I blame him for not wanting to hire someone old enough to be his mother? At his age, I suspect, I'd have done the same thing. My agent tactfully suggested looking for older directors for me to work with, but that presented a new problem: First, few older directors are working in Hollywood at all; and those who are like to surround themselves with younger folk in order to show how hip and cool they are.

I was reminded of the last job I didn't get, also lost to a younger designer, although at least she had worked with the director before. As I was leaving the interview, I saw her striding through the parking lot—a cute girl with spiked black hair, dressed in skintight jeans and a black leather jacket, juggling her portfolio and coffee. The minute I saw her, I knew I'd lost the job, but this time, apart from wanting the income and the prestige of employment, the hardest part was the blow to my vanity. I'd always been the new kid on the block. I'd always dated older men—hell, Jim is eleven years my senior—and now I was the old one, undesirable and invisible. The realization made me uneasy and sad.

When the Costume Designers Guild wrote to request my union dues, I had to think twice about whether I could afford to continue spending a thousand dollars a year on a union whose value became a lot less tangible as the potential for employment grew ever more remote. I called the Guild and explained my situation to a sympathetic and knowledgeable woman. Secretly, I was hoping that she would try to convince me not to leave, that she might promise I would find work eventually. Instead she readily agreed that there were "difficulties facing older designers." She recommended that I apply for "honorable withdrawal status."

As I filled out the papers, I felt like a soldier leaving the army after a long tour of duty. I couldn't say I'd miss getting up at four A.M. in the dark and cold and driving to a distant location in an unknown part of town, following a map that tells you how to get there from the production office, which is nowhere near where you live but does lie just within the union-prescribed forty-mile radius so they don't have to put you up for the night. I wouldn't miss getting lost, finding the location, waiting for the Teamsters to turn on the electricity so we could see the clothing in the truck, setting the clothing out in the actors' trailers, discovering that the director has changed the sequence of scenes, and then resetting the clothing. I wouldn't miss that moment when the director suddenly looks at the outfit the actor is wearing—the outfit he loved two weeks ago—and says, "I loathe it." I wouldn't miss having to act cool and unflustered while rushing back to the wardrobe truck parked three miles away and trying to find a replacement. Or hightailing it to the nearest mall and stuffing my trunk with armfuls of clothing, praying that something would work, speeding back to the set so I arrived before they were ready to shoot the scene, because the one thing in filmmaking that can never, ever happen is for wardrobe to hold up a shoot.

I was trying not to think about the things I would miss—the creative process, the particular camaraderie of a film shoot, the thrill of seeing what you've done up on the screen, the satisfactions of a job well done . . . I was becoming reconciled to closing this twenty-five-year chapter of my life, but it was happening so *quietly*, with nothing to mark the passing, no goodbyes. At least a movie had a wrap party.

And then, a few months later, my agent's assistant called—not with a job but to say that an organization called WIFTS (the Women's International Film & Television Showcase) Foundation wanted to give me their 2010 Visionary Award for Costume Design. I'd never heard of the organization, but their mission, to "celebrate and promote the army of talented women filmmakers who rarely get recognition," sounded tailor-made for me. I said I would be honored to accept, and honored I was.

What does a costume designer wear to receive an award for costume design? I have to admit I felt a bit of pressure, but since the event was in the afternoon, I didn't have to worry about a gown, thank God! Nonetheless, I did try on a bunch of outfits before I came up with something that felt right. It was rather simple: a pair of black pants, a short gray Agnès B jacket, and a black-and-white-striped shirt. Years of costuming had taught me that sometimes it's better not to stand out too much; it's more important to feel comfortable. Frankly, I was more concerned about the speech I had to give than what I looked like.

The award ceremony was held in a small movie theater on Beverly Boulevard, with a red carpet and photographers. Someone from the foundation interviewed me, and I found myself enjoying talking about the work I'd done. I invited close friends and family. I asked Geneviève Bujold (with whom I'd now done three movies) to present the award, and she graciously agreed. My friends and my agent paid for an ad congratulating me that appeared on a screen in the theater. The multitalented Philippe Mora, a French-Australian writer, director, actor, and artist, emceed the event. I gave a short speech called "What Exactly Does a Costume Designer Do?," which was well received— I even got a few laughs. The recipients in the other categories—an architect, the founder of a nonprofit organization in South Central Los Angeles, a documentary filmmaker, and Jennifer Tilly, the actress and poker whiz (who knew?)—were impressive. I felt lucky to be among them. Afterward, there was a small cocktail party. I basked in my fifteen minutes of fame and took home a curious ceramic trophy shaped like a feather. That seemed a fitting end to my costume-designing career. Or so I thought.

At an Academy screening in 2013—in the late '90s I had been inducted—I ran into fellow member Lesley Ann Warren, with whom I'd worked on *Choose Me*. She told me she would be working on a very low-budget film, and would I be interested in doing the costumes? I surprised myself by saying yes.

I worked on the project only ten days, my budget was twenty-five hundred dollars, and one of the actors had sixty-one changes! I managed to pull it off, satisfying both the director and the actors. And myself. I was probably the oldest person on the crew, but it was a reminder of the skills and knowledge I had gained doing costumes over the years. It seemed an appropriate valedictory to a career spent indulging my unregenerate preoccupation with the things people wear.

CHAPTER 35

Glamour Togs

In 2009 Jim and I decided to downsize and move closer to our grandchildren. We bought a loft in downtown L.A. After years of being about to happen, downtown finally seemed to be happening. Former industrial buildings and offices were being turned into lofts; supermarkets and shops were moving in. As with the early days in SoHo, New York, artists and bohemians had lived in the area over the years, but now more middle-class people were moving in. Jim and I were ex-artists and bohemians, now middle-class, so we fit right in.

Although I enjoyed the creative process of designing our new space and exploring a new part of L.A., it was a difficult transition for me. After living in our former house for over twenty-one years, I felt isolated from my friends and my familiar routines. Also, since the kids had truly left home and were living on their own (Ruby in New York and Matthew in L.A.), I think I was suffering from a belated case of empty-nest syndrome, exacerbated by the fact that my costume-designing career, like the water in L.A., had gone from a trickle to a drought. I was depressed and struggling to find a way to reinvent myself. As so often happens, the solution was in my (new) backyard.

DTLA, as it is trendily called, is a strange mix of businesspeople, artists, Latino workers, and the largest concentration of homeless in Los Angeles. Driving past the homeless people on a daily basis not only made me appreciate how incredibly lucky I was to have a roof over my head, a decent income, and, most important, a health-care plan, it also made me want to do something for those who were less fortunate.

After some research, I attended a volunteer orientation at the Down-town Women's Center, one of the few shelters downtown that doesn't have a religious affiliation—and allows the inhabitants to have cats! The residence houses seventy women and feeds more than two hundred a day. I learned how easy it is to become homeless in America. A string of bad luck—the loss of a job or apartment, a marital split, a medical emer-gency—and very quickly, you can lose your home. When you don't have a place to live or a job, the slide into poverty can be rapid. Many of the residents at the shelter are middle-class women who, through a series of unfortunate circumstances, have found themselves adrift. Many have mental-health problems. Women are among the fastest-rising sectors of the homeless in America.

When I first started volunteering at the center, I helped out in the donations area. Sorting through the vast piles of clothing donated to the center was an eye-opening experience—the variety of things cast off by people, from ball gowns to underwear, some of it impeccably clean and some of it filthy, was jaw-dropping but also familiar. It reminded me of being back in the costume houses, going through the bins of shoes. I helped sort and size clothing. Twice a week, clothes were put out in the dining room for women to choose from. Some of the higher-end stuff is kept back for the resale store, where 100 percent of the proceeds goes back to the women and the center.

They had also just started a social enterprise project in which the women make arts and crafts to be sold at the store. I learned candle-making and taught a workshop once a week. The women are all ethnicities, black, white, Latino, and Asian. They struggle to learn skills that can translate into wage-earning jobs. They learn to sew and make jewelry. Occasionally, they talk about their former lives, working in a fast-food restaurant, teaching, assisting a famous movie star, being a mother and a wife. Many of them have been abused and, rather than remain in such relationships, have wound up on the street. One of them who had been homeless for two years recalled with pleasure the softness of the bed after her first night in the residence.

One day, amid a mound of donations, I found a dress that was badly stained and ripped. As I inspected it more closely, I realized that it was an Ossie Clark dress very much like the one I had worn for my twenty-first birthday, the same dress that I had seen years later in a high-priced vintage store. It was bedraggled, down on its luck, but still beautiful. I was stunned that such an item could have found its way into this arena, but I supposed it was no more surprising than the people who had found their way into the residence. I realized that if I cut off the bottom part of the dress—which had sustained most of the damage—I could turn it into a shirt, and it might have some kind of life. I took it home, washed and sewed it, and turned it into a rather lovely wraparound blouse. But I wasn't sure what to do with it.

A few weeks later, through a friend, I met two women—Evvy Shapero, a neuro-feedback therapist, and Kara Fox, a therapeutic photographer—

who had started a nonprofit organization called the Glamour Project. They visit battered-women's shelters, cancer victims, rehab clinics, and veterans' associations and give the women a day of respite from the sometimes gloomy isolation of their lives. They make them up, dress them, light them like movie stars, and take a picture. Evvy does the makeup and Kara takes the photographs. They collect donations of makeup and toiletries, which they give to the women. They've amassed a collection of donated hats, jewelry, and scarves. They were looking for someone to help style the women. I jumped right in.

Working with Evvy and Kara and the women they serve has been an elevating, edifying, and moving experience. Many of the women we visit have such a low opinion of themselves that they avoid looking in mirrors. Often a little pampering and a touch of glamour can have a salubrious effect and help them look at themselves, so to speak, in a new light.

Some women have strong feelings about how they want to look and what they will or will not wear; other times they say, "Do whatever you want." It's fun to encourage them to try things and to reinvent themselves in fanciful ways. The women seem to really enjoy the process, and it's wonderful to see their transformation and the giddy way they show off their new look to friends at the shelter or rehab. Many times women who have resolutely chosen not to participate in the project suddenly change their minds and decide they want to "dress up." This is what frequently happens when I trot out my repurposed Ossie Clark shirt. It's one of those simple, lovely things that can lift a person's spirits just by being worn.

Occasionally, someone will talk about her past life: the drug counselor who became an addict, the army veteran who lost an eye and suffers from seizures, the mother struggling to reclaim custody of her children. As I style these women, I think of my mother and wonder what would have happened to her if she hadn't had the resources to deal with her bipolar craziness and her addictions.

After they are styled and made up, Kara takes glamour shots of them. A couple of weeks later, each woman gets two beautiful eight-by-ten glossies of herself: a reminder that she is acknowledged and cared for despite her current circumstances. Sometimes the women send the photos to their children or other family members with whom they have been out of touch. These women have such severe problems that it's hard to imagine a bit of dressing up can make a difference, but as one woman put it, "If other people can treat me this well and give me this attention, maybe I am not the person I thought I was. Maybe I am someone worthy of attention, love, and care."

What we do isn't anything that's going to shake the world, but it makes people feel good. It makes me feel good, too.

CHAPTER 36

Comfort with Style

After all these years of being obsessed with clothing—whether it's clothing I've worn or clothing I've put on other people—I find these days, when I do most of my work from home, my clothing is a combination of comfort and style. I like wearing things that feel good against my skin, that aren't too tight or too loose, and that flatter my body. I am particularly drawn to clothing and accessories that have a history and tell a story.

A constant staple in my wardrobe is the hoodie. I discovered hoodies in the mid-'90s. I was working on a film (*The Chamber*) in Mississippi, and the only two stores in the town where we were shooting were a Walmart and a going-out-of-business dry goods store. The dry goods

297

store had these hoodies from the '50s, boy sizes in odd faded blues and grays. I think my assistant discovered them hidden away in a dusty box. Anyway, there was something unique about their vintage quality and snug fit, which started what I can only describe as an addiction. Since then I don't think a week passes when I don't wear one at least a couple of times.

Hoodies have this all-American iconic quality, a little bit like blue jeans. The modern iteration is a utilitarian garment that originated in the '30s for workers in cold New York warehouses. Later, they became part of the uniform of high school athletics. Eventually, they were adopted by hip-hop culture, giving them a tough, macho quality. But the main appeal for me is the way they feel. The pockets are situated in the perfect spot for digging in your hands and assuming a nonchalant slouch. They are cozy. The hood, though I rarely wear it up, gives me an extra layer around the neck. The zipper makes them versatile for different temperatures. They look good worn open or closed, although I generally wear mine open. And if you get too warm, you can always tie the arms around your waist—which makes your waist look smaller—and still look chic. And they always remain in style. Over the years I have noticed that barely a season goes by when the hoodie doesn't appear in some designer's collection, reinvented in a different way, using different fabrics, like cashmere, or prints, like leopard skin.

Another obsession that doesn't seem to have abated over the years is my love of shoes. Comfort has always been of paramount importance. I rarely wear heels—or at least anything over a couple of inches. Even though I love the way they look, I just don't feel secure in them, and there is nothing less attractive than someone staggering around in high heels. A few years ago I discovered Sperry Top-Siders. Originally, they were developed for a functional purpose. Paul Sperry, a yachtsman, set out to find a solution for maintaining sure footing on slippery decks.

His aha moment came one cold day in 1935, after he watched his dog dart agilely across ice. He was inspired to carve grooves—like those on his dog's paws—into the bottom of a rubber sole. His shoes were so successful that during World War II, the U.S. War Department named Sperry Top-Sider as one of the official shoes of the U.S. Navy.

Now, I don't use my Sperrys for navigating the slippery decks of boats—I rarely go near boats, as I get horribly seasick—but I love the way they feel on my feet, and I love the adjustable leather laces. They are available in gold (reminding me of my gold lamé jeans), silver, or bronze, as well as colorful leathers. I like that this practical item has crossed over to fashion but remains functional. They are also inexpensive.

Another utilitarian item that I covet are the Coach bags designed by Bonnie Cashin. Cashin was a Hollywood costume designer during the '40s and created the looks for such memorable films as *Laura, Anna and the King of Siam,* and *A Tree Grows in Brooklyn.* She is probably better known as one of the most significant pioneers of designer ready-to-wear in America. She also initiated the use of industrial hardware on clothing and accessories. In 1962 she became a founding member of Coach.

One of my favorite Cashin bags is the cross-body city bag. It's the perfect marriage of style and functionality; it has an exterior pocket, a pocket under the flap, a zippered pocket inside, and a long shoulder strap. It closes securely and conveniently with a brass toggle, which she designed, inspired by the hardware on the roof of her convertible. The bag, though not big, has sufficient room for all the modern-day necessities such as a cell phone and an iPad Mini. You can still find these bags—and other Cashin items—in many colors and in good condition on Etsy and eBay for reasonable prices. Plus, they are so well made that even after thirty years, the leather remains soft and supple.

One more addiction that I have to confess to is any item of clothing with a camouflage print or "disruptive pattern," as it was called by the

British armed forces. I think this started in the '80s, when I was exploring army-surplus stores in Seattle and I became fascinated by the history of camouflage. It developed into an important part of modern military uniforms at the end of the nineteenth century, when the increase in accuracy and rate of fire of weapons required soldiers to be less visible. During World War I in France and England, there were units of *camoufleurs*, made up of painters, sculptors, and set designers who created and hand-painted patterns on military uniforms and equipment.

In the '70s, Vietnam War protesters often wore camouflage clothing from surplus stores; it became, ironically, an antiwar symbol. As so often happens, fashion designers, influenced by street wear, coopted camouflage as a recurring motif in their collections. The artist's influence on camouflage came full circle in the '80s, when Andy Warhol made giant silkscreen canvases of beautifully colored camouflage. His final work was a self-portrait overlaid with camouflage. When I wear a camouflage print, I feel I am part of that history. I like the color combination of the classic woodland pattern: green, black, brown, and beige. It's very versatile and works with many clothing combinations. And it remains a little subversive.

Ideally, clothing should be an expression of who you are, your tastes, and your personality. I do think it is more important to wear what suits you rather than to be a slave to fashion. But all of us, men included, tend to wear a uniform, and sometimes that uniform gets outdated: The skinny jeans that looked so great in your twenties don't look so great in your forties. (I gather that even teens are growing fatigued by the jeans craze and opting for athleisure, dressed-up, stretchy exercise clothing.) So you try different styles and different fits and find something that works better for your current body shape. I was the queen of leggings in the '90s; I wore them all the time, practically slept in them. As my body changed and they went out of style, I had to let them go—only to rediscover them in the mid-'00s. Now, instead of wearing them with crop tops, I layer them under skirts, dresses, or tunics. I get to wear my beloved leggings but in a different configuration.

I don't spend a lot of money on clothing. I appreciate the workmanship that goes into some designer pieces—I like to look at them and feel the fabrics—but I believe you can look good without draining your bank account. The few times I have spent a lot of money on an item of clothing, I feel strangely guilty, as if I've eaten a too-rich meal. Yet I am the first to admit that there are times when retail therapy can be beneficial. A friend of mine who discovered she had inoperable lung cancer waltzed into Prada and bought the bag she had always desired. I thought, Good for her. She didn't have long to live, but she got real pleasure from using that bag. When she died, she bequeathed it to me. And when I use that bag, I think of her.

Maybe it's because I've never had a lot of disposable income, or maybe it's from my training working on low-budget films, but I enjoy the hunt, the challenge of finding a bargain. Discovering a stylish item at Target, Uniqlo, or J. Crew (on sale) can be very satisfying. And today, if you need something special, there are so many discount stores, resale boutiques, vintage stores, and websites where you can find wonderful items at bargain prices. I'll admit it does take a bit of time and effort, but it's so worth it. There is nothing like discovering that great Jil Sander jacket at a fraction of the original cost, as I once did at Filene's Basement in Boston.

Finally, I am not a label whore. I have always eschewed clothing with a blatant logo. I think most logos are ugly, and it's a shame that branding has become such a major part of fashion. Like any fashionista, I enjoy watching the red-carpet parade at award shows, but more and more they seem to be advertisements for brands like Chanel, Dior, and Armani rather than a reflection of the actors' personalities or the designers' imaginations. I miss Cher in her outrageous Bob Mackie confections, or Sally Kirkland in extreme décolleté, or Audrey Hepburn in a delicate white floral dress designed by Givenchy (who claimed that Hepburn was *his* muse). Their clothing was an extension of their unique personalities. Sometimes it worked and sometimes it didn't, but it felt more distinctive and individual.

Furthermore, wearing a designer dress is not a guarantee of looking good. I sometimes wonder whether any of the stylists take into account that most of the time, their clients are seen from the waist up, and very few women over twenty-five look good in a strapless gown. Also, what looks good to the naked eye doesn't always translate to looking good on TV, especially HDTV, which makes patterns (like stripes and herringbone) strobe and certain colors (like red) bleed.

I hope that what I wear will always be a reflection of my personality and my history, and I encourage others to take the same approach. I expect that I will always be opinionated about clothing, and I hope, as I grow older, that I shall continue to be curious and discover new stories to tell.

Acknowledgments

According to the Igbo it takes a village to raise a child. In my case it took a village to create my memoir. Here are some of the friends, teachers, and advisers without whose support and encouragement it would not have been possible. I am deeply grateful to you all. Thank you.

Cheri Adrian, Nancy Bacal, Carol Baum, Tom Baum, Irene Borgia, Mary Ann Braubach, Meredith Brody, Joan Juliet Buck, Clarissa Dalrymple, Susan Dalsimer, Nancy Fasules, Kara Fox, Amy Friedman, Eva Gardos, Ashley Gilliam, Nan Graham, Sandra Harper, Lyndall Hobbs, Sharman Forman Hyde, Ed Kaplan, Sandra Kobrin, Michelle Lang, Diantha Lebenzon, Charlie Levy, Roz Lippel, Adelle Lutz, Jesse McBride, Matthew McBride, Ruby McBride, Jennie Naish, Roberta Neiman, Carolyn Pfieffer, Evelyn Purcell, Toby Rafelson, Ellen Sherman, Irene Skolnick, Evvy Shapero, Matthew Tynan, Roxana Tynan, Lesley Ann Warren, and Michael Attie and everyone at the Don't Worry Zendo.

And to Oliver, my feline companion, who keeps me company at my computer.

Special thanks to Andrea Dietrich who brought the book to life with her beautiful illustrations.

I also owe a considerable debt to my parents and Kathleen Tynan for their invaluable documentation of their lives.

For more information about the Glamour Project please check out www.glamourproject.org.